100 THINGS PHILLIES FANS SHOULD KNOW & DO BEFORE THEY DIE

Bill Baer

TRIUMPH
BOOKS

Library of Congress Cataloging-in-Publication Data

Baer, Bill.
  100 things Phillies fans should know & do before they die / Bill Baer.
    p. cm.
  ISBN 978-1-60078-678-5
1. Philadelphia Phillies (Baseball team)—History. 2. Philadelphia Phillies (Baseball team)—Miscellanea. I. Title. II. Title: One hundred things Phillies fans should know & do before they die.
  GV875.P45B34 2012
  796.357'640974811—dc23

2011044904

This book is available in quantity at special discounts for your group or organization. For further information, contact:

Triumph Books LLC
542 South Dearborn Street
Suite 750
Chicago, Illinois 60605
(312) 939-3330 | Fax (312) 663-3557
www.triumphbooks.com

Printed in U.S.A.
ISBN: 978-1-60078-678-5
Design by Patricia Frey
Editorial production by Prologue Publishing Services, LLC
All photos courtesy of AP Images unless otherwise specified

To Phillies fans everywhere

Contents

Introduction

For a team that had for many years been associated only with failure—becoming the first franchise to reach 10,000 all-time losses—the Phillies have produced many, many great moments. From the 1950 Whiz Kids, to the 1980 championship team, to the 1983 Wheeze Kids, to the 1993 team (which first baseman John Kruk referred to as "24 morons and one Mormon"), to the mostly homegrown 2008 championship team, Phillies fans have been treated to rosters not just with talent, but with unique and diverse personalities, as well.

Every fan who grew up with the Phillies has stories to tell about Connie Mack Stadium, Veterans Stadium, and now Citizens Bank Park. While other teams look at the city with an evil eye, Philadelphia has always been and continues to be the best sports town on the continent. Whether the team wins 65 games or 102, fans expect nothing but greatness from their players on a day-in, day-out basis.

The stars are memorable and, unlike actual stars, will always flash brightly as part of Phillies history. But equally as important, and just as memorable, are the role players or the less-talented players with personality. For every Mike Schmidt homer, there is Tomas Perez giving a teammate a shaving-cream pie; for every Tug McGraw World Series save, there is a Mitch Williams walk-off RBI single at 4:00 AM.

This book attempts to capture the 100 things about Phillies baseball that every fan should know and/or do. Honestly, this book could have been "500 Things" and it still wouldn't have done Phillies baseball justice. Even the players below a bit player like "Pie Man" Perez in popularity have a following. Just think about the Sal Fasano fan group called "Sal's Pals" that camped out in left field.

For a player who played in Philadelphia just one year and never reached 220 at-bats in any season in his career, that speaks to just how much Phillies fans love baseball.

There is a reason that, after emotionally dropping an F-bomb in a speech after the World Series parade in 2008, Chase Utley made sure to thank Phillies fans. He said, with some of the most expressive hand gestures, "Without you, we would not be in this position."

This book has 100 topics that all Phillies fans should know in a general order of importance. I generally dislike ordinal rankings of anything because, whether it is power rankings for teams, a list of favorite bands, or what have you, the list will vary for anybody. While reading, you may disagree with the ordering. Don't fret—I disagree with some of my own ordering, as well. Feel free to rip out the pages of the book and put them in your own order.

1 Harry Kalas

Baseball teams are often thought of in terms of players, coaches, and front-office personnel. It is rare that both the fans and the players will identify the team with someone who does not fit neatly into those three groups. Broadcaster Harry Kalas was that rare breed.

Kalas was unceremoniously hired by the Phillies in 1971 to succeed Bill Campbell. The expectations for Kalas were low, but he quickly won the hearts and minds of Phillies fans for his unique style of play-by-play. In particular, he and Richie Ashburn developed quite a rapport both on and off the air. Their affable personalities worked to make them both legends in the city of Philadelphia.

Doing the play-by-play for nearly every Phillies game from 1971 through 2008, Kalas saw the ups and downs of the Phillies franchise: the boring games and the unbelievably exciting games, the heroes and the villains. He always had a way to put his personal stamp on it all. From Mike Schmidt's 500th career home run ("Swing and a long drive! There it is! Number 500! The career 500th home run for Michael Jack Schmidt!"), to Mitch Williams' 4:00 AM walk-off single against the San Diego Padres in 1993 ("This game is over, on an RBI hit by Mitchy-poo!"), to Chase Utley scoring from second on an infield single ("Chase Utley, you are the man!"), Kalas left an indelible mark on Phillies baseball.

While he quickly earned the respect and admiration of Phillies fans throughout the greater Philadelphia area, the most surprising aspect was how quickly the players grew to accept him and treat

1

*Hall of Fame broadcaster Harry Kalas waves to the crowd during ceremonies
honoring him before the start of a Phillies game against the St. Louis Cardinals
on August 18, 2002, at Veterans Stadium.*

him as one of their own. Frank Coppenbarger, the director of team
travel and clubhouse services, said of Kalas, "He sat in the back of
the plane with them, and that's pretty much unheard of. He was
like a player to them."

Although the Phillies won the 1980 World Series, there was
always a hole in the collective memories of Phillies fans because
Kalas was not able to call the games himself due to contract stipu-
lations with regard to nationally broadcast games. This upset
Phillies fans, who quickly forced the rules to change. The Phillies
reached but lost their next two World Series appearances in 1983
against the Baltimore Orioles and in 1993 against the Toronto Blue
Jays.

It wasn't until 2008 that Kalas got to call the final out of a Phillies championship. You could hear the relief and satisfaction in his voice as Brad Lidge struck out Eric Hinske, dropped to his knees, and waited to embrace catcher Carlos Ruiz. While color broadcaster Chris Wheeler threw his fists around in excitement, Kalas sat in his chair, finishing his call—but he couldn't help cracking a smile.

Kalas passed away in Washington, D.C., on April 13, 2009, at the age of 73. Phillies fans across the nation were in disbelief. The local reporters and broadcasters who had to deliver the news needed every ounce of strength they had to keep from bawling openly on live television. There was also relief and happiness that Kalas got to call his team winning it all once before his passing.

The public swell of support for the Kalas family was incredible. Phillies fans packed Citizens Bank Park as Kalas was memorialized by his family and friends, many of whom belonged to the Phillies organization. The players sought to remember Kalas by wearing a black "HK" patch on their uniforms for the remainder of the season, and by hanging his blue blazer and white loafers in the dugout before every game.

Kalas is still a part of the Phillies fan experience. After a Phillies player hits a home run at Citizens Bank Park, a recording of Kalas' legendary "Outta here!" call plays throughout. After a Phillies win, Kalas' favorite song, "High Hopes," plays as fans exit the stadium to head to their cars or to public transit.

Kalas lives on with the Phillies' current broadcast teams: Tom McCarthy, Chris Wheeler, and Gary "Sarge" Matthews on TV, along with Jim Jackson, Scott Franzke, and Larry Andersen on the radio. McCarthy had the toughest job of all in having to fill Kalas' loafers as the play-by-play broadcaster. McCarthy may never live up to those lofty expectations, but he and the rest of the Phillies' broadcast team strive every day to preserve the memory of the man who, more than any player, was Phillies baseball.

2008 Regular Season

In 2007 the Phillies had cleared their biggest hurdle simply by getting to the playoffs for the first time since 1993. The expectations were low, and it was a good thing as the Phillies were quickly dispatched by the red-hot Colorado Rockies. Going into 2008, though, the team was expected to build on its success. The core needed to take it to another level, and the young players could not use inexperience as an excuse.

GM Pat Gillick, who had predicted a doom-and-gloom period for the Phillies after trading away Bobby Abreu, ensured his team would have an experienced closer as opposed to starter-turned-closer Brett Myers. Über-closer Brad Lidge was acquired from the Houston Astros along with utility man Eric Bruntlett for outfielder Michael Bourn, reliever Geoff Geary, and infield prospect Mike Costanzo. Meanwhile, the Phillies retained the services of lefty reliever J.C. Romero and signed Chad Durbin, So Taguchi, and Pedro Feliz via free agency.

Starting off the regular season, the Phillies had another one of their typically slow starts, finishing the month of April at 15–13 in second place. It wasn't until mid-May that the Phillies finally hit their stride. After a loss on May 19, the Phillies were 24–22 and had fallen to third place. However, they won 15 of their next 19 games, retaking control of the division and staking themselves to a 3½-game lead.

The biggest surprise in the first half was right fielder Jayson Werth. Geoff Jenkins started the season as the everyday right fielder, but as Jenkins' offensive problems became more and more of an issue, Werth's playing time gradually increased. At the end of

June, Werth's OPS (on-base + slugging percentage) was nearly 200 points better than Jenkins'.

On the rubber, Cole Hamels emerged as the ace the front office had always envisioned when they drafted him and nurtured him throughout the minor leagues. Hamels finished the first half with a 3.15 ERA and averaged nearly eight strikeouts per nine innings. With a 93 mph fastball and a devastating change-up, the young lefty was making a habit out of making seasoned veterans look foolish.

A surprising challenger emerged in the second half. The New York Mets, who were reeling from a collapse of epic proportions in the 2007 season, spent much of the first half bouncing between third and fourth place. They held first place for a week at the end of July before giving it back to the Phillies. On August 13, the Mets won the series opener against the Washington Nationals, the start of a stretch in which the Mets would win 10 of their next 11 games.

On September 10, the Phillies had lost three of four and fell 3½ games behind the Mets, their largest deficit of the season. Fans turned toward the wild-card to gauge the Phillies' chances, assuming the odds of another September collapse for the Mets was far too unlikely. The Phillies had 16 games left. If the Mets played roughly .500 baseball (8–9), the Phillies had to go at least 11–5 to win the division.

As fate would have it, the Phillies won 13 of their final 16 games. The Mets didn't exactly collapse, but a 7–10 record over their final 17 games was not helpful.

Ryan Howard came up with an incredibly productive month of September, catapulting the Phillies to the top of the division. In 102 plate appearances, Howard hit 11 home runs and drove in 32 runs while posting a 1.274 OPS. No surprise to anyone, he won National League Player of the Month honors.

Three left-handed starters propelled the Phillies to their success, as well. Cole Hamels and Jamie Moyer each made five starts in September, posting respective ERAs of 2.84 and 3.26, while J.A. Happ had five appearances (including two starts) with a 2.41 ERA. In the bullpen, Brad Lidge clinched a perfect season—41 for 41 in save opportunities—earning eight saves with a 0.71 ERA in the final month for the Phillies.

The Phillies had done the improbable for the second season in a row. Everything that could have gone right for them did. The team suffered relatively few major injuries, and nearly everyone who needed to perform well did. Happ was an emergency fill-in who seemed more like a godsend in the way of Marty Bystrom in 1980. The many rag-tag veteran players filling out the bullpen and the bench performed above and beyond their meager expectations.

For the first time in nearly 30 years, Phillies fans had reason to believe their team was legitimately good enough to bring home a championship. They had passed the toughest test in the regular season but had to prove themselves once more by winning 13 more games in the playoffs.

3 Phillies Take Advantage of the Mets in 2007

On August 25, 2007, the Phillies lost their fourth game in a row and sat seven games back in the division. Their season was slipping away, and the clock was ticking.

The next day, the Phillies smashed the San Diego Padres 14–2, salvaging the finale of a three-game series before the division-leading Mets came into town for a four-game series. The rout gave the Phillies just the jolt of energy they needed with 33 games left in the season. The Mets were on a roll, having won nine of their previous 13 games. When talking heads talk about a "must-win" series for a team, this was it for the Phillies.

The Phillies continued to hit in the series opener. Mets starter Brian Lawrence failed to get through the fifth inning, surrendering 10 hits. Meanwhile, J.D. Durbin surprisingly turned in a quality start, allowing only two runs through six and one-third innings. The series was off on the right foot, but the Phillies would need to keep their foot on the gas.

In Game 2, an early two-run home run by Carlos Delgado staked the Mets to a lead. Tom Glavine was dominant through seven innings, holding the Phillies scoreless. However, he did not come out for the eighth inning, having crossed the 100-pitch plateau. With a switch-hitter and two lefties due up, the Mets opted to go with lefty reliever Pedro Feliciano. After working the count to 2–1, leadoff hitter Jimmy Rollins took a typically hefty swing, made solid contact, and deposited the Feliciano offering into the stands in left field.

Feliciano got Chase Utley to ground out weakly to second before issuing a four-pitch walk to Pat Burrell. Shane Victorino trotted out to first to pinch run, an overt admission by the Phillies they would attempt to manufacture a run in the event Ryan Howard could not do the damage himself. Howard tried, but to no avail, as his fly ball to deep left field was caught by Moises Alou.

Mets manager Willie Randolph brought in right-handed reliever Aaron Heilman to try to close out the inning. Victorino promptly broke for second, then careened for third base as catcher Paul Lo Duca's throw was way off-target. As the baseball gods were smiling upon the Phillies that evening, Aaron Rowand hit a grounder weakly down the third-base line. His reputation as a gritty ballplayer was evident as he ran hard all the way down the line, earning his second hit of the evening as Victorino scored the tying run. Heilman would finish the inning without relinquishing any more runs.

Brett Myers came in to keep the score tied and did just that. In his two 1-2-3 innings, he induced five ground-ball outs and one strikeout. Meanwhile, the Mets asked Guillermo Mota to give them two quality innings. His first inning was clean, but he ran into problems in the bottom of the 10th. Victorino, who stayed in the game, laced a line drive to center. Mota, perhaps distracted by the potential for Victorino to steal, left a change-up (his fourth in four pitches) over the middle of the plate. Howard took his trademark swing, hitting a walk-off two-run home run to left field. The Phillies had clinched at least a series split and had won their third game in a row.

Game 3 started off as a pseudo–home run derby. Phillies starter Jamie Moyer surrendered a first-inning home run to David Wright and Mets starter Oliver Perez surrendered two first-inning homers to Jimmy Rollins and Pat Burrell. They were not omens of things to come, fortunately, as both pitchers settled down. The Mets tied the game at two in the fourth on a Carlos Delgado RBI single. The Phillies took the lead back in the fifth on a Pat Burrell sacrifice fly. From that point forward, both teams' starters and their bullpens posted goose eggs. The Phillies won without drama, climbing to within three games of first place.

The August 30 game is forever burned in the memories of Phillies fans, as it became a motif for the Phillies' season. The game featured 21 runs on 27 hits while 12 pitchers and 25 position players were utilized. Most importantly, the game featured five lead changes.

As the previous game appeared to be a pseudo–home run derby, so did this game. Ryan Howard launched a two-run home run in the bottom of the first off of Mets starter Orlando Hernandez. Pat Burrell tacked on a two-run shot of his own in the bottom of the third, followed by a solo home run from Aaron Rowand. Quickly, the Phillies were up 5–0 and appeared to be on their way to a series sweep.

Phillies fans, through many years of conditioning, had become accustomed to the other shoe dropping. The shoe dropped in the top of the fourth for Phillies starter Kyle Lohse. He surrendered three runs on two doubles, a single, a walk, and a hit batter. Geoff Geary came on in relief and ended the threat, but things did not improve for the Phillies. In the fifth, Geary allowed two runs on three hits, and the score was tied.

The Phillies, ever resilient, stormed back for three runs in the bottom half of the fifth against Aaron Sele. Four singles and a walk later, the Phillies were up 8–5. After two solid innings of relief from Clay Condrey, the Phillies brought in J.C. Romero to start the eighth. Romero got the leadoff batter in Shawn Green but walked Ruben Gotay. Not confident that Romero could conquer Moises Alou, Charlie Manuel strode to the mound to bring in Antonio Alfonseca. Little did he know he would open the floodgates.

With good plate discipline and good hitting, the Mets took Alfonseca to the cleaners. Alfonseca did not retire a single batter, allowing four runs on two hits and three walks. Jose Mesa came in to stop the bleeding, and did as much as could have been expected with runners on first and second and no outs. He allowed one walk and one more run to score, but got the final two outs of the inning.

Mets manager Willie Randolph, realizing his team's division lead was disintegrating, asked Billy Wagner for a two-inning save. In the bottom of the eighth, he faced Pat Burrell, whom Wagner referred to earlier in the season as having a "one-path swing." As he had previously, Wagner grooved a fastball into Burrell's "path," which was subsequently hit to the fans in the left-field stands. The Phillies, in this seesaw game, were within one run at 10–9. Wagner got through the eighth without any more trouble, and Tom Gordon pitched a 1-2-3 ninth, giving the Phillies one last try in the bottom-half.

Jayson Werth led off the inning with a single. The fans at Citizens Bank Park could sense a victory was in their grasp. Carlos Ruiz flied out, bringing some tension back to the ballpark. At this point, all the focus was on Werth. Two factors were at play: Werth

September 2007

After game No. 145 in the 2007 regular season, the Phillies were 76–69, seven games behind the 83–62 New York Mets in the NL East. From that point on, though, the Phillies played eight games better than the Mets, taking sole control of first place for the first time all season on September 28, after the 160th game. According to baseball genius–turned–political pundit Nate Silver, the odds of the Mets forking over their division lead were nearly 500-to-1.

Game No.	PHI	NYM	Game No.	PHI	NYM
146	W	L	155	W	W
147	W	L	156	L	L
148	W	L	157	L	L
149	W	L	158	W	L
150	W	L	159	W	L
151	W	W	160	W	L
152	L	L	161	L	W
153	W	W	162	W	L
154	W	W		13–4	5–12

was a smart, efficient base runner, and Wagner was inept at holding runners on base as his pickoff move was subpar. As a result, Werth not only stole second, but he stole third, as well—on consecutive pitches, no less.

Tadahito Iguchi, who pinch hit for third baseman Abraham Nunez, drove in the tying run on a single to left. Wagner's problems did not end there. Iguchi stole second base, taking advantage of Wagner's inattentiveness. To set up a double play and get the favorable lefty-on-lefty matchup, Jimmy Rollins was intentionally walked to bring up Chase Utley. After a tense seven-pitch at-bat, Utley lined a single to right field, scoring Iguchi for the game-winning 11th run. The crowd erupted. Fans watching on TV listened to Harry Kalas exclaim into his microphone.

The idea of a season turning around on a single event is more mythical than anything, but it was quite real in the case of the 2007 Phillies. The Phillies engaged with the Mets again on September 14 for a three-game series and swept them again. From September 13 to the end of the season, the Phillies went 13–4; the Mets, 5–11. The Phillies took control of first place in the NL East for the first time all season on September 27 and never looked back. They earned their first postseason berth since 1993, winning the division by one game.

4 Jim Bunning's Perfect Game

Jim Bunning accomplished quite a lot in his life. The Kentucky native was a great pitcher, tossing more than 3,700 innings in his 17-year career. His consistency from 1957 to 1967 earned him a spot in the Baseball Hall of Fame in Cooperstown, New York. A man could rest on his laurels on that alone, but Bunning also began a long and prosperous political career starting in 1977. Bunning won each of six elections from 1986 to 1996 for Kentucky's Fourth Congressional District, and also won two elections to the U.S. Senate in 1998 and 2004.

Those accomplishments do not stick in the memories of most people when they think of him, however. Remarkably, Bunning is one of only seven pitchers to throw both a no-hitter and a perfect game. That is quite special by itself, but Bunning, a father of seven, threw his perfect game on Father's Day, 1964.

It was June 21, and the visiting Philadelphia Phillies were at Shea Stadium to play the New York Mets for the first game of a doubleheader. Bunning was slated to start the first game and Rick Wise, the back end. The 37–23 Phillies were on a roll, having won three of their previous four games while the 20–46 Mets had lost eight of their previous nine games.

The Phillies scored a run in both the first and second innings to give Bunning an early cushion, then tacked on four more in the

Jim Bunning strikes out New York Mets pinch-hitter John Stephenson to complete his perfect game on Father's Day, June 21, 1964, at Shea Stadium. It was the first perfect game thrown in the National League since 1880.

sixth. Bunning seemed to get stronger as the game progressed, notching six of his 10 total strikeouts in the game's final three innings. Overall, he threw 69 of 90 pitches for strikes.

During the ninth inning, Bunning and his catcher, Gus Triandos, conferred on the mound. Asked later what they had discussed, Triandos said, "He said I should tell him a joke, just to get a breather. I couldn't think of anything. I just laughed at him." Even under the intense pressure of completing one of the rarest feats in baseball, Bunning wanted to keep it light. He later told reporters, "In a game like that, the pressure not only builds on the pitcher but on the fielders, as well. I was just trying to relieve it by talking."

To reach the finish line, Bunning needed to get through short-stop Charley Smith and pinch-hitters George Altman and John Stephenson. Bunning got Smith to pop out to shortstop Bobby Wine in foul territory, then buckled down and struck out Altman to bring him to within one out of history. The fans at Shea Stadium put aside their rooting interest as they stood up and cheered for the final out.

Bunning fed Stephenson, who was batting .074 at the time, a steady diet of curveballs. Stephenson worked the count to 2–2, having seen four consecutive curves. Most hitters would expect a different pitch after seeing the same one so many times in a row, but Bunning went to the curve for a fifth time. Stephenson was ill-prepared and swung through it for the 27th and final out.

Phillie after Phillie sprinted from the dugout to mob Bunning in celebration on the baseline halfway between third base and home plate. Hurling the first perfect game in the National League in 84 years earned Bunning an appearance on the *Ed Sullivan Show* the same night, and plenty of advertising deals soon followed. On the postgame television interview, Bunning said of his performance, "Wow, one of them days."

Yes, indeed, "one of them days" that will forever be remembered in major league baseball.

5 1980 Regular Season and NLCS

The Phillies got their start in 1883 as the Philadelphia Quakers. In 1890 the team name was changed to "Phillies." To that point, there were only eight teams in the league and 17 overall, but the Phillies had not made the postseason even once. In fact, it was not until 1915 that the Phillies would win a pennant, but they lost the World Series in five games to the Boston Red Sox.

The 1883–1915 years were simply a microcosm of what was to come for Phillies fans. The Phillies did not reach the postseason again until 1950, when they were swept by the New York Yankees in the World Series. The years 1951–1975 comprised yet another playoff drought. It was in the mid-1970s, though, when a new era of Phillies baseball was ushered in.

Most importantly, Mike Schmidt made his major league debut in 1972 and became a regular part of the Phillies lineup by '74. The third baseman needed just two seasons in the minors to convince the front office he was ready. Going into the '75 season, the Phillies traded for reliever Tug McGraw, then acquired center fielder Garry Maddox in early May.

This was the start of the first run of consistently competitive baseball in franchise history. The core stayed the same while the front office patched the rest of the holes with prospects, free-agent signings, and small trades. The Phillies would make the playoffs in 1976, 1977, and 1978, losing in the playoffs to the Cincinnati Reds (in '76) and the Los Angeles Dodgers ('77 and '78).

The 1980 team did not have a magical feel to it, as most championship teams typically do. Dallas Green had taken over as manager in the previous season, but he was harsh and was frequently at odds with his players. The team was almost at the end of its rope, as well: the youngest players in the lineup were Manny Trillo and Greg Luzinski, both 29 years of age. The biggest contributors in the starting rotation and bullpen, Steve Carlton and Tug McGraw, were 35 years old. If the Phillies were going to win a championship, 1980 very well might have been their last shot.

Earning first place in the NL East was an extremely difficult task. The Phillies hovered around .500 for most of the season and never had control of first place for longer than five days. A hot September and October (23–11 record) propelled them ahead of the Montreal Expos by one game. In fact, the Phillies played the Expos in the final series of the season, winning two of three.

Mike Schmidt would go on to win NL Most Valuable Player honors while Steve Carlton would earn the Cy Young Award. Both were incredibly vital to the Phillies' regular season success. Prior to 1980, both players had trouble turning it on in the postseason, however. Schmidt hit an unflattering .182 with no home runs in 50 plate appearances, while Carlton posted a 4.78 ERA with just one win in five starts and two relief appearances spanning 37⅔ innings. For the Phillies to succeed in the playoffs, they would need both players to show up and produce.

The Phillies matched up against the Houston Astros in the best-of-five NLCS, which would turn out to be one of the most exciting playoff series in baseball history. Game 1 was comparatively very ordinary. Steve Carlton held the Astros to one run over seven innings, while Greg Luzinski hit a two-run home run in the sixth inning to give the Phillies a 2–1 lead. The Phillies tacked on one more run, and Tug McGraw tossed two scoreless innings to seal the victory.

Game 2 was the real start of the party. The game was back-and-forth through nine regulation innings, but the score stood at 3–3 going into the 10th. The Astros strung together several hits, including a two-run triple by Dave Bergman, to take a 7–3 lead. The Phillies scored an unearned run in the bottom-half, but lost 7–4 as the series evened to 1–1 and moved from Veterans Stadium to the Astrodome. Manager Dallas Green was unfazed. "We had to win two out of three last week in Montreal to get here," he said. "We're not scared of playing in the Dome or anywhere else on the road."

Game 3 had so much palpable tension, you could have cut it with a knife. Runs were at a premium as the score was tied at 0 going into the 11th inning. Joe Niekro had tossed 10 scoreless innings, at the time only the seventh time that had been accomplished in the postseason since 1903. Larry Christenson, Dickie Noles, and Tug McGraw had done their part to keep runs off the board, as well, allowing just five hits through 10. After the Astros'

Dave Smith kept the Phillies off the board in the top half of the 11th, Joe Morgan led off the bottom of the inning with a triple. McGraw intentionally walked the next two batters to set up a force at every base, but it was to no avail as Denny Walling hit a sacrifice fly to left field for the walk-off win.

The Phillies earned their pinstripes in Game 4. They were down 2–0 going into the eighth inning, having been shut down by Vern Ruhle. The right-hander came out for the eighth but was out of gas as Lonnie Smith, Greg Gross, and Pete Rose each singled; the final hit put the Phillies on the board at long last. Ruhle was lifted for Dave Smith, who had been holding the Phillies silent all series long. Mike Schmidt drove in a run (his first of the series) with an infield single to second base, which also had the reward of knocking Smith out of the game. Southpaw Joe Sambito was brought in to face the left-handed Bake McBride. The managerial tactic paid off as McBride struck out to bring up Manny Trillo. Trillo hit a line drive to right fielder Jeffrey Leonard. Schmidt, at first, thought Leonard trapped the ball, so he took off for second, but umpire Bruce Froemming ruled it a catch. Pete Rose tagged up and scored the go-ahead run just ahead of Schmidt being doubled up at first base.

Rose's heads-up base running appeared to be the game-winning play, but the Astros played small-ball in the ninth to tie the game up. A walk, a sacrifice bunt, and a single brought the score to 3-all going into the 10th inning. With runs coming at a premium all series long, fans settled in for what could have been a long, long game. However, the Phillies wanted to get to the ace match as fast as possible, so they mounted a two-out rally in the top of the 10th. RBI doubles by Greg Luzinski and Manny Trillo gave the Phillies a 5–3 lead, and Tug McGraw nailed down the bottom half of the inning for the save. The Phillies were one win away from the World Series.

After the game, McGraw was exasperated. "There has never been a game to compare with that one," he said. "There has never been a game I've ever witnessed that has been more exciting, more controversial, more interesting than the game I just saw. It was like a motorcycle ride through an art museum. You see the pictures but afterward you don't remember what you saw."

Game 5 was quite an uneven match-up. Future Hall of Famer Nolan Ryan toed the rubber for the Astros while rookie Marty Bystrom had the fate of the Phillies resting on his arm. Twenty-four runs were scored between the two teams in the first four games; the two teams would combine for 15 in Game 5 alone. Pitching was not the theme of the day; rather, it was the resiliency of both teams' offenses.

The score was tied at 2 going into the bottom of the seventh. Bystrom had pitched admirably, allowing two runs in five and one-third innings. The sixth inning was finished off by Warren Brusstar, then Larry Christenson took over in the seventh. The Astros managed a first-and-second with two outs. What happened next was a crushing blow to the Phillies' chances of reaching the World Series. The Astros scored three runs: one on a Denny Walling single to right field, one on a wild pitch, and one on an Art Howe triple to right. Ron Reed, who had come in to face Howe, ended the bleeding by getting Alan Ashby to fly out to left, but the damage was done. Phillies fans' heads were in their hands as they lamented yet another postseason failure.

If the Phillies were to come back, they would have to do it against Nolan Ryan. However, Ryan had logged 233⅔ innings in the regular season and an additional 13⅓ already in the postseason, so he was running on fumes. The Phillies jumped on him quickly in the top of the eighth with three consecutive singles and chased him out of the game with a bases-loaded walk, cutting the Astros' lead to 5–3.

Joe Sambito was brought in to face McBride again, but Dallas Green remembered how his lefty was dominated earlier in the series, so he chose to pinch-hit with Keith Moreland. Moreland grounded out to second base, but Bob Boone was able to score, bringing the Phillies to within one run at 5–4. Sambito was quickly lifted for Ken Forsch, a right-hander, to face Mike Schmidt. Schmidt struck out looking on three pitches. The Phillies' best chance to tie the game rested on the bat of Del Unser. Unser came up to the plate aggressively as he swung at the first pitch and laced a single to right field, scoring Greg Gross. The Phillies laughed in the face of long odds as the score knotted up at 5–5. They were not done—Manny Trillo tacked on two more runs with a triple to left field.

All Tug McGraw had to do was pitch two scoreless innings, and the Phillies were in the World Series. McGraw, at 36, had pitched nearly 100 innings in 1980 up to this point; he had very little left in the tank. Just as quickly as the Phillies evened the score, the Astros did the same. After two singles and two strikeouts, the Astros had first and third with two outs. RBI singles by Rafael Landestoy and Jose Cruz brought the score to 7–7 going into the ninth. The offenses took a breather as Frank LaCorte held the Phillies scoreless in the top and Dick Ruthven silenced the Astros in the bottom.

The series had already become one of the most epic in the history of baseball, but it still lacked a resolution. Both teams were dog-tired and running out of tricks (and players). The Phillies were up first in the 10th inning. Del Unser, who had played hero earlier, doubled with one out. La Corte got the second out on a Trillo fly ball to center, but Garry Maddox got the most memorable hit of the series: a double to center that scored the eighth and eventual series-winning run. Ruthven came back out for his second inning of work, notching a 1-2-3 10th inning. The Phillies had done it: they had overcome tremendous adversity and insurmountable odds—they were in the World Series.

6 1980 World Series

The first game of the 1980 World Series, between the Philadelphia Phillies and Kansas City Royals, took place on October 14. The Phillies had won 91 regular season games and just barely got through a grueling five-game series against the Houston Astros in the Championship Series. With the weight of a near-100-year championship drought on their shoulders, the 1980 Phillies could not take anything for granted, even with the presence of the eventual Cy Young Award winner in Steve Carlton and NL Most Valuable Player in Mike Schmidt.

Meanwhile, the Royals were as threatening as any opponent the Phillies had faced to that point. Third baseman George Brett had one of the best regular seasons in the modern era (he finished with a .390 batting average and an OPS of 1.118!), and Dan Quisenberry appeared to be on his way to a long and prosperous career as a closer. If the Phillies were to vanquish the Royals, it would take everything in their power to do so.

Game 1 was typical 1980 Phillies: fall behind, scratch and claw back to a lead, and hold on for dear life. They fell behind 4–0 after three innings on a pair of two-run home runs, but scored five in the bottom of the third when six consecutive batters reached base, punctuated by Bake McBride's incredible three-run home run to deep right field. The Phillies tacked on a couple more runs as starter Bob Walk settled down, notching three straight 1-2-3 innings in the fourth, fifth, and sixth innings. He tired in the eighth, serving up his third two-run homer of the game, before handing it off to Tug McGraw. Tugger made short work of the Royals in his two innings, giving the Phillies their first World Series game win since Game 1 of the 1915 Series against the Boston Red Sox.

In Game 2, the Phillies saved their rallying for late. Through six innings, the Phillies had a 2–1 lead as Royals starter Larry Gura matched Steve Carlton pitch-for-pitch. Carlton was uncharacteristically wild, allowing three of his six total walks in the seventh, with each eventually coming around to score. The Phillies were behind 4–2 after seven, requiring them to rally against Quisenberry for any hope of a 2–0 series lead. They did just that, singling and doubling their way to four eighth-inning runs, handing Ron Reed a two-run lead in the ninth, which was more than enough breathing room for the right-hander.

The Phillies were up two games to none. It couldn't be this easy, could it? Phillies fans, with years upon years of conditioning, braced for the worst as the series moved to Kansas City.

Game 3 was another pitchers' duel. Phillies starter Dick Ruthven had the start of his life while the Royals limited the Phillies' offense with a combination of starter Rich Gale and relievers Renie Martin and Quisenberry. The score was tied 2–2 after six. Each time the Royals scored, the Phillies immediately answered back in the following inning, reaffirming the tie. The same happened in the seventh as an Amos Otis solo home run was answered by a Pete Rose RBI single. In a game destined for extra innings, it was 3–3 at the end of regulation.

Tugger was tired. He had thrown 92 innings in the regular season, his highest total in five years. Tack on an additional 10 innings in the postseason to this point, and you can understand why the lefty was running on empty. Still, the Phillies needed him to keep the score tied while they waited for a Royals mistake, so Tugger went in for the 10th inning. The Royals had runners on first and second with two outs. Tug had thrown 20 pitches and needed to get through Willie Aikens, who had been near-impossible to

Phillies closer Tug McGraw leaps into the air after the Kansas City Royals' Willie Wilson strikes out to end the game and give Philadelphia its first-ever World Series title. In the background is Series MVP Mike Schmidt.

retire. Ahead 2–1, Aikens singled to left-center, scoring Willie Wilson for the walk-off win at Kauffman Stadium.

Game 4 was forgettable for the Phillies. The Royals victimized Phillies starter Larry Christenson, jumping out to a 4–0 lead, one they would not relinquish. There was no magical Phillies rally, though sacrifice flies in the seventh and eighth made it interesting. The Phillies lost 5–3, and the series was even at two games apiece. One more game remained in Kansas City before returning to Philadelphia.

The Phillies mustered up another magical rally in Game 5. Behind 3–2 in the ninth, they would once again have to bowl over the Royals' closer to take a series lead. Mike Schmidt led off with a single and scored on Del Unser's double, a hit that later became iconic of the series. Unser would later score on Manny Trillo's infield single, a line drive that hit Quisenberry. McGraw came in for the save, still on fumes. Still shaky, Tugger walked three but finished the inning without allowing a run. With one win to go, the Phillies returned home.

Game 6 had the feeling you get after a *Rocky* montage, as if the previous five games were just practice for this sixth and hopefully final game. Nearly 66,000 people packed themselves into Veterans Stadium for the potential clinching game, as Steve Carlton squared off against Rich Gale. By comparison, Game 6 was easy. The Phillies held a 4–0 lead through seven. Tugger relieved Carlton in the eighth, and got through the inning with minimal damage. The dogged lefty worked a strenuous ninth, with his final confrontation coming against Willie Wilson with the bases loaded and holding a three-run lead. On the fourth pitch of the at-bat, Wilson swung and missed. Tug jumped off the mound, arms extended as high as they would go as the Phillies relieved 97 years of tension. They had done it after all the trials and tribulations: they won the World Series. See you in another 97 years, right?

7 Start a Phillies Blog

According to a study by Forrester Research from December 2010, Americans now spend as much time on the Internet as they do watching television. The Internet has been a big part of American culture for the past decade, and it is no different within the sports community.

Before the rise of the Internet, if sports fans wanted to have their opinions heard, they would have to call in to talk radio stations or send letters to the editor. The vast majority of people who made the effort would never get noticed. Now, on the Internet, anyone can start a blog at no cost whatsoever and immediately share with the world their thoughts on any subject. In a matter of minutes, your thoughts on the Phillies could reach thousands of other people.

There are countless communities within the blogosphere, but there is something special about the Phillies' blog community— there is something for everybody. If you like humor, you gravitate toward The Fightins (www.thefightins.com) and Zoo with Roy (www.zoowithroy.com). If you just want the news, game recaps, and a place to chat with other fans during games, Phillies Nation (philliesnation.com) has you covered. Or, if you need a dose of Sabermetric analysis, you stop by Crashburn Alley (crashburnalley.com—created by yours truly), Brotherly Glove (www.brotherlyglove.com), or The Good Phight (www.thegood-phight.com). The common denominator is that all of these blogs work with each other rather than against each other for the good of the community.

While many bases are covered, there is always room for more. Every day, someone new joins the Phillies blogosphere, and everyone brings something unique to the table. No one can be turned away at the door.

The blogosphere is a meritocracy, meaning it does not matter in the least what your credentials are; your success and popularity as a blogger will be determined by what you can provide to the community. It is a truly unique experience, as you will work with like-minded people, whether it is debating a subject or collaborating on a project, or simply sharing thoughts on a game.

It is a truly engaging way to watch the game, and you meet people you never would have known about otherwise. Never before have fans watched the great game of baseball while having immediate interaction with other people. If you are a passionate Phillies fan with basic computer skills, start up a blog and put yourself out there. Your enjoyment of the Phillies will increase manyfold.

8 Connect to the Phillies on the Internet

If you are not one for large amounts of writing, perhaps blogging is not for you. You can still interact with the Phillies and other Phillies fans on the Internet, however. Most Americans are on Facebook, according to a study by Arbitron and Edison Research. Fifty-one percent of Americans over the age of 12 have a Facebook profile. That is a great place to start. During games, cheer for your favorite players and go crazy on Facebook when the Phillies make a dramatic comeback . You would be surprised how many other people are doing the same.

If you want to venture out of your already established social circle, Twitter is the place to go. Not only can you follow your favorite players and ask them questions directly, such as Vance Worley (@VANIMAL_49), you can follow beat writers for the latest news, bloggers for unique takes on the team, as well as other fans.

I have been on Twitter for more than two years now, and I could not imagine life without it. Almost every day, I am parked in front of my computer during a game screaming my online head off when Carlos Ruiz drives in a run or throws out a runner. Getting an immediate pulse for what the community is thinking is an incredible experience.

The community on Twitter is large and growing every day. Blogs, such as The Fightins, have organized tailgate parties at Phillies games through Twitter. Fans give away tickets they cannot use, or look to meet up with other fans at local bars. The possibilities are endless.

Just as with blogs, the Twittersphere is a meritocracy. You are not judged by who you are, but rather by what you can offer the community. Even if you are just nice to other people, you will have a bunch of followers in no time. No one can be turned away at the door, so there is absolutely nothing to lose. Go to Twitter.com, create an account, and check out the Tweeters listed in the sidebar.

9 Cliff Lee

Cliff Lee's career with the Cleveland Indians prior to 2008 can best be described as schizophrenic. At his best, he looked like ace material. At his worst, he could not harness his control problems. The lefty also dealt with injuries and a fan base that did not have the patience to wait for him to figure it out.

He persevered through it all, winning the AL Cy Young Award in 2008. There was no doubt the lefty, who finished 22–3 with a 2.54

Cliff Lee came to the Phillies in a trade in 2009 and pitched brilliantly in the second half of the regular season and all the way through to the World Series. The left-hander was traded for Roy Halladay in a three-team, multiplayer deal after the season, only to be reacquired prior to the 2011 season.

ERA, was the most dominant in the league that year. It was a tough time for the Indians, though. Lee was a year and a half away from free agency in the summer of '09, and the organization was going nowhere fast. The Phillies were a contending team looking for another ace after the Roy Halladay talks fell through with the Toronto Blue Jays. In a move that shocked everyone, GM Ruben Amaro sent four of the Phillies organization's top 10 prospects (per *Baseball America*) to the Indians for Lee and outfielder Ben Francisco.

Phillies fans immediately fell in love with their new lefty ace. He made his debut in red pinstripes on July 31 in San Francisco against the Giants, holding them to one run in nine impressive innings of work. Fans embraced his lackadaisical attitude and the speed at which he worked while toeing the rubber. Lee finished the regular season with a 3.39 ERA as a Phillie, helping his new team reach the postseason again to defend its title.

The way Lee pitched, one had to think he was tailor-made for the postseason. He opened Game 1 of the NLDS against the

Colorado Rockies with a one-run, nine-inning performance. He closed the series out in Game 4 with a quality start, and the Phillies moved on to the NLCS against the Los Angeles Dodgers. Lee took the bump in Game 3; the Dodgers had no chance. From the start, Lee was on the mark. He finished with 10 strikeouts and no walks, shutting the Dodgers out through eight innings on just three hits. It was one of the most dominant starts in a playoff game by a Phillies starter ever. The Phillies got through the NLCS in five games, returning to the World Series for a second consecutive year.

The pressure was on Lee as the Phillies opened Game 1 of the World Series in New York against the Yankees. The Phillies' new ace took his place on the pitcher's mound. From his mannerisms and demeanor, you'd have thought he was relaxing at home as opposed to pitching in a stadium holding 50,000 hostile fans in the most important series of the season.

Lee was unhittable from the start. He twirled a complete game, striking out another 10 batters with zero walks, while allowing just one unearned run. During the game, he made a play that forever endeared him to Phillies fans. In the bottom of the sixth with a runner on first and one out, Johnny Damon hit a pop-up back to the pitcher's mound. In such an important game, most pitchers would make certain that the ball didn't drop, but Lee nonchalantly stuck his glove out at the last second and snatched the ball like a frog catching a fly with its tongue. It was the baseball equivalent of saying "whatever." Lee was more interested in snapping his chewing gum than catching the ball.

The Phillies ended up losing the World Series and, just as quickly as he'd arrived, Lee was gone. In a surprising turn of events, Amaro made essentially a three-team trade that sent Lee to Seattle for a handful of prospects, while the Phillies acquired Halladay from the Blue Jays for a handful of their own prospects. Basically, the Phillies swapped aces and prospects. While fans were happy to get Halladay, they were sad it came at the expense of Lee.

Roy Halladay and Cliff Lee

Roy Halladay and teammate Cliff Lee have made some history recently with historically great strikeout-to-walk ratios. In 2010 Halladay struck out 219 hitters and walked just 30 in 250⅔ innings of work. Meanwhile, with both the Mariners and Rangers, Lee struck out 185 and walked a paltry 18 in 212⅓ innings.

Player	SO/BB	Year	Team
Bret Saberhagen	11.0	1994	NYM
Cliff Lee	10.3	2010	SEA/TEX
Curt Schilling	9.6	2002	ARI
Pedro Martinez	8.9	2000	BOS
Greg Maddux	8.9	1997	ATL
Pedro Martinez	8.5	1999	BOS
Ben Sheets	8.3	2004	MIL
Carlos Silva	7.9	2005	MIN
Greg Maddux	7.9	1995	ATL
Curt Schilling	7.5	2001	ARI
Roy Halladay	7.3	2010	PHI

(Source: Baseball-Reference.com)

Lee would return, however. Teams don't often acquire aces, let alone the same one twice. Lee was a free agent after the 2010 season and was expected to cash in with either the New York Yankees or Texas Rangers. The Phillies weren't on the radar. Rumors flew back and forth during the off-season, but the baseball world's jaw was left agape when, on December 15, the Phillies announced they had agreed with Lee on a five-year, $120 million contract.

The Lee signing gave the Phillies a four-headed-monster rotation with Halladay, Lee, Cole Hamels, and Roy Oswalt, each the ace of a rotation in his own right. Along with the hype, though, came great expectations—the Phillies would have to have a lot of success for the rotation to live up to what the fans expected of them.

Lee certainly did his part. He finished with career bests in innings pitched (232⅔), complete-game shutouts (six—three times his previous career-high of two), strikeout rate (9.2 per nine innings), and ERA (2.40). Two other pitchers, teammate Halladay and Los Angeles Dodgers ace Clayton Kershaw had equally great seasons, so Lee did not walk home with the NL Cy Young hardware.

10 Mike Schmidt

Few players personify an entire franchise the way Mike Schmidt personified the Phillies. Drafted in the second round of the 1971 amateur draft, Schmidt was an instant hit when given an every-day job in 1974. Along with leading the league with 36 home runs that year, he played stellar defense at third base. After six straight seasons in which the Phillies finished with fewer than 80 wins, Schmidt became the one who could take them to the promised land; all GM Paul Owens had to do was give him a decent supporting cast.

In 1976 the Phillies ended their 25-year postseason drought, in large part due to Schmidt leading the league in home runs for the third consecutive year. It was at this point that Phillies fans began to realize the unlimited potential of this team. The Phillies had turned into an offensive juggernaut, finishing in the top three in almost every major offensive category, including second in batting average, on-base percentage, and slugging percentage.

Unfortunately for the Phillies, they began to grow in the era of two powerhouse teams in the Cincinnati Reds and Los Angeles Dodgers. Despite Schmidt's impressive regular season production and the team's franchise-record 101 wins in both 1976 and 1977, they were quickly dispatched in the NLCS three years in a row. The "Big Red Machine" Reds swept them in '76, while the Dodgers beat the Phils 3–1 in both '77 and '78.

Schmidt began to receive criticism about his postseason production. His regular season numbers were incredible, but in 50 postseason plate appearances from 1976 to 1978, Schmidt mustered a lackluster .513 OPS with zero home runs and a paltry four runs batted in. Theories began to fly in from every angle: he was pressing too much; he wasn't clutch enough; he didn't have the capability of being a star player, and so on. In addition, Schmidt had a down year throughout all of 1978, finishing the regular season with a .798 OPS, more than 100 points below his normal level of production.

Although Schmidt rebounded in a big way in 1979, the Phillies regressed. Schmidt hit a career-best 45 home runs and won his fourth consecutive Gold Glove at third base, but the Phillies were a team in transition. They won 84 games and finished in fourth place in the NL East, 14 games behind the eventual world champion Pittsburgh Pirates. Manager Danny Ozark was fired at the end of August, when the Phillies had lost eight of their last nine games. Dallas Green was named the interim manager, and the Phillies were in store for some changes.

Nineteen eighty was the pinnacle for the Phillies, the result of many failed experiments and careful tinkering. For Schmidt, it was a career year—he set career-highs in home runs (48), RBIs (121), slugging percentage (.624), and OPS (1.004), leading the league in those categories, as well. He won the NL Most Valuable Player award unanimously, taking all 24 first-place votes. He was named to the All-Star Game for the fifth time, took home his fifth consecutive Gold Glove, and earned the Silver Slugger award at third base the first time the honor was given.

Most importantly, though, he showed up in the postseason. He posted an .820 OPS throughout the playoffs and hit two important home runs in the World Series: a fifth-inning, game-tying solo home run in Game 3 and a fourth-inning, go-ahead two-run home run in Game 5. As a surprise to no one, he took home World Series

Mike Schmidt launches a two-run home run in the fourth inning of Game 5 of the 1980 World Series off of Royals starter Larry Gura in Kansas City. Schmidt was later named Series MVP as the Phils took the title in six games.

MVP honors. Any concerns that followed Schmidt into the 1980 season were effectively erased with his production from April through October. Everything Schmidt was expected to be, he became; he took the Phillies to the promised land and back.

Schmidt would lead the Phillies to two more postseasons: to the first NLDS in 1981 (losing to the Montreal Expos) and to the World Series in 1983 (losing to the Baltimore Orioles). He would win the NL MVP award two additional times and take home five more Gold Gloves and Silver Sluggers and be named to seven more All-Star teams.

Unfortunately, Schmidt's story with the Phillies did not end on a high note. In 1988 Schmidt injured his rotator cuff and had to

Mike Schmidt

Mike Schmidt currently sits in 15th place on the all-time home run leader-board, but when he retired, he ranked much higher—seventh, to be exact. Since then, Barry Bonds, Ken Griffey Jr., Alex Rodriguez, Sammy Sosa, Jim Thome, Mark McGwire, Rafael Palmeiro, and Manny Ramirez have surpassed him. Here's a look at the leader-board when Schmidt retired.

Player	Home Runs
Hank Aaron	755
Babe Ruth	714
Willie Mays	660
Frank Robinson	586
Harmon Killebrew	573
Reggie Jackson	563
Mike Schmidt	548

(Source: Baseball-Reference.com)

miss the last month and a half of the season. The Phillies had become a cellar-dweller with just 65 wins, and the storybook era was drawing to an abrupt close. Schmidt regained his health to start the 1989 season, but he hit a wall in the month of May.

After an 0-for-3 game on May 28, his 14th hitless game in 19 May games, Schmidt announced his retirement in San Diego. Schmidt rarely showed emotion either on or off the field, but as he stood in front of the media, he broke down in tears as he publicly announced his retirement: "Some 18 years ago, I left Dayton, Ohio, with two very bad knees." He paused, choking up. "And I dreamed of becoming a major league baseball player. I thank God that dream came true." Schmidt broke down into tears, left the podium, and did not finish his speech—a surprisingly human moment for an otherwise superhuman player.

Not only had Schmidt become the best player in Phillies history, he had become the best third baseman in baseball history.

At the time Schmidt retired, his 548 career home runs was the seventh-most in the history of major league baseball.

In 1995, in his first year of eligibility, Schmidt was inducted into the National Baseball Hall of Fame with 96.5 percent of the vote, which was the most of any inductee at the time. Since retiring, Schmidt has tried his hand at broadcasting, managing a minor league team, and writing. In addition, he became a leader in raising money to fight cystic fibrosis with a fishing tournament known as Mike Schmidt Winner's Circle Invitational.

11 Jimmy Rollins' 2007 MVP Season

As a prospect progressing through the Phillies' minor league system in the late 1990s, Jimmy Rollins was never known for his offense. Scouts and prospect gurus regarded him as a defense-first shortstop who would be able to hit just enough to keep a job in the majors. Rollins' speed was expected to be a big part of his offensive package; home runs and RBIs were not.

That was the case as Rollins began his major league career. From 2001 to 2005, Rollins averaged fewer than 12 home runs per 700 plate appearances and was 7 percent worse than the National League average in OPS. However, he played outstanding defense at shortstop and stole 168 bases in that span. Rollins was progressing exactly as expected.

Something happened in 2006, however. While he was still the slick-fielding shortstop with blistering speed Phillies fans had grown to know and love, Rollins had developed incredible power. He hit 25 home runs that season, easily surpassing his previous career high of 14. Rollins also hit 45 doubles, another career high.

Jimmy Rollins smacks his 20th triple of the season against the Washington Nationals in Philadelphia on September 30, 2007, adding to his 30 homers, 38 doubles, and 41 stolen bases and punctuating his MVP season.

Somehow, some way, Rollins became one of the rare five-tool players in baseball, joining the likes of Carlos Beltran and Grady Sizemore. Even better, Rollins played at a position where it is and has always been difficult to find five-tool players. Could Rollins keep it up, though? Or was his 2006 season a fluke? To add to the excitement, Rollins proclaimed that the Phillies were "the team to beat," a direct challenge to the division rival New York Mets, who were one Yadier Molina home run away from going to the World Series in the previous season.

Rollins started off the 2007 season in style, hitting a home run on Opening Day off of John Smoltz of the Atlanta Braves. The trend would continue as he hit two more home runs in the first week and finished April with nine homers. Not only did he appear to be silencing the non-believers, but he was making good on his preseason boast.

Still, the skeptics remained, questioning the sustainability of Rollins' run. As the season moved through May, Rollins cooled off. In fact, Rollins didn't hit a single home run in May and went a total of 36 consecutive games without a homer before ending the skid on June 6. Fans had become frustrated with Rollins' schizophrenic offense, referring to him as "Good Jimmy" when he was on a hot streak and "Bad Jimmy" when on a cold streak.

Rollins seemed to flip a switch in July. Not only did he hit for prodigious power, he was getting on base frequently. At the end of July, Rollins had 26 doubles, 14 triples, 20 homers, and 19 stolen bases. Fans and analysts alike wondered if he could compile a few more triples, as he would be the third player with a 20/20/20/20 season in baseball history, joining Frank Schulte (1911) and Willie Mays (1957). That, no doubt, would place him in the conversation for the NL Most Valuable Player award.

While Rollins made a run for the MVP award, the Phillies were in serious contention for their first playoff berth since 1993. Entering August, the Phillies were three games behind the New

York Mets, sitting in second place in the NL East. Rollins' great season was timed perfectly with those of Chase Utley, Ryan Howard, Pat Burrell, and Cole Hamels. Rollins continued to hit in August, adding eight doubles, a triple, four homers, and eight stolen bases as the Phillies inched ever closer to first place in the division. Following a four-game sweep of the Mets at the end of August, the Phillies were two games behind with 29 games left to play.

As if the Mets were trying to help the Phillies end their playoff drought, they went on a skid through most of September. From September 11 to 28, they lost 13 of 19 games, relinquishing their hold on first place for the first time since May 13. During the same span of time, the Phillies won 13 of 19 games and took control of the division after game No. 160.

Rollins kept up his offensive game in September, seeking to join the exclusive 20/20/20/20 club. He sat on 19 triples entering the final day of the season. The Phillies had been keeping their eye on the scoreboard as the Florida Marlins were playing the Mets. If the Mets and Phillies both won, the division would be tied, and both teams would have had to play a tie-breaker in Philadelphia to determine the division winner.

Mets starter Tom Glavine imploded early, surrendering seven runs in one-third of an inning. The Phillies had the early and priceless knowledge that if they won, they were in the playoffs. They had increased their lead over the Nationals to 4–1 in the bottom of the sixth inning when Rollins strode to the plate to take what was his last at-bat of the regular season. He needed one triple for 20 and for entrance into the quadruple-double club.

Rollins worked a seven-pitch at-bat against Luis Ayala before lacing the eighth pitch down the right field line into the corner. Fans stood up and screamed, hoping that Rollins could take third base safely. He wheeled around second, sped toward third, and dove in safely for the milestone. Most importantly, the Phillies went on to win the game and the division, earning their first playoff berth in 14 years. The iconic moment is forever remembered with Brett Myers throwing his glove in the air and waiting to embrace catcher Chris Coste.

Although the Phillies were quickly swept out of the NLDS by the Colorado Rockies, that the Phillies made the postseason at all was considered a good first step for the organization. That was not forgotten among MVP voters from the Baseball Writers Association of America. Citing his 20/20/20/20 season, his 162 games played, and various franchise marks challenged and broken, the BBWAA awarded Rollins the MVP over Matt Holliday, Prince Fielder, and David Wright. Rollins received 16 first-place votes and 79 percent of the voting share. With the previous winner, Ryan Howard, the duo became the first teammates to win back-to-back MVP awards since Jeff Kent and Barry Bonds in 2000 and 2001.

20/20/20/20 Club

On the last day of the 2007 regular season, Jimmy Rollins joined the 20/20/20/20 club. The numbers refer to a player hitting at least 20 doubles, 20 triples, 20 home runs, and stealing at least 20 bases in the same season. Entering 2007, only two players were members, but Rollins and Detroit Tigers center fielder Curtis Granderson both joined Willie Mays and Frank Schulte in the club in 2007. Rollins went on to win the National League Most Valuable Player award, his 20/20/20/20 season no doubt playing a critical role. Rollins' great season helped the Phillies end a playoff drought going back to 1993, but they were unfortunately vanquished in the NLDS by the red-hot Colorado Rockies.

Player	Team	Year	2B	3B	HR	SB
Frank Schulte	CHC	1911	30	21	21	23
Willie Mays	NYG	1957	26	20	35	38
Curtis Granderson	DET	2007	38	23	23	26
Jimmy Rollins	**Phillies**	**2007**	**38**	**20**	**30**	**41**

12 Randy Wolf's Fireworks Display

Aside from his early successes on the pitcher's mound, Randy Wolf had built up a reputation as one of the rare pitchers who could handle himself in the batter's box. He had homered once in Triple A Scranton/Wilkes-Barre as a 22-year-old and once again in the majors at the age of 25. He was no Mike Hampton who, entering the 2004 season, had hit 12 home runs, but managers around the league took caution with the No. 8 hitter in the Phillies' lineup because Wolf was not an automatic out like so many other National League hurlers.

Wolf homered early in the 2004 season, on April 24 in a 7–0 rout of the Montreal Expos. But between then and mid-August, Wolf was silent with the bat. He pitched well, but elbow tendinitis forced him onto the disabled list after his June 2 start against the New York Mets. The Phillies, at the time, felt they had enough to compete for a playoff spot, especially coming off a disappointing 2003 season where their wild-card hopes were dashed in late September at the hands of the eventual world champion Florida Marlins.

Wolf figured to be an integral part of the playoff push the Phillies hoped to put together, but little did they know their crafty lefty would put on a show with his bat late in the season. Heading into an August 11 game against the Colorado Rockies at home, the offense had been sputtering, averaging less than 3.8 runs per game in the past 23 games. They had recently returned home from a tiring 13-game road trip that took them from Florida to Chicago to San Diego and, finally, Los Angeles. They hoped to recollect themselves on a 10-game homestand.

The Rockies were headed nowhere, entering the series at 49–62, in fourth place and 16½ games out of first place. They had swiped the first two games of the four-game series from the Phillies, taking advantage of a tired and under-performing Philadelphia bullpen.

In the third game of the four-game set, the Phillies took a 1–0 lead into the bottom of the third inning against Rockies starter Jason Jennings. Of the eight batters who had faced Jennings in the first two innings, only Bobby Abreu appeared to have Jennings squared up properly, as he drove in Jim Thome from first base with an RBI double to deep right-center.

Wolf led off the inning and worked the count against Jennings surprisingly well. He took a first-pitch called strike, followed by a ball to even the count. On the third pitch, Wolf ripped Jennings' offering to right field, depositing it in the stands for a solo home run. Excluding the two other home runs he hit previously in his career, he was the first Phillies pitcher to homer since Robert Person hit two on June 2, 2002.

From there, the floodgates opened. The Phillies scored three more runs in the inning on an RBI double from Placido Polanco and a two-run homer from Thome. Wolf figured in the scoring in the fourth inning, as well, reaching base on a well-struck single up the middle, then scoring on a two-run homer by Jimmy Rollins. The Rockies had touched Wolf up for four runs, though, so the game was still tense. The exhausted Phillies led 7–4 going into the bottom of the sixth.

The Rockies brought in Adam Bernero to keep the score close. To make matters worse, the Phillies hadn't been disciplined at the plate. Bernero was averaging nearly five walks per nine innings, but two of the first three hitters he faced swung at the first pitch, both flying out to center field. However, as Randy Wolf stepped to the plate, he had Jason Michaels on first base and an opportunity to pad his own lead.

Wolf, as he did before, worked the count well, earning a 3–0 count. He kept the bat on his shoulders as Bernero's fourth pitch crossed the plate for the first strike. Thinking Wolf would be taking again, Bernero grooved a batting practice fastball over the plate. Who could fault him? Ninety-nine percent of pitchers would be looking for the walk there. Wolf, representing the 1 percent, whipped the bat around and laced the ball over the right-field stands for his second home run of the game and the fourth of his career. The Phillies were up 9–4 and would go on to tack on six more runs for an easy 15–4 rout of the Rockies.

Wolf joined the aforementioned Person, as well as Randy Lerch, Larry Christenson, and Rick Wise, as the only Phillies pitchers since 1931 to homer twice in a game. The fireworks show from Wolf wasn't enough momentum for the Phillies, as they went on to lose their next seven games and eventually faded out of the playoff picture, but it was certainly one of the most memorable moments of the decade for the Phillies. Many National League pitchers go an entire career without coming close to homering; Wolf hit two legitimate homers in the span of three at-bats.

13 Robert Person Owns the Show

Before Randy Wolf, there was Robert Person. A 25th-round draft pick of the Cleveland Indians in 1989, Person spent time with the New York Mets and Toronto Blue Jays before being sent to the Phillies in exchange for reliever Paul Spoljaric. On the mound, Person showed glimmers of potential with bat-missing ability, but poor control contributed to a 5.16 ERA in his first four full years in the majors.

Even with the bat, Person wasn't impressive. In the minors, he hit zero homers and hit a meager .161. In his first six years in the majors, he never homered and hit .123. Somehow, in 2001, it started to click. He hit a solo home run on July 20 against the New York Mets, then added another solo shot to his résumé on September 1 against the Montreal Expos.

At the same time, he was starting to realize some of the potential the Phillies saw when they acquired him from the Jays. He posted a 3.63 ERA in 2000 and, although his ERA rose to 4.19 in 2001, Person lowered his walk rate significantly. As a team, the Phillies had been struggling amidst a youth movement, but with Person, the fans had someone with whom they could identify. Soon enough, a fan group called "Person's People" started showing up at Veterans Stadium for each of his starts.

Little did they know that June 2, 2002, would be the pinnacle of Person's career and little of it would have to do with his pitching. At the time, the Phillies had lost 12 of their last 17 games and looked to reverse their fortunes in the series finale against the Montreal Expos.

Expos starter Britt Reames struggled immensely, unable to find anything that could fool the Phillies' hitters. He would face only six Phillies, retiring just one of them, before being removed from the game. A double, infield pop-out, walk, three-run home run, and two more walks later, Rheames had allowed three runs and was on the hook for two more as Bruce Chen entered the game.

The bloodletting would continue. After Tomas Perez fouled out for the second out of the inning, the Expos intentionally walked Todd Pratt to bring Person to the plate. Person took a pitch out of the strike zone before ripping Chen's second offering over the fence in left field for a grand slam. After nine batters, the Phillies had scored a whopping seven runs.

It was just not the Expos' day as things got exponentially worse in the third inning. Chen sandwiched two walks around a single to load the bases with no outs. A two-run double by Abreu and a two-run single by Jeremy Giambi brought the Phillies to 14–1. Chen would sandwich a fly out around two more walks before being lifted for Masato Yoshii.

Person strode to the plate with the bases loaded for the second time in three innings, ready to take his third at-bat and second of the inning. With a 1–2 count, Person took a healthy cut at Yoshii's offering, sending the ball down the left-field line with home run distance, but it barely cut foul. Phillies fans in attendance for the game stood up and gave Person a brief standing ovation. Unfortunately, Person couldn't deliver, striking out swinging to end the inning.

Having just been activated from the disabled list, Person knew he wasn't going to be in the game long but had held the Expos in check through five innings. Manager Larry Bowa let Person know his day was done, but that he was not going to hit for him if his turn in the lineup came around. As fate would have it, the Phillies tagged Yoshii for two singles, enough to bring Person to the plate with runners on the corners with one out.

Person was clearly out to make history, as he swung at four of the first five pitches he saw from Yoshii. As what seemed to be par for the course, at least for the day, Yoshii threw a cookie to Person, who powered the pitch into the seats in left field for his second home run of the day. The Phillies were up 17–1 and their pitcher, their nine-hole hitter, was responsible for seven of them. Person's seven RBIs set a franchise record for a pitcher. Going all the way back to 1919, only three pitchers have driven in seven runs or more in a game: Person and Vic Raschi (1953) with seven, and Tony Cloninger with nine (1966).

Offensive achievements aside, Person also finished the day with a pitching line of five innings pitched, three hits, one unearned run, four walks, and five strikeouts. Not bad for his first start back from the disabled list, but it was the least interesting news of the day. While Person didn't hit his home runs in high-pressure situations, they were certainly impressive nonetheless and represent a feat unlikely to be seen again in our lifetimes.

Unfortunately, Person's story didn't end happily. He finished the 2002 season with a 5.44 ERA and made only seven starts the following year, the last we saw of him in the major leagues. Nevertheless, he gave the Phillies something—and someone—to be excited about after many years of dormancy following the magical 1993 season.

14 Bobby Abreu's 2005 Home Run Derby

To help promote Major League Baseball's new global baseball tournament called the World Baseball Classic, the All-Star Game festivities were altered to create a more worldly atmosphere. The Home Run Derby, held in Detroit's Comerica Park, had each of its eight contestants from different parts of the world.

In previous seasons, Abreu was never asked to compete. That was mostly because he was never among the most prolific power hitters in baseball, despite hitting 25 or more home runs in three of his previous five seasons. Rather, Abreu was thought of more as a contact hitter due to his finishing with a .300 or better batting average in six of his seven full seasons entering 2005. However, among representatives from Venezuela, few could argue with Abreu's selection.

Other contestants included Ivan "Pudge" Rodriguez from Puerto Rico, Jason Bay from Canada, Carlos Lee from Panama, Mark Teixeira from the United States, David Ortiz from the Dominican Republic, Andruw Jones from Curaçao, and Hee-Seop Choi from South Korea. Clearly, Abreu would be in for a fight if he wanted to advance to the second round of the tournament, let alone win it.

With bullpen coach Ramon Henderson lobbing batting practice fastballs, Abreu took a healthy cut and hit a home run deep into the right-field seats for his first home run of the Derby. After a few more cuts, Abreu stood with three homers and three outs. The general thought was that, if he got hot, he might eke his way into double digits. Then he had 10 homers with six outs and was at least assured of a spot in the second round. Surely, he wouldn't break Miguel Tejada's record of 15 homers in the first round, set the previous year.

Several minutes later, Abreu had 14 homers and seven outs, just one long ball away from tying the Derby record. Henderson threw the most batting-practice-ish fastball there ever was, and Abreu launched it into the second deck at Comerica, above the railing adorned with Pepsi signs. The crowd roared, causing Abreu to step back and humbly smile at the fans in attendance. Other Venezuelan All-Stars holding their country's flags yelled words of encouragement for their fellow countryman.

Abreu wasted no time in setting the new record, hitting his 16th homer on his next swing. From there, the Phillies' right fielder went on a tear, smashing an additional eight home runs before logging his 10th out. Few of them were wall-scrapers, many of them reaching distances of 425 feet and beyond.

Another magic moment came after smoking his 21st home run out to deep center field: Abreu broke his bat. He held the bat up to a nearby TV camera to show where the bat split, saying he hit the ball "too hard." Jimmy Rollins then came out with two new bats and pretended to test each one for quality, holding each one up to his ear and smacking it, as if he could tell how good a bat was by the sound it emitted. As if his résumé weren't good enough going in, Abreu officially put himself on the map with his performance in the first round of the 2005 Home Run Derby, earning a legion of new fans outside of Philadelphia.

Going into the second round, Abreu's goal was simply to make sure he advanced to the finals. The worry was that he sapped too much of his energy hitting too many first-round home runs, which

Bobby Abreu, one of the most productive hitters in Phillies history, set new records in winning the 2005 Home Run Derby during the All-Star break in Detroit, hitting 24 dingers in the first round and 41 overall.

don't carry over into the semifinals. In addition, between the time Abreu made his last out in the first round and when he took his first cut in the semis, over an hour had passed, giving some the added concern that he had gone cold or lost his momentum. Abreu wasn't quite as impressive in his next set, but his six homers were just good enough for second out of the four remaining sluggers, moving him into the finals with Pudge Rodriguez.

Abreu had the honor of going first ahead of Rodriguez, so he could put a lot of pressure on the Tigers catcher by taking a big lead. Phillies fans were biting their nails as Abreu made six outs and had just three home runs, but he went on a hot streak at that point. He hit six home runs in a row and finished the final round with 11, forcing Pudge to hit 12 or lose the tournament. Pudge could only muster up five home runs, and the Phillies' starting All-Star was crowned the champion.

As Abreu received his trophy, Johan Santana—then the best pitcher in major league baseball—stood behind him waving the

Venezuelan flag. In the post-derby interview with ESPN's Sam Ryan, Abreu said, "We [are] all together, we stay together," adding "we [will] never be alone."

15 Ryan Howard at the 2006 Home Run Derby

By the time the 2006 Home Run Derby came around, Ryan Howard was already kind of a big deal. Howard, at the time, was an über-prospect who had been road-blocked by Jim Thome at first base. The Phillies traded Thome after Howard earned 2005 National League Rookie of the Year honors with 22 home runs in little more than 300 at-bats. Few players can replace Thome, but Howard was one of them.

It was no surprise to see him among the contestants at Pittsburgh's PNC Park on July 10, 2006. He had 28 homers at the All-Star break and was overall having an MVP-caliber season; it would have been a travesty if Howard had not been invited. The Phillies first baseman was joined by David Wright, Miguel Cabrera, David Ortiz, Jermaine Dye, Miguel Tejada, Lance Berkman, and Troy Glaus.

Bobby Abreu, the Phillies' representative in the 2005 Derby, left Howard with a high bar to reach. Abreu set records with 24 first-round homers and 41 overall, along with taking home the trophy. But, if anyone could steal the show, it was Howard. After all, he had brought along Phillies bullpen coach Ramon Henderson to feed him batting-practice fastballs, which Henderson had done the previous year for Abreu. If Howard could win, it would be the first time a team won back-to-back derbies since Ken Griffey Jr. of the Seattle Mariners won in 1998 and 1999.

In the first round, Howard had the unfortunate job of hitting last among all eight contestants, meaning he had the added pressure of knowing exactly how many homers he needed to hit to advance. Through eight outs, Howard had just two home runs, and it looked like a disappointing appearance for the young slugger. However, he turned it on just in time to finish the round with eight home runs. One of his home runs, measured at 471 feet, cleared the seats in right field entirely and landed in the Allegheny River.

Howard eked into the second round, trailing David Wright, David Ortiz, and Miguel Cabrera with 16, 10, and nine, respectively. Wright, with 16 homers, quickly became the star of the contest, but he lost steam just as fast. In the second round, Wright could only muster two home runs, opening the door for Howard.

While other players soon tired, Howard seemed to get better the more he swung. He finished up his turn with four home runs in five swings, good for 10 dingers overall and giving him 18 total, tied with Wright. As a result, Howard and Wright were the finalists competing for the Home Run Derby hardware.

Wright hit just four homers in the final round. As long as Howard could hit five home runs, he would win the tournament. Howard needed only five of his 10 available outs to reach the summit, his final home run smacking against a "Hit It Here 500 Flights" sign that won a prize for a lucky fan in attendance at PNC Park. Howard did not bother to watch the flight of his final home run, instead choosing to celebrate with his son, Darian.

While the Derby doesn't help a team win a World Series, it was important for the Phillies, who were on the road to respectability. If Howard winning the ROY award the previous year didn't do it, winning the 2006 Derby certainly made him a nationwide celebrity. Of course, that would become a fact after the season, when Howard won NL MVP honors with 58 home runs and 149 RBIs.

Howard would go on to participate in the '07 and '09 Derbies, but did not have as much success. In '07 he failed to make it out of the first round with three homers; in '09 he made it to the semifinals but was narrowly bumped out by Prince Fielder and Nelson

Cruz. As he is still among the premier power hitters in baseball, Howard could yet win another Derby. For now, everyone still remembers the legend of the '06 Derby.

16 Brad Lidge's Perfect Season

GM Pat Gillick got serious about the bullpen as he was putting together his team for the '08 season. Starter-turned-reliever Brett Myers was going back into the starting rotation, so Gillick needed to strengthen the bullpen as the Phillies began their quest to reach the postseason again. On November 7, 2007, it was announced that the Phillies had reached an agreement with the Houston Astros that would bring closer Brad Lidge and utility infielder Eric Bruntlett to Philadelphia in exchange for reliever Geoff Geary, outfield prospect Michael Bourn, and infield prospect Mike Costanzo.

Lidge had found a lot of success in Houston, even helping them reach the World Series in 2005. Overall, he posted a 3.30 ERA with the Astros and notched one of the highest strikeout rates in history for a reliever, averaging 12.6 strikeouts per nine innings. His mid-90s fastball helped set up his devastating slider that could be put anywhere—even in the dirt, intentionally.

Lidge gave the Phillies' bullpen a legitimate ninth-inning weapon. As long as they could get to the ninth with a lead, the Phillies felt strong. Of course, they had to fill in around the edges and did so all season long, adding mid-season acquisitions J.C. Romero and Scott Eyre to a bullpen that already included Chad Durbin, Ryan Madson, and Clay Condrey.

At the time, the Phillies were typically slow starters, so Lidge did not get a chance to earn a save until the team's seventh game of the season on April 7, when they were in Cincinnati to play the

Reds. In his inning of work, Lidge allowed two base runners via walk, but struck out one and notched the save, anyway. It was save No. 1 of what would be 41 historic regular season saves.

Lidge quickly became a fan favorite in Philadelphia as he did not allow an earned run until game No. 40 of the regular season, played on May 13 against the Atlanta Braves—and Lidge still got the save, his 10th. His only adversity came in July, when he posted a 5.14 ERA for the month, but still did not blow any saves. Entering August, he was 26-for-26 in save opportunities with a 2.15 ERA.

The Phillies, meanwhile, felt good about their postseason chances. They took control of first place at the end of July and needed to keep their foot on the gas as the regular season waned. Lidge was an important part of the Phillies' success. The Phillies finished out the season winning 17 of 25 games. Meanwhile, Lidge posted a 0.71 ERA in the final month and converted each of his final eight save opportunities, giving him 41 total and a 100 percent success rate on the season. It was the first time a reliever had earned 30-plus saves with a perfect success rate since Eric Gagne did so in 2003 with the Los Angeles Dodgers.

Lidge's success carried into the postseason. He saved the first two games of the NLDS against the Milwaukee Brewers and three of the Phillies' four wins in the NLCS against the Dodgers. Most importantly, though, he got the Phillies off on the right foot in the World Series with a perfect ninth inning against the Tampa Bay Rays in Game 1. He became forever embedded in Phillies history by saving the fifth and final game with a strikeout of Eric Hinske. Lidge dropped to his knees and held out his arms, waiting to be embraced by catcher Carlos Ruiz. As the Phillies won the World Series, Lidge also clinched a true perfect season, converting 48 of 48 save opportunities. Not only was Lidge's 2008 the best ever by a Phillies reliever, it easily ranked among the best in baseball history.

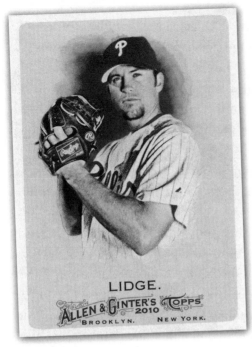

Closer Brad Lidge will always be loved in Philadelphia for his perfect 48-for-48 season in 2008, which helped the Phillies reach and win the World Series that year.

Since then, Lidge has not been able to match his success and he has been demoted in the Phillies' bullpen. Ryan Madson took over the closer's role late in the 2009 season and quickly became a dominating force in the National League. Still, any reliever who passes through Philadelphia will be trying to live up to the extremely high standards Brad Lidge set in 2008 en route to the franchise's second championship in nearly 130 years of existence.

17 Pitcher in the Outfield

On August 24, 2010, the Phillies and Astros played what all assumed to be your typical run-of-the-mill regular season game between a major league superpower and a perennial underachiever. Bud Norris opposed Cole Hamels, both contributing to a pitchers' duel. Hamels allowed two runs on a fourth-inning Carlos Lee home run; Norris allowed one run on a sixth-inning RBI double by Raul Ibanez.

The Phillies entered the ninth inning behind one run and facing reliever Wilton Lopez. Quickly, Carlos Ruiz and pinch-hitter Mike Sweeney were retired on weak ground-outs to shortstop. These games happen, sometimes you lose to inferior teams—such is life during a grueling 162-game schedule. That was the rationalization, anyway, as the Phillies' chances of winning dwindled.

Jimmy Rollins had other things on his mind. Lopez struggled to find the strike zone, falling behind 3–1. Catcher Humberto Quintero set up on the outside corner, but Lopez missed his spot, lobbed a batting practice fastball on the inside corner to Rollins, who took his traditionally short swing and drove the ball over the right field fence to tie the game. The crowd, up to that point, had been lethargic despite the largest sellout of the season on Carlos Ruiz Bobblehead Night. Rollins' home run resuscitated the crowd, and electricity filled Citizens Bank Park once again.

The score would remain tied at 2 going into the 14th inning. With two outs in the bottom of the 14th, however, the Phillies began to mount a two-out rally with the middle of the lineup. Placido Polanco had singled to right field, and Chase Utley drew a walk, putting pressure on reliever Mark Melancon with the Phillies' most-feared hitter up at the plate.

Howard fouled off Melancon's first offering. The second pitch, a slider in the dirt, tempted the slugger but he checked his swing. The appeal went to the third-base umpire, a minor league fill-in named Scott Barry, who ruled that Howard had swung. Howard put his hands on his hips in disbelief. Barry returned the favor, putting his hands on his own hips, mocking Howard. Howard was furious, pleading his case to home-plate umpire Greg Gibson to no avail.

Howard took a ball to bring the count to 1–2. Melancon threw another slider in the dirt, equally as tempting as his second pitch, getting Howard to check swing again. The appeal went to Barry, who immediately decreed that Howard had swung, and threw Howard out of the game before he could even put his arm down after the strike "fist-pump," glaring at Howard all the while.

With the inning over, Howard wanted to let Barry know how he felt, so he took off his helmet and strode toward Barry as only an angry 6'4", 240-pound man can do. Gibson walked along with him attempting to restrain him, but Howard started to trot to create some distance. As he closed in on Barry, third-base coach Sam Perlozzo, Polanco, and Utley teamed up to create a gate between the angry player and the angry umpire. They succeeded, and the worst Howard was able to do was shout some choice words and direct some angry hand gestures Barry's way. All the while, Barry stood there, arms folded with the smuggest of smug looks on his face.

With Howard ejected, the Phillies had no other position players to take Howard's spot. It was unfortunate timing, as back-up catcher Brian Schneider was double-switched into the game and had led off the bottom of the 14th. Manager Charlie Manuel moved Ibanez from left field to first base, and Roy Oswalt took Howard's place in the batting order and went out to left field.

Fans went crazy with laughter and cheer as the pitcher trotted out to take his position in left. Oswalt, typically humble, couldn't help but enjoy the situation in which he found himself. The legend in baseball goes that, if you are replacing someone in the field, the ball typically finds you quickly. Such was the case for Oswalt, who was immediately tested when leadoff hitter Jason Castro weakly hit a David Herndon sinker to left field on the fly. Oswalt lined up the ball, settled under it, and made the catch.

Of the 45,000-plus still in attendance, all rose to give Oswalt a standing ovation. As the TV cameras on the Phillies broadcast zoomed in on Oswalt, he cracked a smile as only an introverted farm boy from Mississippi could, a memory that still makes Phillies fans break down in laughter. The top of the 15th ended with no runs scoring, despite the pitcher in left field. Unfortunately, though, Herndon broke down in the 16th, allowing two runs for a 4–2 Astros lead—none of it Oswalt's fault, of course.

The controversial ejection of Howard played a vital role in the Phillies' offensive shortcomings as they tried to rally in the bottom of the 16th. Schneider and Rollins both made quick outs, but Polanco walked and Utley was walked intentionally to bring up Oswalt in the No. 4 spot in the batting order—Howard's spot. Unsurprisingly, Oswalt grounded out weakly to third base to end the inning and the game.

More than a year has gone by since that game, and fans still refer to it as "the Scott Barry game" or "the game where Ryan Howard freaked out." Most couldn't tell you who won or lost, but it is remembered all the same.

18 Eat a Cheesesteak at Pat's or Geno's

Watch any national broadcast of a Phillies game at Citizens Bank Park and you can bet on being inundated with cheesesteak trivia once every five minutes. Just as New York is known as "the city that never sleeps," Philadelphia is known for being the breeding ground for quality cheesesteaks.

The label is not without merit. Philadelphians just know how to make cheesesteaks, an art crafted to perfection after many, many years. The two places most well known for cheesesteaks are Pat's and Geno's, located opposite each other at the intersection of Passyunk Avenue, just a 10-minute drive from the Phillies' ballpark.

Passersby will typically notice Geno's first, particularly at night, as its signs are in bright neon above the shop. Founded by the late Joey Vento in 1966, Geno's became a direct competitor of Pat's, but both companies have benefited more from the rivalry than they would without it.

Unlike Pat's, Geno's became politically active, showing support for slain police officer Daniel Faulkner and the death sentence of Mumia Abu-Jamal. Pictures of fallen officers are posted on the shop windows. In 2006, when immigration was a hot-button political issue, a sign was posted on the shop window reading, "This Is AMERICA: WHEN ORDERING Please SPEAK ENGLISH." Vento's activism sparked a heated controversy, resulting in court hearings and even an appearance for Vento on Fox News, where he spoke with host Neil Cavuto.

Comparatively, Pat's is tame. Founded in 1930 as a hot dog shop by brothers Pat and Henry Olivieri, Pat's began selling cheesesteaks in 1933. The legend goes that the brothers were bored at lunch and wanted to experiment with something new. They went to the market for ingredients, cooked themselves some lunch, and thus the cheesesteak was born. Allegedly, they sold the first cheesesteak to a cab driver for 10¢. Pat's eats up the Philadelphia accent stereotype, insisting that customers order their sandwiches simply by stating the name of the cheese they would like and whether or not they would like onions on their sandwich. For instance, if you wanted Cheez-Whiz but no onions, you would say, "Whiz witout"—the *h* intentionally omitted in "without."

Pat's and Geno's are both affordable, at about $7 for a cheesesteak. On a Friday or Saturday night, lines typically wrap around the shop, spanning as many as 50 people, even in cold or inclement weather. Many Philadelphians are such cheesesteak aficionados that they have moved on from Pat's and Geno's, feeling that they cater too much to a tourist clientele. Every Philadelphian has his or her favorite place, rating higher than Pat's and Geno's. Ultimately, every place has its own style. With enough "experiments," you too can find your own niche in the cheesesteak world, so try it all.

19 Fans in Philly Are Good People

Despite what you may have heard, most fans of Philadelphia sports teams are good people. They are loyal, hard-working people who try not to ruffle any feathers. Over the years, though, Philadelphia has gained a reputation as a hotbed for malcontent fans, a very select minority of people that has been used to illustrate the public at large.

Ask any non-Philly fan, especially those in New York, and they will happily read you a list of all of the bad things fans have done in the past. From throwing snowballs at a fake Santa Claus, to booing Michael Irvin's spinal cord injury, to throwing batteries at J.D. Drew, to fans vomiting on each other, they have the goods on us. After all, why do you think Veterans Stadium needed an in-house court and jail?

As with anything, using the exceptions to prove the rule is always faulty reasoning. Worse incidents have occurred in other cities, but their sports fans have never garnered the negative reputation that Philly fans have. For example, on June 28, 1987, at County Stadium, the Brewers hosted the Toronto Blue Jays. In the seventh inning, a fan threw a cherry bomb on the field, interrupting the game. The offender was arrested by the ninth inning. Similarly, in 2003 a fan at an Oakland A's game threw a cherry bomb from the upper deck. In September 2002 two fans at Comiskey Park in Chicago ran onto the field and attacked Kansas City Royals first-base coach Tom Gamboa. Fortunately, Gamboa escaped with only minor cuts and the two fans were quickly dealt with and punished for their crime. In April 2003, during a game between the Texas Rangers and Oakland A's, a fan threw a cell phone at Rangers outfielder Carl Everett from the second deck of

Oakland Coliseum. The phone hit Everett in the back of the head. The fan was charged with assault with a deadly weapon and was held on $15,000 bail.

Without running through a list of every incident that has occurred outside of Philadelphia, suffice it to say that there are bad apples in every bunch, and to single out Philadelphians for their bad apples is short-sighted. As a result of this misappropriated reputation, people avoid attending sporting events in Philadelphia for fear of their safety. If they do take the leap and show up at Citizens Bank Park or Lincoln Financial Field, they show up in regular clothing rather than in team attire, fearing that overt support of an opposing team is enough of a trigger for violence against them.

Recently, as a result of the Phillies' success and the rapidly growing fan base, fans have been flocking to Washington, D.C., for road games when the Phillies play the Nationals. To this date, there have been no reports of egregiously rowdy behavior on the part of Phillies fans, and any unique behavior qualities of the Phillies-heavy crowds do not disappear when other teams come in to play.

Ultimately, the reputation of Philly fans is completely undeserved and is only exacerbated by national writers looking for a headline, and by opposing fans looking for a reason to trash-talk other fans. If you are a fan of Philadelphia sports teams, show others you are not as the media has depicted you: be kind, courteous, and welcoming when you are at the ballpark.

20 Shane Victorino Gets Doused by Cubs Fans

On August 12, 2009, the defending World Series–champion Phillies were in Chicago to play the second game of a three-game set with the Cubs. They had taken the first game by the score of

4–3 in 12 innings. Center fielder Shane Victorino went 0-for-4 and did not play any important role in the final outcome of the game.

Why is that an important thing to know? In the bottom of the fifth inning, with the Cubs down 12–2 with the bases loaded against Phillies starter Pedro Martinez, Cubs third baseman Jake Fox hit a fly ball to deep center field. Victorino, who became a household name when he won the All-Star Game Final Vote for the National League a month prior, ranged back to make what appeared to be an easy catch. He stepped on to the warning track, put his glove up, and prepared to make the grab.

At the time the ball landed in his glove, beer rained down on him and a plastic cup fell to the ground. Victorino quickly looked up to see what was the cause of his shower, then alertly relayed the ball back to the infield. The Cubs scored a run on the play and still threatened with runners on the corners with two outs. More importantly, Victorino was fine following the incident.

Left fielder Raul Ibanez, who had sprinted toward Victorino to back up the play, pointed up at the stands, presumably to identify the culprit. Unfortunately, the wrong person was grabbed and locked up in the stadium's security area. The real offender, a 21-year-old named John Macchione, turned himself in later and was charged with two misdemeanor counts, one count of battery, and one count of illegal conduct within a sports facility.

Surprisingly, Victorino was very positive despite being the very undeserving recipient of a beer shower. "I think he needs to be held accountable. But for the most part, I just see it as the guy thought it was fun. It is what it is. It didn't cost me in any way and it didn't hurt me in any way. It's part of the ballgame," he said.

As mentioned in the previous chapter, there have been some incredibly dangerous antics pulled off at ballparks over the years, so it was fortunate that the extent of the tomfoolery was a doused uniform. It was, however, another incident that sparked the age-old ballpark security debate.

The Phillies went on to win the game 12–5 and also took the final game of the series for the sweep. The Cubs finished at 83–79, 7½ games behind the division-winning St. Louis Cardinals in the NL Central, so it is quite possible that Macchione was acting out of frustration. After all, the Cubs had lost five of six entering the night and were beginning to fade away in the division. The Phillies were heading in the exact opposite direction as they would go on to win 11 of 13 games from August 11 to 24.

Thankfully, Phillies players were not made the target of any more fan outrage, despite their immense success since 2007. Victorino earned a spot on the NL All-Star roster for the second time in 2011 and has not had to worry about plastic cups of beer being tossed at him while he attempts to catch fly balls.

21 J.D. Drew Spurns the Phillies

Ask baseball fans outside of Philadelphia about outfielder J.D. Drew and you will get a shoulder shrug. They may tell you he never lived up to expectations or that injuries ravaged a once-promising career. Ask fans in Philadelphia about him and you will get a completely different story.

J.D. Drew first entered the amateur draft in 1994 as an 18-year-old. The San Francisco Giants selected him in the 20th round, but he did not sign, choosing instead to attend college at Florida State University. As a college baseball player, Drew flourished, finishing his career with a trophy case full of honors, including becoming a member of Team USA in the 1996 Olympics, winning the 1997 Dick Howser Trophy (the Heisman Trophy of college baseball), and earning 1997 *Sporting News* Player of the Year. He entered the 1997 amateur draft again with agent Scott Boras. The Phillies, well on their way to another losing season, were very interested in Drew as an impact player to get them back on the road to respectability. Boras, however, warned the Phillies—and the rest of baseball—that Drew would not sign for less than $10 million. That was then, and still is now, an extremely large amount of money for an unproven player. By comparison, Gerrit Cole, the No. 1 overall pick in the 2011 amateur draft, received $8.5 million from the Pittsburgh Pirates.

Nevertheless, the Phillies, under general manager Ed Wade, drafted Drew thinking they could drive down his price. They offered him $2.05 million, about one-fifth of what Drew and Boras expected. They refused the offer. Boras spoke to a *Philadelphia Inquirer* reporter about the offer, saying, "[Drew] doesn't want to work for people paying dramatically less than what other teams on the market were willing to pay."

Negotiations reached a standstill. Boras guided Drew to the St. Paul Saints of the independent Northern League. Drew would play out the year there and, Boras assumed, would become a free agent a week before the 1998 draft. Thus began a historic court battle in which Boras fought Major League Baseball for his client's employment rights. Eventually, arbitrator Dana Eischen ruled that, because Drew wasn't a member of the MLBPA, his rights weren't subject to arbitration. Thus, Drew was forced to enter the 1998 amateur draft, as opposed to being able to choose his employer at his price.

In 1998 Drew was chosen in the first round, fifth overall, by the St. Louis Cardinals. He began his major league career the same year after briefly cutting through minor league pitching like a hot knife through butter. He made his debut on September 8, the same night Mark McGwire broke Roger Maris' single-season home run record.

Phillies fans, however, remained bitter, feeling as though they were cheated as a result of Drew's greed. When he played in

Philadelphia for the first time on August 10, 1999, he was booed loudly and was pelted with D-batteries by two fans. As Drew's career went on, Philadelphia's passionate hatred of Drew remained.

Drew found himself on the disabled list in each of his five full seasons in St. Louis and drew the ire of manager Tony LaRussa. In the off-season following the 2003 season, he was traded to the Atlanta Braves, with whom he accrued 518 at-bats in the '04 season. That was then and still is now a career-high. As his career waned, injuries continued to be a problem and made him toxic to all but the richest teams.

In December 2004 the Dodgers signed him to a five-year, $55 million contract. The contract included an escape clause that allowed Drew to opt out of the contract and become a free agent after two years. Naturally, Drew exercised his option and signed with the Boston Red Sox in January 2007 to a deal worth $70 million over five years.

From 2008 to 2011, Drew averaged fewer than 400 at-bats per season, becoming an afterthought in baseball conversations. People no longer talked about the über-prospect from Florida State with the world at his fingertips, but instead referred to him with a sense of disappointment, wondering what could have been if he had played his cards differently.

To this day, Drew is still reviled in Philadelphia. Hell hath no fury like Philadelphia scorned.

22 Phillies Lend a Helping Hand in Colorado

Community service is a big part of being a major league baseball player. As public figures, players can help the less fortunate by donating their own money, raising money with the general public, or using their off-the-field talents for the greater good. By and large, this is a calculated effort by both players and their teams to establish a good relationship with their paying customers. What the Phillies did on July 8, 2007, was a completely unplanned, spontaneous act of good will.

The Phillies were at Coors Field in Colorado, wrapping up a three-game series with the Rockies. They had dropped the previous two games and were in the midst of a dry spell, having lost seven of their previous nine games. Forecasts called for heavy winds and rain, but the two teams hoped to get their game in before the brunt of the storm rolled through. After six innings, the Phillies were up 5–4, but time was running out—the storm was on its way.

The umpires called the grounds crew out to place the tarp on the infield in the seventh inning. Rain was falling at a brisk pace and the wind was whipping violently, making the job of getting the tarp rolled out and secured on top of the infield monumentally more difficult. With one strong gust of wind, Rockies groundskeeper Keros Johnson was trapped under the tarp. Members of the Phillies dugout, including Shane Victorino, Ryan Howard, Michael Bourn, and Adam Eaton, rushed out to rescue Johnson and help get the tarp down safe and secure.

Within minutes, the job was done, and the Phillies walked off the field to a standing ovation from the Rockies fans who had stayed in the rain to watch the Phillies' act of good citizenship. When asked about the event afterward, Eaton remarked, "One guy flew 10 feet in the air. We were just hoping they're not hurt."

Head groundskeeper Mark Razum was surprised both at the strength of the wind and by the unexpected help he received. "The wind was so strong, we couldn't hold it," Razum said. "When it draped over the guys, I was worried that somebody might suffocate. It was really cool the Phillies came out and gave us a hand."

After play resumed, Shane Victorino hit a two-run home run to boost the Phillies' lead to three runs, at 7–4. They would go on to win 8–4, but the results of the series were an afterthought as the talk centered around the rain delay.

Ironically enough, the Rockies would be the Phillies' undoing in the playoffs, the Phillies' first appearance there since 1993. As the Phillies made their exit from the playoffs, the theory of karma was disproven.

23 Ryan Howard Reaches New Heights

Ryan Howard has hit a lot of home runs in his career, many of them of the aesthetically impressive variety. None can match the one Howard hit off of New York Yankees starter Mike Mussina on June 20, 2006.

The Yankees were in Philadelphia for a three-game interleague series. Mussina took the bump for the Yankees while Cory Lidle toed the slab for the Phillies. Mussina found himself in trouble early, allowing two base runners on a single, a stolen base, and a walk after retiring the first two batters he faced. On the first pitch, Mussina threw a fastball he intended to start inside and tail toward the plate, but he missed his location.

Howard took his Ruthian cut and launched the ball down the right-field line. Unlike many other home runs hit at Citizens Bank Park, then considered a very homer-friendly park, this ball had incredible loft. When it landed, it had reached the third deck, the first time in the park's three-year history a ball had ever been put at that level.

The site HitTrackerOnline.com measured the impact at 390 feet from home plate and estimates that if the ball had been allowed to follow its full trajectory, it would have landed 437 feet away. Howard has since hit home runs measuring nearly 500 feet, but this

After belting two homers off of New York Yankees starter Mike Mussina in the first and fourth innings, Ryan Howard hits a two-run triple off of Mike Myers in the seventh on June 20, 2006, in Philadelphia. In only his second full major league season, Howard would go on to win NL MVP honors in 2006.

home run has and always will register in the memories of Phillies fans. In fact, the Phillies commemorated the home run by painting a white *H* on the seat the ball hit in the third deck.

Later asked about his homer, Howard replied, "I didn't think it was humanly possible to do something like that."

Howard put the Phillies up 3–0 early, but the Yankees battled back to 3–3 in the fourth inning. In the bottom half, Pat Burrell led off with a single to bring Howard back to the plate. Howard quickly fell behind 1–2 to Mussina. Perhaps reading that Mussina did not want to repeat what had happened earlier, Howard looked for an off-speed pitch on the outside part of the plate. Mussina obliged, and Howard drove the pitch to left-center for his second home run of the game. His fourth and fifth runs batted in put the Phillies up 5–3.

Again, the Yankees clawed their way back to 5–5 in the top of the seventh. With two outs and runners on first and second, the Phillies once more looked to their cleanup hitter to give them back their lead. Chase Utley had reached after being hit by a Ron Villone pitch, and Pat Burrell drew a walk from Scott Proctor. Favoring the platoon split, Joe Torre opted to bring in yet another reliever, this time side-winding lefty Mike Myers.

On the second pitch of the at-bat, Myers made a mistake to Howard. Breaking character, Howard kept the ball in the yard. However, it rolled all the way to the wall down the right-field line, allowing both runners to score and Howard to trot into third base for a triple. Phillies legendary broadcaster Harry Kalas could not contain his excitement calling the play: "Line drive, and that's going to be a fair ball! Down in the corner. Utley scores! Burrell is being waved around. The relay throw home—not in time! Ryan Howard does it again! What a night!"

The Phillies retook the lead 7–5; Howard was responsible for all seven runs. Dating back to 1919, Howard is the only Phillie to have at least two home runs, one triple, and seven RBIs in one game.

Unfortunately, the Phillies' bullpen could not hold, allowing four runs in the top of the eighth, putting them behind 9–7. The offense could not muster up another rally, and the Phillies lost the game. Of the 378 instances of a player hitting at least two home runs and driving in at least seven runs in one game, only 21 have resulted in a loss for that player's team. Howard's incredible night may have had an unfortunate ending, but it created a lasting memory for every Phillies fan who tuned in that night.

24 Brett Myers Brings the Lumber

Throughout his career with the Phillies, Brett Myers was a jack-of-all-trades. As he went through the minor leagues and made his mark in the majors, he was a part of the starting rotation. He did quite well, posting a 3.72 ERA in 2005 and showed ace potential. He moved to the bullpen in May 2007 when Tom Gordon suffered a rotator cuff injury. Before and after Myers suffered an arm injury in Florida the same year, Myers was an effective reliever, posting a 2.87 ERA with 21 saves. In the off-season, the Phillies acquired closer Brad Lidge from the Houston Astros, so Myers humbly returned to the rotation.

One way Myers never contributed was with the bat. From 2002 to 2008, Myers' career OPS was .302 with eight doubles in 390 plate appearances. He was not an offensive threat, to say the least. In the 2008 postseason, though, that all changed.

In Game 2 of the NLDS, the Phillies squared off against CC Sabathia and the Milwaukee Brewers. After the first inning, the Brewers had taken a 1–0 lead and Sabathia looked strong. In the second, though, the Phillies mounted a rally. Jayson Werth and Pedro Feliz hit back-to-back doubles to tie the game up at 1. After Carlos Ruiz grounded out, Myers came to the plate to continue the rally with a runner on third base and two outs.

Myers quickly fell behind 0–2 to Sabathia, and Phillies fans slumped in their seats, accepting there would be nothing more to this rally. Myers continued to battle. Ball one. Foul. Ball two. Foul. Ball three. Foul. Suddenly, after eight strenuous pitches from Sabathia, Myers had the count at 3–2.

Sabathia whizzed a 97 mph fastball low and inside, which Myers took for ball four. He happily tossed his bat and took first base. Little did he know what he'd started. Phillies fans stood up and cheered the tough at-bat Myers completed. Sabathia continued to labor, walking Jimmy Rollins on four pitches, loading the bases for Shane Victorino. Victorino fell behind 1–2, then lined a fastball down the left-field line for a grand slam. Not only did that home run, which Myers helped create, put the Phillies up 5–1, it set the tone for the entire series.

Myers got another shot at Sabathia in the bottom of the fourth. Ruiz had grounded out on the first pitch, but Myers wanted to make the lefty work. He took the first three pitches he saw, falling behind 1–2. Myers then fouled off four of the next five pitches he saw, drawing even at 2–2. He took a ball on the ninth pitch, earning a full count, before flying out to center field on the 10th pitch. As he jogged back to the dugout, Phillies fans again applauded him, for he had seen 19 pitches against Sabathia in his two at-bats. For any hitter, let alone a pitcher, that is outstanding work.

Myers was not done. In the fifth inning, with runners on first and second with two outs, Myers faced Brewers reliever Seth McClung. He swung at McClung's first offering, an outside fastball, lining it to right field in front of Corey Hart. Myers again had loaded the bases, but Rollins was unable to do anything with it. Regardless, the Phillies took the game 5–2 and eventually took the series in four games.

There was no way Myers could do an encore in Game 2 of the NLCS, right? After all, the Los Angeles Dodgers were sending Chad Billingsley, a hard-throwing right-hander, to the hill.

As in Game 2 of the NLDS, the Phillies fell behind 1–0 early. The Dodgers scored on an RBI ground-out in the top of the second, forcing the Phillies to respond in the bottom of the inning. Both Pat Burrell and Jayson Werth struck out, but a single by Greg Dobbs and an RBI double from Carlos Ruiz tied the game and brought Myers to the plate. At the very least, they got the pitcher out of the way.

Myers' game plan must have been "swing at anything" because for his second straight at-bat, he swung at the first pitch. He lined Billingsley's 88 mph fastball back through the middle to center field, scoring Ruiz and putting the Phillies up 2–1. The Phillies would tack on two more runs when Victorino singled to center.

The Phillies continued to put the pressure on Billingsley in the bottom of the third. A single, double, and an intentional walk, followed by a Ruiz fielder's choice force-out at home, brought Myers back to the plate. The Dodgers' battery of Billingsley and catcher Russell Martin wanted to take advantage of Myers' aggressiveness by getting him to put a bad swing on an unfavorable pitch.

Billingsley threw a 93 mph fastball that was at least six inches off the plate outside, but Myers took his usual first-pitch hack and laced it past first baseman James Loney into right field, scoring Werth and Dobbs. Fox broadcaster Joe Buck said with evident shock in his voice, "Brett Myers has done it again with his bat." The camera panned to Myers on first base. Hearing shouting from his dugout, Myers peered in and shrugged his shoulders—he had no idea how he was hitting this well, either. The inning ended several minutes later, but not before Victorino padded the Phillies' lead with a two-run triple.

Myers got another at-bat in the bottom of the fourth. He had let the Dodgers back in the game by allowing a three-run home run to Manny Ramirez in the top of the fourth, but with a three-run lead, the Phillies still felt confident, so they let Myers hit against reliever James McDonald. Myers again swung at the first pitch, a 71 mph curveball low and outside, and hit a weak chopper down the third-base line, perfectly placed between McDonald and third baseman Casey Blake. Myers reached first base easily.

The right-hander finished the 2008 postseason with four hits, a walk, and three RBIs in six plate appearances. For the first time in his career, his hitting completely overshadowed his pitching, sparking the Phillies to two surprising postseason victories.

25 Phillie Phanatic

For as much as fans of other teams have disliked Phillies players, one member who has always been exempt from criticism is the team mascot, the Phillie Phanatic. Created after the 1977 season, the Phanatic has been as vital to each and every Phillies home game as the players themselves.

Describing the Phanatic is, well, difficult. He is just *a bit* overweight, covered in green fur with a cylindrical beak. Most days, he can be seen wearing a typical Phillies home jersey with a star on the back where a number would be found.

During a game, the Phanatic goes through several routines to keep the fans interested in the game. Most notably, he whizzes around the stadium in an all-terrain vehicle, usually his method of escape after mocking a member of the opposing team. Sometimes in his travels, he makes stops around the stadium to shoot hot dogs into the crowd with a pneumatic gun attached to the back of his ATV.

Always loyal to his team, the Phanatic attempts to vex the opposing pitcher from time to time by doing the "Phanatic Dance." Studies are inconclusive as to whether this actually works. However, the Phanatic has attempted to seduce umpires on the job. In the rare instances where he succeeds, the Phillies usually come out on top.

His acts have made him not only a fan favorite, but the most well-respected mascot in all of sports according to a market research study reported by *Forbes* in January 2008. After hearing of the results of the study, Tom Burgoyne, the Phanatic's "best friend," said, "The Phanatic is kind of reveling in the fact that he's been listed as the No. 1 guy and to be on such a list. He really does think it's great."

Other mascots, such as Billy the Marlin, the San Diego Chicken, and Mr. Met have become well-known across the country, but none are as well-liked and respected as the Phillie Phanatic. Next time you are at a Phillies game, make sure you find the furry green creature. He may be on top of the dugout dancing, stretching with the players before the game starts, or in the booth bringing treats to the broadcast crew. But beware—he may ask you to dance with him or, worse, smooch you after you get your picture taken with him!

26 Billy Wagner and the Radar Gun

From 1996 to 2003 with the Houston Astros, Billy Wagner rose to prominence as one of the best closers in the game. He used a high-90s fastball that, at times, reached triple digits and a devastating, biting slider to rack up the swinging strike threes. Most years, he could be found with one of the lowest ERA marks among relievers, even finishing with a 1.57 ERA in 1999 and 1.78 in 2003—in the midst of the so-called "steroid era."

The Astros did not see themselves retaining Wagner's services as he was eligible for free agency soon, so they traded him to the Philadelphia Phillies after the 2003 season. The Phillies sent three prospects—Ezequiel Astacio, Taylor Buchholz, and Brandon Duckworth—to Houston to complete the deal.

The Phillies, at the time, felt that they could compete for a post-season spot and believed adding Wagner to the back of the bullpen would give them the necessary boost they needed. Phillies fans, who hadn't been able to get behind a closer since Mitch Williams, instantly grew fond of the small, flame-throwing southpaw.

In his first year with the Phillies, Wagner posted a 2.42 ERA with a ridiculously high 9.83 strikeout-to-walk ratio. He missed some time with a hand strain, but when he was on the mound, he was mostly cheered for his immense success, but was also booed, and not for the reasons one would think, considering the reputation of Phillies fans.

Wagner, on occasion, was able to throw his fastball at 100 mph. When "Fastball 100 MPH" flashed on the LED screen in right field, fans would cheer raucously. However, when it flashed "FASTBALL 99 MPH," fans would boo. To most observers, the booing is blatantly ironic and evidently supportive, but Wagner did not see it that way.

After a career year in 2005, Wagner signed with the rival New York Mets as a free agent. In an interview, Wagner expounded on the phenomenon of fans paying attention to the radar gun. To the *Newark Star-Ledger*, he said, "Those people, it doesn't matter how successful you are. I don't get it. They boo you. They scream at you. Anybody who's going to boo you when you don't hit 100 miles per hour, what does that tell you?"

Wagner, a farm boy raised in Tannersville, Virginia, was clearly not comfortable with the dynamics of a large sports town. As a result of those remarks, other comments he made in the media since, his general aloofness, and one soul-crushing blown save on September 7, 2005, Wagner quickly went from one of the most well-liked players to ever don Phillies red to one of the most reviled.

27 Tempers Flare Between Phillies, Reds

There have been many bench-clearing brawls over the years, but at least for the Phillies, none was more memorable than what occurred on June 13, 2003. The 33–32 Cincinnati Reds hosted the 34–31 Phillies, with Jimmy Haynes opposing Kevin Millwood.

Millwood wasn't sharp, and it was very evident early. He allowed six runs by the fourth inning before being lifted for reliever Carlos Silva. Silva allowed three more runs before the inning mercifully ended, putting the Phillies behind 9–0. As they say, it was just one of those days.

Silva was still in the game in the fifth inning, trying to squirm out of a second-and-third, one-out jam against the legendary Ken Griffey Jr. With a 1–1 count, Griffey ripped a line-drive single to right field, scoring Haynes. Reds left fielder Adam Dunn rounded third and headed home as right fielder Bobby Abreu made a strong and accurate throw to catcher Mike Lieberthal. Lieberthal corralled the throw and braced for impact with Dunn, a 6'6", 240-pound player who could easily have been mistaken for a football player. Dunn bowled Lieberthal over, but the ball remained in the glove, and the second out of the inning was recorded. Alas, the Reds were up 10–0.

Baseball has many rules in an "unwritten rulebook," one of which is to take your foot off the gas when you have the game in hand. According to Baseball-Reference.com, the Reds were virtual locks to win the game, with a win expectancy of 100 percent entering the inning. Following these rules, the leading team does not attempt to steal any bases or go above and beyond to put another run on the scoreboard. Dunn's collision with Lieberthal went against this unwritten rule, and the Phillies were livid.

Dunn came to the plate again in the bottom of the sixth with Silva on the mound. The first pitch came in toward Dunn's knees for ball one. Sensing trouble, home plate umpire Doug Eddings issued a warning to the reliever. Silva disregarded the umpire's warning, throwing a fastball behind Dunn's back. As Eddings ejected Silva, Dunn dropped his bat, tightened his batting glove, and dashed toward the pitcher's mound.

Lieberthal sprinted behind Dunn and tackled him by the legs just before he reached the mound to attack Silva. As Dunn sprawled on the ground, Silva stepped toward Dunn and took a heavy swing at his head, grazing Dunn's helmetless head. Naturally, Dunn was ejected as were Reds first baseman Sean Casey and Phillies reliever Jose Mesa and manager Larry Bowa.

Speaking to reporters after the game, Dunn said, "He threw the first pitch, and you say, 'Okay, maybe he's just trying to come inside.' But when a big-league pitcher throws one behind you, it's obviously a purpose pitch."

Asked about Dunn's base-running aggression, Millwood was not happy: "I didn't like it. If it's a close ballgame, that's what should happen. But when it's 10–0, you stop or give a courtesy slide. You don't run over a guy."

The Phillies went on to lose in demoralizing fashion by a score of 15–1, but fans in attendance at Great American Ballpark walked away with a great story to tell. Lieberthal's open-field tackle of Dunn remains one of the most iconic moments in a brawl involving the Phillies.

28 Aaron Rowand's All-Out Effort

On May 11, 2006, the second-place Phillies hosted the division-leading New York Mets. They had split the first two games of the three-game set, playing the rubber match on a Thursday evening with rain on the horizon.

Newcomer Aaron Rowand was patrolling center field once again. The right-hander had been great defensively and was an offensive threat, as well, for the Phillies, hitting six home runs and driving in 17 runs in 32 games entering the game that evening.

Starter Gavin Floyd found himself in trouble early after getting two quick outs. Carlos Beltran, Carlos Delgado, and David Wright all walked to load the bases for Xavier Nady. The count went to 3–2 before Nady sent a fly ball to deep center field toward the bullpen. Rowand ranged back, tracking the ball the entire way.

As he strode closer and closer to the wall, it became evident he was not going to slow down, even when he hit the warning track. With his back almost directly to home plate, Rowand caught the fly ball like a wide receiver. In that same split-second, he collided face-first with the fence—which, to that point, was not padded—and recoiled back and to the ground.

Rowand had made the catch—holding up his glove triumphantly—ending the stressful inning for Floyd, but the crowd of 28,000-plus at Citizens Bank Park feared more for his safety. Right fielder Bobby Abreu, who had moved toward center field to back up the play, rushed to Rowand's side as the Phillies' medical staff burst from the dugout.

As Rowand kneeled on the ground, TV cameras were not able to pick up to what extent he was injured. After a few minutes, Rowand returned to his feet and was helped off of the field, clutching what appeared to be a bloody nose with a hand towel. He was replaced in the lineup and in center field by Rule V pick-up Shane Victorino.

The Phillies took a 1–0 lead in the bottom-half of the inning thanks to a Chase Utley home run and added a second run in the bottom of the fourth on an RBI single by David Bell. Floyd took the mound for the top of the fifth, retiring the Mets in order just as the rain began to fall heavily. The game was put on hold and eventually called, the Phillies emerging victorious by a 2–0 score in five innings.

The postgame talk, naturally, centered around Rowand's catch and his status. He had been admitted to Thomas Jefferson University Hospital, and the damage was relatively minimal—just a few broken bones in his face; he was not concussed nor was there any potential for brain damage. Rowand went into surgery the next day, landing on the Phillies' 15-day disabled list.

Rowand spoke about his catch and his motivation several days later. "I play hard," Rowand said. "That's how I played as a kid. My coaches and my father taught me to play like that."

As a result of Rowand's injury, the Phillies immediately installed padding on the center-field fence while the team went on a six-game road trip to Cincinnati and Milwaukee. At the same time, they went on a winning streak, emerging victorious in 13 of 14 games between April 30 and May 14, partly inspired, they say, by Rowand's catch.

Unfortunately, Rowand was not quite the same after he returned 15 days later. From May 27 until the end of the season, the center fielder could only muster a .689 OPS with six home runs and 30 RBIs. However, he rebounded the next year—his final year in red pinstripes—helping the Phillies reach the postseason for the first time since 1993.

Although Rowand's stay in Philadelphia was not long, fans quickly grew to idolize the gritty outfielder, and his catch on May 11, 2006, was a big reason for that. Entering free agency after the '07 season, Rowand signed a five-year, $60 million contract with the San Francisco Giants. Rowand returned to Philadelphia with the Giants on May 2, earning a rousing standing ovation in his first plate appearance.

Rowand is an example that, to be loved in Philadelphia, a player need not win a World Series championship or the MVP (though those certainly don't hurt). Rather, he simply has to play his hardest on a daily basis and wear his heart on his sleeve. Rowand certainly exemplified the former, and that is why he will always be welcomed back in Philadelphia with open arms.

29 Brett Myers Uses His Noggin

Pitchers are often thought of as the cerebral players on the field. Between the pitcher and catcher, there is a lot of thought that goes into each and every pitch, whether it's pitch type, speed, or location, there are an infinite number of variables that must be considered after each and every pitch. To be a successful pitcher, you must use your noggin.

On May 8, 2005, however, Brett Myers used his head in a totally different manner. The Phillies were in Chicago, finishing up a three-game set in which they had taken the first two games. Myers was squaring off against the up-and-coming Carlos Zambrano in what figured to be a low-scoring affair between two middling ballclubs.

Myers had a perfect bottom of the first inning after the Phillies were unable to capitalize on some shakiness on Zambrano's part. In the second, Myers recorded two easy outs, inducing weak fly balls from Aramis Ramirez and Jeromy Burnitz, bringing the right-handed-hitting catcher Michael Barrett to the dish.

After falling behind 1–0, Myers threw a waist-high 95 mph fastball outside. Barrett, whose stance was straight and closed, was able to reach out and make solid contact, sending a line drive screaming back toward Myers. Myers did his best to protect himself as best as his reflexes would allow, but the ball hit him square on the right side of his head and ricocheted into the hole between short and third, reaching left fielder Placido Polanco with momentum to spare.

Most players would have been incapacitated after being struck with such force, but Myers never even went to a knee. As the ball was returned to the infield, Myers circled the pitcher's mound as if nothing had ever happened—just your typical, run-of-the-mill single, right?

If that had happened today, given Major League Baseball's much more stringent policy regarding potential concussions, Myers would have been immediately removed. This was 2005, though, so he remained in the game with no argument, getting through the inning without any further damage. In the bottom of the fourth, however, both Neifi Perez and Aramis Ramirez hit solo home runs to put the Cubs up 2–0. Still, Myers continued to pitch brilliantly, the home runs notwithstanding.

Meanwhile, Zambrano was having yet another great outing. After Bobby Abreu singled in the first inning, the Phillies were silenced until the sixth, when Abreu hit a solo home run of his own to bring the score to 2–1. From that point, there was no more offense; the Cubs managed just two more hits while the Phillies mustered only one hit and one walk. Both starters finished the game, Zambrano allowing one run over nine innings, while Myers allowed two runs in eight innings, earning the tough-luck loss with 10 strikeouts and just one walk.

Speaking to the media after the game, Myers was not interested in talking about the line drive, instead focusing on the team's loss and what it meant for them going forward. "One day I'm going to give up six runs and get the win," he said. "That's the way things go. Right now, it just so happens that we're not scoring as many runs as we'd like. It's going to turn around."

Fortunately, there were no lasting side effects. Myers was indeed fine and finished the season with his best marks to date, sporting a 3.72 ERA in over 215 innings of work. It was the first step in what the Phillies hoped was a promising career for a potential future ace.

30 The Infinite Wisdom of Davey Lopes

First-base coaches tend to be forgotten about when discussing a team's successes and failures. What could they possibly contribute? They just hold the runner's batting gloves, right? When Davey Lopes joined the Phillies after the 2006 season, he had the responsibility of working with the Phillies' infield as well as coaching first base.

Lopes had a unique style, meticulously measuring the pitcher's movements with a stopwatch and relaying that information to the runner on first base. On many teams, the decision to steal is given by the dugout, but with the Phillies, Lopes and the runners were able to collaborate and decide by themselves on which pitch to attempt to steal.

The Phillies had talented base runners both before and after Lopes joined the team, but they noticed a dramatic improvement in both aggressiveness (attempts to steal) and efficiency (stolen base success rate).

From 2004 to 2006, the three years prior to Lopes' arrival, the Phillies stole bases with a success rate between 79 and 81 percent, while the league average hovered between 70 and 71 percent. In 2007, Lopes' first year on the job, the Phillies' swiped bags at an 88 percent clip, which was not only the best in the league, but a major league record. The Phillies led the majors with an 84 percent success rate in '08, when they won the World Series, and were second-best in '09 with an 81 percent rate.

As for aggressiveness, the Phillies' total stolen-base attempts ranged between 117 and 143 from 2004 to 2006, while the league average rested between 121 and 129. Under Lopes' tutelage, the Phillies attempted 157 steals in '07, 161 in '08, and 147 in '09.

Most importantly, though, Lopes specifically made the Phillies more aggressive in taking third base. They attempted a total of 31 steals of third in the three years before he joined the club; in the three years after, they attempted 13, 19, and 29 steals, with the latter two years ranking among the best in baseball. In addition, the Phillies were efficient in doing so, succeeding at a rate of 85, 89, and 72 percent, respectively.

During his tenure with the Phillies, Lopes dealt with a lot of adversity. He was diagnosed with prostate cancer during spring training before the 2008 season, but was treated and made a full recovery. Nearly two years later, Lopes lost his brother Michael in a Rhode Island house fire. Through all of the hardships, Lopes remained a critical part of the team, as much if not more so than some of the players on the 25-man roster.

Lopes left after the 2010 season when he requested but was not granted a raise by the Phillies. Shortly thereafter, he signed with the Los Angeles Dodgers, where he imparted his seemingly infinite wisdom. Particularly, he impacted Matt Kemp, who had an MVP-caliber season, raising his stolen-bases total from 19 in '10 to 40, while his success rate jumped from 56 to 78 percent.

Nonetheless, the Phillies retained what Lopes had taught them, stealing bases with an 80 percent success rate as a team. In particular, their top three base-running threats—Jimmy Rollins, Shane Victorino, and Chase Utley—were caught just 11 times and stole 63 bags total. The Phillies have learned firsthand just how much of an impact a good first-base coach can make on a team.

31 Veterans Stadium

Every longstanding team has an iconic stadium in its history. Since the turn of the 20th century, the Phillies have called the Baker Bowl, Shibe Park (aka Connie Mack Stadium), Veterans Stadium, and Citizens Bank Park home. Each stadium had its own quirks and features that made it stand out, but none had the reputation of the Vet.

The Vet opened on April 10, 1971, amid a long-running streak of failure for the Phillies franchise. They had not reached the postseason since 1950, when they were swept out of the World Series by the New York Yankees, but the Phillies were hoping a change of scenery could reignite the fan base and give the team an impetus to turn things around.

Overall attendance had been below 1 million in the previous four years for the Phillies, but the Vet's inaugural season saw more than 1.5 million fans walk through the turnstiles. The players, however, did not quite have what it took to compete in the National League, finishing with just 67 wins.

In the off-season, the Phillies got serious, trading Rick Wise to the St. Louis Cardinals for 27-year-old Steve Carlton. The Phillies lagged behind the rest of the league offensively, however, causing them to finish with a paltry 59 wins despite Carlton winning the NL Cy Young Award.

There was a prospect the Phillies were excited about, though: third baseman Mike Schmidt. They took him in the second round of the 1971 draft, and he raked minor league pitching in '72. He did not impress in his first full season in '73, but the Phillies felt that, with Carlton and Schmidt, they had the potential for greatness if they could fill in around the edges.

And so the era of Phillies greatness began. Nearly 2.5 million fans showed up in 1976, the result of the Phillies increasing their win total in four consecutive seasons. They won 101 games in '76, snapping a lengthy playoff drought and rewarding the organization's renewed commitment to winning. The Cincinnati Reds, a juggernaut team known as the Big Red Machine, made mincemeat of the Phillies in the NLCS, sweeping in three games.

Although the end of the '76 season was disappointing, the city of Philadelphia knew it was the dawning of a new era, made possible largely thanks to their new stadium, which gave the team additional revenue and the impetus to continue bringing in quality players.

As the years went on, the Vet became an outmoded sports facility, especially since it had been home to not only a baseball team, but a football team, as well. Many players would complain about the turf, whether it caused burns on slides or caused back problems (in the case of Scott Rolen), while visiting fans and media types found the stadium's aesthetics unappealing. Others were victimized by the stadium's aging infrastructure, like an Army cadet whose neck was broken after a fall when a railing collapsed during a 1998 Army-Navy game. Like an older brother protecting his bullied younger brother, Philadelphia sports fans only grew to love the Vet more for all of its flaws.

The Phillies and Eagles, along with the Pittsburgh Pirates and Steelers, worked together in the late 1990s and early 2000s to have the Vet and Three Rivers Stadium replaced with individual facilities for all four teams. Pittsburgh's proposal was accepted quickly, but Philadelphia spent a lot of time debating the logistics of two new stadiums. Eventually, though, the Phillies and Eagles got their wish, and it was soon announced that the era of the Vet was drawing to a close.

Two stadiums, which would later be known as Citizens Bank Park and Lincoln Financial Field, were built near the Vet. The Eagles played their last game at the Vet in the NFC Championship

Game, losing 27–10 to the Tampa Bay Buccaneers on January 19, 2003. The Phillies lost to the Atlanta Braves 5–2 on September 28.

Veterans Stadium was imploded on March 21, 2004, just a couple weeks before the inauguration of Citizens Bank Park. As the stadium crumbled in just over 62 seconds in front of a live television audience, so did a piece of an entire generation of Philadelphia sports fans. For 33 years, it was home to some of the best—and worst—teams the city ever saw, creating plenty of lasting memories for millions in the City of Brotherly Love.

32 Citizens Bank Park

The end of the Veterans Stadium era was the beginning of a new kind of Phillies baseball. Between 1994 and 2002, the Phillies were criticized by fans, the media, and even their own players for not being committed to winning. As the Phillies prepared to move into their new stadium, expecting at least a brief surge in revenue, ownership allowed general manager Ed Wade more freedom with resources.

The Phillies signed free agent Jim Thome to a six-year, $85 million contract on December 6, 2002. Two weeks later, the Phillies sent highly touted catching prospect Johnny Estrada to the Atlanta Braves for established starter Kevin Millwood. In the final year of the Vet, the Phillies showed the fans they wanted to try their hardest to bring home a World Series championship. Going into the 2004 season, the Phillies acquired closer Billy Wagner from the Houston Astros and later traded for Eric Milton from the Minnesota Twins. As a result, the team's Opening Day payroll jumped from $58 million in 2002 to $71 million in '03 and $93 million in '04.

Over 3 million fans showed up at the gate in '04, justifying the resources the Phillies had put into the team. It marked only the second time that the Phillies had 3 million or more fans in attendance in a season, joining the 1993 team.

Citizens Bank Park was more than just a place with a baseball field and some seats. Joining the more modern ballparks in major league baseball, CBP offered a variety of new features. Along with the usual concession stands and merchandise stores, the new stadium has a large scoreboard behind the seats in left field and a very open, outdoorsy feel, especially compared to the Vet.

In fact, CBP was so outdoorsy that you could feel it in the concourse area on any given day, as large gusts of wind swirled throughout. The way the ballpark was configured, especially in left field, wind flowed through, creating heavy gusts that helped lift and carry fly balls. Citizens Bank Park ranked as the fifth-most homer-friendly park in all of baseball in its first year. This was something not accounted for when the park was designed. The stadium could not be redesigned, so president David Montgomery made the next-best modification: the fence in left field was moved back five feet.

Meanwhile, fans continued to show up to the stadium even after that new ballpark smell faded. In the '05 and '06 seasons, the Phillies saw a combined 5.4 million fans go through the turnstiles. The Phillies were very competitive, as well, winning 88 and 85 games, respectively. With a playoff-caliber team and a family-friendly stadium, Phillies fans were as energized as ever.

Two thousand seven marked the culmination of years of effort within the Phillies organization. Draft picks acquired since the turn of the millennium, such as Cole Hamels, Chase Utley, and Ryan Howard, established themselves as legitimate major league stars. Pat Gillick, the architect of many extremely successful ballclubs, took over as GM of the Phillies after the 2005 season and was able to fill in around the edges with players like J.C. Romero, Shane Victorino, and Greg Dobbs.

The Phillies ended another playoff drought, winning the NL East on the last day of the 2007 season. The crowd at Citizens Bank Park was electrified, and the golden era of Phillies baseball began. Since 2007, the Phillies haven't looked back. Season attendance has been above 3 million ever since, and the Phillies currently have a sellout streak of more than 200 games. They won the World Series in 2008, reached the World Series again in '09, and have won the NL East division crown five years running.

Just as Veterans Stadium helped create the great Phillies teams of the mid- and late 1970s, Citizens Bank Park was a motivator for the Phillies' current run of success. Unlike the Vet, though, players love to play on the field. It consistently rates among the cleanest, most aesthetically pleasing, and fan-friendliest in all of baseball. Even fans of visiting teams, including the Mets, have a hard time finding bad things to say about "the Bank."

If you have not yet visited Citizens Bank Park, make some time in the summer to take your family into Philadelphia to catch a Phillies game. For out-of-towners, if you happen to find yourself in Philadelphia for work or visiting family, you will want to set aside a few hours to take a trip to Citizens Bank Park. You will be glad you did, as it is nearly impossible not to have a good time there.

33 Ryan Howard's 2006 Season

Mike Schmidt aside, the Phillies have had very few legendarily great offensive seasons to speak about in the modern era. Schmidt, of course, won three NL MVP awards and led the league in home runs eight times, retiring with 548 of them. Before Ryan Howard came along, Del Ennis was second in Phillies history with 259 home runs.

HOWARD.

Replacing injured slugger Jim Thome in 2005, Ryan Howard never looked back, putting up incredible numbers in his first season in the majors, on his way to being named Rookie of the Year. In 2006 he surpassed his rookie year, hitting 58 homers with 149 RBIs and a 1.084 OPS, winning MVP honors.

Howard was selected in the fifth round of the 2001 draft and became an instant hit in the minors, culminating in an eye-popping, 46–home run, 131-RBI season between Double A Reading and Triple A Scranton/Wilkes-Barre. With future Hall of Famer Jim Thome at first base in the majors, Howard's road appeared to be blocked, but then-GM Ed Wade resisted the onslaught of trade offers over the years.

When Thome succumbed to injury in 2005, Howard was quickly recalled from the minors and given an everyday job at first base in the majors. He rewarded the Phillies with a breakout season, finishing with a .924 OPS en route to earning the NL Rookie of the Year award. The Phillies traded Thome, in the middle of a six-year contract, to the Chicago White Sox in the off-season to make room for the up-and-coming Howard.

Howard started off the 2006 season in style, homering on Opening Day in a 13–5 loss to the St. Louis Cardinals. He finished the month of April with five homers and 12 RBIs, but he hadn't even started to heat up yet. May 5 marked the time when Howard went from pretty good to elite. He homered twice against the Giants, bringing his OPS up to .971. He would never look back. Howard homered in 11 of 27 May games, finishing the month with 13 total, along with 35 RBIs and a 1.018 OPS.

He stayed hot in June, homering nine times in total with two more multi–home run games. Howard became a folk hero on June 20 when the Phillies hosted the Yankees at Citizens Bank Park. In the first inning, Howard took a Mike Mussina fastball and deposited it in the third deck in right field, where no other player had yet gone—and none has since. At the All-Star break, Howard had 28 home runs, 71 RBIs, an All-Star selection, and was named as a participant in the Home Run Derby, which he ended up winning in dramatic fashion.

If the All-Star break offered pitchers anything, it was some extra time to watch some video and read some scouting reports on Howard. In the event that the allotted time was used in that fashion, it didn't help. Howard continued to victimize National League pitching with reckless abandon, homering in his first two games after the break. At the end of July, the first baseman had 35 home runs, and he showed no signs of slowing down.

As August rolled around, Phillies fans began to talk about Howard not only surpassing the Phillies' single-season home run record, set at 48 by Mike Schmidt in 1980, but about him surpassing Babe Ruth's 60 home runs as well as the 61 hit by Roger Maris. Given the performance-enhancing-drug controversy surrounding Barry Bonds, Mark McGwire, and Sammy Sosa, Ryan Howard had the potential to be viewed as the legitimate holder of major league baseball's single-season home run record.

If there was any added pressure on Howard, he sure didn't show it. He homered in nearly half of the games in August, even hitting one in four consecutive games from August 25 to 29. The one

Howard hit on the August 29 marked his 48th, tying Schmidt's single-season franchise record. On August 31, Howard broke the tie, smashing his 49th home run into the upper deck at RFK Stadium in Washington. Howard finished the month of August with 14 home runs, 41 RBIs, and a monstrous 1.214 OPS. All told, he was sitting on 49 homers with a month to go.

It appeared Howard was well on his way to 60 home runs when he hit three home runs in one game against the Atlanta Braves on September 3, all against Tim Hudson. Howard tacked on an additional four homers through September 8, giving him 56 with 21 games left in the season. Unfortunately, Howard was only able to hit two more home runs in his final 21 games, but he did not slump—he batted .328 with a .540 on-base percentage (thanks in part to 14 intentional walks) and a .507 slugging percentage.

Howard finished at 58 homers, 149 RBIs (both MLB bests), and a 1.084 OPS. In the off-season, he received a shopping cart full of awards, including the *Sporting News* Player of the Year, National League Hank Aaron Award, Player of the Year, and the National League Outstanding Position Player in the Players Choice Awards voting, Series MVP in the Major League Baseball Japan All-Star Series, and—most prominently—the NL Most Valuable Player award. Howard became the first Phillie to win the MVP award since Schmidt in 1986 and the first player in baseball to win the Rookie of the Year and MVP awards in back-to-back seasons since Cal Ripken Jr. did so in 1982–1983.

Howard would show that his 2006 season was no fluke, hitting 140 home runs and driving in 423 runs in the next three seasons, finishing in the top five in MVP voting each year. Known for his great work ethic, as long as Howard stays healthy, he should become at least the second-best hitter in Phillies history behind Schmidt. Howard's 2006 season is one very memorable part of an enthralling career.

34 Catch Spring Training in Clearwater

For die-hard baseball fans, the off-season is torture. There is no baseball to be found on *SportsCenter*, and the regular season seems millions of miles away. If you can make it through those arduous four baseball-free months, reward yourself with a vacation down to Clearwater, Florida, in March to catch some spring training baseball.

Bright House Field comfortably seats 7,300 with an additional 1,500 grass berm seats. With just a minimal amount of effort spent on planning ahead, you should have no problem finding room. The warm Florida weather in March is a welcome reprieve from the snow and ice of a typical Philadelphia winter, a perfect foreword to the regular season.

Should you choose to step away from the game for a bit, Bright House Field offers plenty of family-friendly fun. If you are lucky enough to be sans kids, relax with a drink at the tiki hut pavilion in left field. Down the foul lines, you can camp out and wait for players to make their exit, as they will usually spend a considerable amount of time signing autographs for fans young and old alike. It is a great opportunity for you and your kids to meet a future star—or, perhaps, an already established star like Ryan Howard.

When you get back to your seat, you can catch some interesting spring training strategy. Where else can you see a Double A prospect pitching to a hitter with more than 200 career home runs in the majors? The younger players will be trying to prove themselves and win one of those rare roster spots.

Meanwhile, the veterans will be taking spring training in stride, picking specific areas to work on each day. Early in spring training, you will likely see veteran pitchers throwing nothing but fastballs in an effort to see just how much they've lost in the off-season. With a few weeks left to go, pitchers will start to gradually mix in more and more of their off-speed pitches.

You may even find yourself witnessing a once-in-a-lifetime moment. Once such moment happened in mid-March 2010 when top prospect Domonic Brown went up against Detroit Tigers ace Justin Verlander. Brown came into spring training with a lot of hype as the Phillies made a concerted effort not to trade the kid. Facing Verlander was his first legitimate major league test.

Verlander threw everything in his arsenal to Brown, but couldn't get him to swing and miss with two strikes, whether it was a 98 mph fastball or a 12-6 curve ball, Brown battled and battled. Eventually, with the count 3–2, Verlander threw a fastball belt-high and inside. Brown took his trademark graceful swing and demolished the pitch, sending it to right-center, where it cleared the seats easily and nearly landed on Route 19. Brown finished the day with two homers and four RBIs, giving the fans a lasting memory of their trip to Bright House Field.

There is no guarantee you will see something as awesome as that, but you never know. After all, you really could use a vacation.

35 Chooch

When you think of a typical professional baseball player, you think of someone who has earned a truckload of money coming out of a top-tier college in the United States. For many players, like former UCLA Bruin Chase Utley, this holds true. But other players take a much more arduous path to the major leagues.

In 1998 the Phillies signed a Panamanian by the name of Carlos Ruiz for the low price of $8,000. Ruiz, a failed second baseman and pitcher, had to prove himself at the Phillies' Latin American baseball academy in the Dominican Republic before he joined the Gulf Coast League Phillies (rookie ball) in 2000 as a catcher.

As Ruiz moved from Class A to Double A, scouts worried about his bat. While he possessed strong defensive skills behind the plate, his OPS never went above .698 in his first four years in the minors. The Phillies viewed him as a potential backup catcher if he ever got to the majors. By the time Ruiz made the jump to Triple A in 2005, the Phillies were bringing along another catcher with a brighter future named Jason Jaramillo.

It was at that point, though, that the switch went on for Ruiz. He had hit 17 home runs for Reading in 2004 and continued his offensive surge at Triple A in 2005, finishing with an .812 OPS. In 2006 veteran catcher Mike Lieberthal was nearing the end of his career as a Phillie. Ruiz was called up to the majors at three different points in the season: once in May, once in July, and once in September. It was the third stint in September that cemented his stay in Philadelphia. In 29 plate appearances, Ruiz hit .360 with four extra-base hits and seven RBIs.

Out of spring training in 2007, Ruiz earned the everyday job as the Phillies' catcher. Not only was he expected to hit and play solid defense, he had the responsibility of handling a hodge-podge starting rotation that included veterans Jamie Moyer and Jon Lieber, as well as newcomers Cole Hamels and Kyle Kendrick. Ruiz handled it all with relative ease. Quickly, the pitchers grew to trust and respect Ruiz's game-calling; it was a rare sight to see a pitcher shake him off.

In the off-season, the Phillies traded for closer Brad Lidge, who lived and died on his slider. Lidge's success relied, in part, on his catcher's ability to block sliders in the dirt. Fortunately, Lidge had the best catcher in baseball for that particular task. The sight of Ruiz sacrificing his body to keep a slider in front of him prevented many a base runner from advancing throughout the 2008 regular season. Subsequently, Lidge finished the season a perfect 41-for-41 in save opportunities, thanks in large part to Ruiz.

The 2008 World Series couldn't have ended in a more perfect fashion. The Phillies, facing the Tampa Bay Rays in Game 5, were on the verge of winning their first championship since 1980. Lidge was on the mound, ahead 4–3 in the ninth. The Rays had a runner on second with two outs, resting their hopes on pinch-hitter Eric Hinske. With an 0–2 count, Ruiz gave Lidge the sign for a slider low and away. Lidge immediately concurred, throwing it directly to Ruiz's glove, missing Hinske's bat for the 27th and final out.

A kneeling Lidge, arms extended, waiting for a celebratory hug from his catcher, remains the most memorable sight from the World Series. Lidge had all of the fame for a perfect season (including 7-for-7 in the postseason) but he couldn't have done it without Ruiz.

As the years went on, the Phillies assembled one of the greatest starting rotations of all time. They opened the 2011 regular season with Roy Halladay (Cy Young winner in 2003 and 2010), Cliff Lee (Cy Young winner in 2008), Cole Hamels, Roy Oswalt (five top-five finishes in Cy Young balloting), and Joe Blanton. Despite the big names, each and every one of them deferred to Ruiz on pitch selection. Each felt confident intentionally throwing a pitch in the dirt because they knew Ruiz would block it.

All of this respect from baseball's best for $8,000. The Phillies may never find another bargain as good as Ruiz!

36 Pat Gillick

You may as well call Pat Gillick the King Midas of baseball, because every team he took over turned into a winner. A former minor league player himself, Gillick guided the Toronto Blue Jays,

Baltimore Orioles, Seattle Mariners, and Philadelphia Phillies to new levels of success.

Gillick took over as GM of the Blue Jays, an expansion team, in 1978. In the franchise's first five years, their winning percentage never exceeded .414, but the team took big strides in 1982–1984. In 1985 the Jays won 99 games, losing the ALCS in seven games to the eventual World Series–champion Kansas City Royals. From 1989 to 1993, the Jays reached the postseason in four out of five years, winning the World Series in back-to-back years in '92 and '93.

After the strike, Gillick moved to the Orioles in 1996. The O's hadn't reached the postseason since winning the World Series in 1983, but they won the AL wild-card in Gillick's first year, advancing to the ALCS. They were dispatched in five games by the New York Yankees, but the O's weren't a one-hit wonder. They won 98 games in 1997 and reached the ALCS again, losing to the Cleveland Indians.

Gillick moved to the Mariners in 2000, another team with little postseason experience. Prior to Gillick's arrival, the Mariners had reached the postseason just twice since 1977. In Gillick's first year, the Mariners won 91 games, reaching the ALCS. The Mariners improved by 25 wins the next year, tying the major league record for single-season wins with an incredible 116 wins. What made it more incredible was that the Mariners did this after losing franchise icons Alex Rodriguez and Ken Griffey Jr. Unfortunately, in the ALCS the Mariners matched up against the Yankees—who were attempting to win a fourth-consecutive World Series—and lost in five games. The Mariners won 93 games in each of the next two seasons, but missed the playoffs. Gillick left after the '03 season.

In 2005 the Phillies were once again staying home in October. The fan base had grown impatient with GM Ed Wade, as the team had not reached the postseason during his tenure. Wade was fired, and the Phillies began their search for a new GM. Many names came up in rumors, including a lot from within the organization, but the Phillies wanted an outsider's perspective. On November 2, 2005, the Phillies informed the media that they had selected Gillick to be their new GM.

Three weeks later, Gillick made his presence felt. Confident that first baseman Ryan Howard could handle an everyday job in the majors, Gillick traded the immensely popular Jim Thome to the Chicago White Sox for center fielder Aaron Rowand and two pitching prospects, Gio Gonzalez and Daniel Haigwood. The Phillies, with some new blood, were still expected to be contenders in the National League.

Going into June, the Phillies were 27–25, in third place, but still very much in the thick of things. But the month of June was just absolutely abysmal for them. The Phillies won just nine of 27 games, losing 15 of 18 at one point from June 8 to 28. By the time July rolled around, the Phillies were eight games under .500 and 12 games out of first place in the NL East. At the end of July, Gillick recognized the Phillies' situation and decided to trade cornerstone outfielder Bobby Abreu to the New York Yankees. In return, he received four prospects, none of whom ended up making an impact at the major league level for the Phillies.

Gillick spoke in pessimistic terms about the Phillies' future. After the Abreu trade, Gillick said, "It would probably be a stretch to think we're going to be there [as a contender] in 2007. It's going to be a little slower. I don't want to mislead anyone." The Phillies, however, were thinking more about the present than the future. They won 18 games each in August and September 2006, finishing just three games out of the wild-card.

The Phillies had even more new blood in 2007. Carlos Ruiz won the everyday job at catcher, Shane Victorino was the everyday right fielder, and a slew of castoffs joined the bullpen and bench. With this infusion of new blood, the Phillies ended their 13-year playoff drought, winning the NL East on the last day of the season thanks to a historic collapse by the New York Mets in the final three weeks. The Phillies had completely defied Gillick.

Many of Gillick's *Moneyball*-esque acquisitions, such as Jayson Werth and Greg Dobbs, paid huge dividends for the team. In 2008 Gillick added closer Brad Lidge and starter Joe Blanton to the team, an attempt to strengthen the team in time for another playoff push. It was just what they needed. Lidge had a perfect season, completing 41 of 41 save opportunities while Blanton didn't get saddled with a loss in any of his 13 starts. The Phillies reached the postseason again, making quick work of the Milwaukee Brewers and Los Angeles Dodgers en route to beating the Tampa Bay Rays in five games to win the World Series.

Much to the dismay of the Phillies fan base, Gillick resigned from his position after the city finished celebrating. He was 4-for-4 in taking a floundering franchise and resuscitating it back to prominence. The Phillies owe their success in the late 2000s and early 2010s to many people, particularly the scouts who helped draft Jimmy Rollins, Chase Utley, Ryan Howard, and Cole Hamels. And, of course, the players themselves deserve a lot of credit. However, it cannot be underscored enough just how much Gillick's watchful eye played a role in the Phillies' rise to prominence.

37 Smuggy

Ruben Amaro Jr. took over for Gillick after the Phillies won the World Series in 2008. He had worked under both of the team's previous general managers, Ed Wade and Pat Gillick, learning many tricks of the trade. Amaro himself was a former player in the Phillies organization, playing for the major league team in two different stints from 1992 to 1993 and 1996 to 1998. He did not have much success, finishing his career as an outfielder with a .663 OPS.

Going into the 2009 season, the expectations for the Phillies were high. They had just won the World Series and their so-called window of opportunity was as wide open as ever. Due to the huge influx in ticket and merchandise sales, the Phillies had financial flexibility for the first time in the history of the franchise. The team's Opening Day payroll increased from $98 million in 2008 to $113 million in '09.

Amaro did not make his presence felt immediately upon taking over. He made several low-key trades, entering the '09 season with essentially the same team that had just won the World Series. However, as the trade deadline approached and the Phillies were looking primed for another postseason run, the starting rotation remained a big question mark. Amaro wanted more assurance in the postseason beyond Cole Hamels, so he went shopping for an ace in late July. Rumors had linked Roy Halladay with the Phillies, but when the Toronto Blue Jays decided to hold on to their ace, Amaro quickly traded for Cliff Lee with the Cleveland Indians. It was arguably the biggest trade in franchise history, as Amaro sent four of the Phillies' top 10 prospects (according to *Baseball America* circa January 2009) over to Cleveland.

Lee was an instant hit in Philadelphia. The reigning AL Cy Young Award winner let his performance on the field do the talking for him, and he was loud. Lee worked fast, rarely issued walks, and was very economical with his pitches. In the postseason, Lee posted a 1.56 ERA with a 5.5:1 strikeout-to-walk ratio, notching complete games in Game 1 of the NLDS and Game 1 of the World Series. Although the Phillies didn't successfully defend their championship, Amaro showed he had no problem sacrificing the future for better odds at winning the World Series.

Amaro had become known as "Smuggy" in the Phillies fan base because he appeared to be very arrogant. He was often seen wearing

Ruben Amaro's Trade History

It can be argued that Ruben Amaro has made the most high-profile transactions in a three-year period as any GM in baseball history. He acquired three aces (Cliff Lee twice) en route to assembling one of the greatest starting rotations baseball has ever seen. He also signed former superstar pitcher Pedro Martinez in 2009 and traded for superb right fielder Hunter Pence in 2011. Very few of Amaro's moves have flown under the radar, showing that the Phillies GM will do whatever it takes to compile an elite baseball team.

Date	Traded	Received	Team
11/20/2008	Greg Golson	John Mayberry	Rangers
12/10/2008	Jason Jaramillo	Ronny Paulino	Pirates
3/27/2009	Ronny Paulino	Jack Taschner	Giants
7/29/2009	Carlos Carrasco, Lou Marson, Jason Knapp, & Jason Donald	Cliff Lee & Ben Francisco	Indians
12/16/2009	Cliff Lee	Phillippe Aumont, Tyson Gillies, & J.C. Ramirez	Mariners
12/16/2009	Kyle Drabek, Michael Taylor, & Travis d'Arnaud	Roy Halladay	Blue Jays
7/29/2010	J.A. Happ, Jonathan Villar, & Anthony Gose	Roy Oswalt	Astros
8/4/2010	cash	Mike Sweeney	Mariners
9/29/2011	Jarred Cosart, Jonathan Singleton, Josh Zeid, & Domingo Santana	Hunter Pence	Astros

Sources: Baseball-Reference.com and www.mlbtraderumors.com.

designer sunglasses with a Blackberry in his hand, often refusing to divert his attention away from his handheld device to acknowledge reporters. In fact, a Phillies blog called The Good Phight devised what they titled a "smug advisory system" for the GM, with the highest rating labeled DISGUST, with the subtitle "Infuriated by Your Idiocy." Of course, it was done in a complimentary, prideful way.

Amaro lived up to his billing in the off-season. He missed out on Halladay in July, but he made sure he got his target. In what played out as two separate trades but may as well have been a three-team trade, Amaro sent Lee to the Seattle Mariners and prospects to the Blue Jays in exchange for Halladay and prospects from the Mariners. Fans were puzzled as to why Amaro couldn't have simply kept Lee and traded for Halladay, anyway, but the trade was done and fans had to live with the consequences.

Halladay was having a great season, but by the trading dead-line, Amaro wanted to add another ace. No, he was not going to reacquire Lee (who ended up getting traded to the Texas Rangers). Rather, he traded J.A. Happ and two prospects to the Houston Astros for Roy Oswalt. The former ace of the Astros found imme-diate success with the Phillies, posting a 1.74 ERA in 82⅔ innings. The Phillies looked unstoppable going into the playoffs, but after sweeping the Cincinnati Reds in the NLDS, the streaky-hot and eventual world-champion San Francisco Giants won the NLCS in six games.

Amaro was not content after the 2010 season. Cliff Lee was a free agent for the first time in his career, but was linked with only two teams throughout the winter: the Texas Rangers and New York Yankees. The Phillies were not in the picture. After weeks of spec-ulation, it was announced on December 15 that Lee was rejoining the Phillies, signing a five-year, $120 million contract. Lee joined an already stacked rotation that included Halladay, Oswalt, and Cole Hamels, foreboding doom for the rest of the National League.

The Phillies had Amaro at the helm for just over two seasons, and he had already dealt for four aces, including Lee twice. Going into the 2011 season, the Phillies had very few question marks, but the health of the team was in doubt. Jayson Werth left the Phillies as a free agent, so right field was also a work in progress, which was at first patched with prospect Domonic Brown and outfielder Ben Francisco. When the offense slumped, including those right fielders, Amaro made his fourth big deal, trading two mega-prospects in Jarred Cosart and Jonathan Singleton and two lower-tier prospects to the Astros for right fielder Hunter Pence.

What will Amaro do in the future? Time will only tell, but you can rest assured it will not go unnoticed.

38 Jayson Werth

Jayson Werth has sports in his blood. His grandfather, Ducky Schofield, and uncle, Dick Schofield, both had long careers in the major leagues. His mother, Kim, competed in the Olympic Trials in the 100-meter dash and the long jump, and his father, Jeff, was a wide receiver for Illinois State University. His two sisters earned scholarships to UCLA and the University of Nebraska for track and volleyball, while his brother played soccer for Syracuse University.

You can understand why Werth was a highly touted prospect when he was taken in the first round of the 1997 draft by the Baltimore Orioles. He originally played catcher but moved to the outfield in 2002 as part of the Toronto Blue Jays organization. In 2004 the Jays traded Werth to the L.A. Dodgers for a relief pitcher.

With the Blue Crew, Werth was expected to blossom, but his career was nearly ended when A.J. Burnett hit him with a fastball during a spring training game on March 2, 2005. Werth didn't return until late May, but his power was gone. He hit just seven home runs in 395 plate appearances and slugged a paltry .374. The wrist problems persisted, causing him to miss the entire 2006 season.

Werth says he saw many doctors, but none could properly diagnose his wrist problem. "No matter who I saw for my wrist, it was always the same old thing: as long as you can tolerate it, you can play," he said.

Fate very well may have intervened when Werth went home to Springfield, Illinois. He ran into a friend of the family, an orthopedist. Werth detailed his wrist injury and was quickly referred to the Mayo Clinic. There, his wrist injury was properly diagnosed as a split tear of the ulnotriquetral ligament. Werth had surgery, then made his way into free agency.

Phillies GM Pat Gillick signed Werth to a one-year, $850,000 contract in early December. The Phillies had an outfield that consisted of Pat Burrell in left, Aaron Rowand in center, and Geoff Jenkins in right, so Werth was simply a backup outfielder at that point in time. However, Jenkins struggled while Werth impressed with great plate discipline and bat control. After spending a month on the disabled list (with an injury not related to his wrist), Werth returned to a job as the Phillies' everyday right fielder.

From Werth's return from the DL until the end of the 2007 season, Werth hit for a .329 average and an incredible .438 on-base percentage, helping the Phillies overcome the New York Mets for the NL East title on the last day of the season. After the season, Jenkins retired and Werth maintained his job in right field. In 2008 Werth regained his power, hitting 24 home runs and finishing with a slugging percentage just a shade under .500. It was in 2009, though, that Werth truly broke out. He finished the regular season with 36 homers and 99 RBIs, along with 26 doubles.

Werth entered spring training in 2010 with a new look. Over the winter, he had cultivated a full beard and let his hair grow, looking more like Jesus Christ than a major league ballplayer. Perhaps, though, it was the Phillies' equivalent to the mullets that became such a staple of the 1993 team. The fans and media adored his new look as Werth entered the 2010 season looking to build upon what he accomplished in '09.

Jayson Werth was an integral part of the Phillies' division-winning teams of 2007–2010, hitting for power and average while playing right field. In the 2008 World Series, he batted .444, with a homer, three doubles, and three RBIs.

WERTH, PHILADELPHIA

Werth didn't hit as many home runs (merely 27) but led the league in doubles with 46. He improved his on-base percentage to .388 and his slugging percentage to .532, finishing the season as one of the top five offensive outfielders in all of baseball. The Phillies were in a predicament, though. The outfielder was about to become a free agent, and they were already very close to hitting the luxury tax, which was set at $178 million for the 2011 season. If the Phillies were to retain Werth's services, they would have to make some tricky financial maneuvers.

GM Ruben Amaro did not make room for Werth, allowing the outfielder to enter the free agent pool. Instead, Amaro signed ace Cliff Lee to join the starting rotation, feeling that prospect Domonic Brown could adequately fill Werth's shoes. As a result, Werth signed with the Washington Nationals for a highly controversial, seven-year, $126 million deal.

In retrospect, it was great that the Phillies did not overpay for Werth, as he had an abysmal 2011 season, while the Phillies—and Lee—reached new levels of success. It will never be forgotten, though, that Werth was one big reason why the Phillies were so successful from 2007 to 2010. Without him, they may not have reached the postseason in '07 or won the World Series in '08.

39 Go to Washington, D.C., for a Phillies-Nationals Game

When the Washington Nationals opened up their self-titled Nationals Ballpark in 2008, they did not know the fury they would unleash when the Phillies came into town. Since the Phillies won it all in 2008, they have seen a surge in popularity across the nation. Much like the New York Yankees, the Phillies even help attendance figures when they are on the road.

Nowhere is that more evident than at Nationals Park. Because of its proximity to Philadelphia, fans have been making the trip down to the nation's capital to infuse the stadium with Phillies red and show their support for their team. Understandably, the broadcasts on both sides are encapsulated by this phenomenon; when they pan the camera across the crowd, it is breathtaking to see the Phillies-to-Nationals fan ratio, which often comes out well in favor of the Phillies.

Michelle O'Malley, a resident of Virginia who runs the Phillies fan website Baseball-Ladies.com, is one of the fans who helps invade Nationals Park. O'Malley has enjoyed her time at "Citizens Bank Park South." On her experience, she said, "I enjoyed the experience so much I purchased a mini ticket plan from the Nationals."

The fans even get into the game the same way they do back in Philly. O'Malley spoke about the fans, recalling that "they booed

Citizens Bank Park South

Since the Phillies won the World Series in 2008, their fan base has grown immensely across the nation. Not only has attendance increased dramatically at home—helping the Phillies sell out more than 200 consecutive games—the fans have helped improve attendance figures at other stadiums. In particular, fans have made the effort to congregate at Nationals Park, which has been dubbed "Citizens Bank Park South" among Phillies fans. In 2009 the Nationals drew about 1,000 more fans on average when they hosted the Phillies; in 2010, that improved to about 6,500 more fans; and in 2011, about 4,000 more fans.

Attendance:

Year	Non-PHI	Phillies
2005	34,209	29,699
2006	26,894	24,358
2007	24,034	25,679
2008	29,108	28,190
2009	22,318	23,374
2010	21,936	27,627
2011	24,559	28,862

the Nationals relentlessly, they led their sections in various renditions of 'High Hopes' after a win…you almost forget you're not in your home ballpark after a while."

It is surprising that the two teams have a rivalry of sorts, as the Nationals have not been competitive against the Phillies. Since 2009, the Nationals are 19–35 against the Phillies. Speaking strictly about the two teams, the rivalry has been a snoozefest—but don't tell that to the fans at Citizens Bank Park South.

In 2011 the two highest-selling games of the season for the Nationals involved the Phillies, drawing 44,685 and 41,727. The game with the third highest attendance included the lowly Pittsburgh Pirates, but it was on July 2 and the fans were treated to a fireworks show after the game. The Phillies were responsible for the most popular game at Nationals Park in 2010, as well, enticing 41,290 fans.

If there is any worry about aiding the enemy by helping with ticket sales, it isn't apparent. The Nationals used their influx of money after the 2010 season to sign free agent Jayson Werth away from the Phillies on a seven-year, $126 million contract. In recent years, the Nationals have also seen the rise of top draft picks Stephen Strasburg and Bryce Harper, so they will certainly have the potential to compete with the Phillies down the road.

For now, Nationals Park remains the hot spot for fans just out of earshot of Philadelphia. Fans get to see their team and, as O'Malley put it, get "the same hometown feel" that they would at their own stadium. See and feel the phenomenon for yourself— take a trip to Nationals Park for a Phillies-Nationals game sometime, and feel free to wear your team colors.

40 Chase Utley

The way Harry Kalas spoke of Chase Utley, you'd have thought Kalas himself had adopted Utley into his family. The legendary Phillies broadcaster had an inflection in his voice that let you know which players he found most special—ask anyone who ever heard him talk about Michael Jack Schmidt, as Kalas called the three-time MVP.

Utley found his way into the hearts and minds of Phillies fans as soon as he came up to the majors in 2003. He hit his first career home run in his second game, a grand slam off of Colorado Rockies starter Aaron Cook on April 24, 2003. Even when he made outs, Utley impressed by going full-throttle. Most players run up the first-base line at half-speed on a routine ground out, but Utley would bust it until he hit the bag, no matter how easy the out was.

The Phillies' second baseman exemplified work ethic. Even as a prospect, he willingly moved from second to third base when he was road-blocked by Placido Polanco. Fortunately for everyone involved, the Phillies were not impressed by his arm strength, moving Utley back to second and trading Polanco to Detroit in June of 2005.

Utley quickly became one of the most productive players in baseball. In his first full season in 2005, he hit 28 home runs and drove in 105 runs, leading all second basemen in Wins above Replacement (WAR), a Sabermetric statistic that measures a player's overall value relative to his position. In fact, Utley led all second basemen in WAR for five consecutive years, from 2005 to 2009. The Phillies' second baseman did it all. Not only could he hit, he played outstanding defense and ran the bases extremely well thanks to a sky-high baseball IQ.

One particular play in 2006 made Utley the jewel of Harry the K's eye. The Phillies were in Atlanta for the series finale on August 9, having split the previous two games. Entering the seventh, the Phillies were down 3–1 going up against the Braves' bullpen. Tyler Yates faced five hitters, allowing four to reach base. He exited with the bases loaded and one out, having already allowed a run, as lefty Macay McBride entered the game in relief. Utley had what they call a grinder's at-bat, fouling off several tough pitches. On the sixth pitch, McBride threw a slider that was too high and caught too much of the strike zone. Utley pummeled the ball to left-center, clearing the bases with a double and giving the Phillies a 5–3 lead.

Howard strode to the plate next. McBride threw him a low fastball to start the at-bat. Howard swung wildly, hitting a high-chopper down the first-base line. Most runners at second base on that play lightly jog toward third base and stop there. Utley, however, ran at full-speed the entire time. As McBride, whose back was to third base, made the assist to first base, Utley had rounded the third-base bag and raced toward home.

Kalas couldn't contain his excitement. He yelled, "Chase is gonna keep going…" as first baseman Scott Thorman made the

Chase Utley watches his solo home run against the Boston Red Sox in Philadelphia on May 20, 2006. In only nine seasons, Utley has become the greatest second baseman in Phillies franchise history, putting up impressive offensive numbers while playing stellar defense.

throw to catcher Todd Pratt "…and he's safe at home plate!" With an enthusiastic rhythm, Kalas exclaimed, "Chase Utley, you are the man!"

What is likely the most memorable play of his career occurred in Game 5 of the 2008 World Series against the Tampa Bay Rays.

The Phillies were up 3–1 in the Series and looking to clinch. The game had been delayed due to rain, starting on October 27 and resuming on the 29th. When play resumed, the Phillies had to play what became known as "three innings for the championship." The Phillies took a 3–2 lead in the bottom of the sixth, but Ryan Madson allowed a solo home run in the top of the seventh to bring it back to a tie game.

The Rays kept threatening. With two outs in the seventh, the speedy Akinori Iwamura came to the plate with Jason Bartlett (who also had above-average speed) at second base against Phillies left-handed reliever J.C. Romero. With an 0–1 count, Iwamura hit a grounder up the middle. Utley ranged to his right, corralling the ball on the lip of the infield grass just to the left of second base. Knowing he couldn't get Iwamura, Utley faked a throw to first. Bartlett rounded third toward home as Utley whipped the ball to catcher Carlos Ruiz. Bartlett leaned to the inside of the baseline as Ruiz dove forward and made the tag a split-second before Bartlett touched the plate. The umpire gave the out signal, and Citizens Bank Park erupted with cheers. Utley's heads-up defensive play saved Game 5, which the Phillies eventually won for their first championship since 1980.

The Phillies had a championship parade on October 31, which went through Philadelphia and ended in Citizens Bank Park, where various members of the team addressed the fans. Most took the opportunity to thank the fans for their support and offer optimism for the future, but Utley took a less conventional route. Utley took the microphone and said, with audible emotion, "World champions." He paused. "World fucking champions!" The crowd went raucous with cheers and applause.

Utley is already the greatest second baseman in Phillies franchise history, but he may go down as one of the top 10 or even five second basemen of all time, joining the likes of Ryne Sandberg, Roberto Alomar, and Joe Morgan.

Chase Utley

While most Phillies fans adore Chase Utley, his greatness often flies under the radar. Already in his career, he is among the top five among all Phillies players in career Wins above Replacement (WAR). WAR is a Sabermetric statistic that factors in a player's contributions on offense, defense, and on the bases, as well as his playing time and his position, then compares him to a replacement-level player who would play for the league-minimum salary.

Phillies Top 10 Leaders in Career Wins above Replacement (WAR):

Player	Pos.	WAR	Years
Mike Schmidt	3B	108.3	1972–1989
Richie Ashburn	CF	52.3	1948–1959
Sherry Magee	LF	47.6	1904–1914
Bobby Abreu	RF	46.6	1998–2006
Chase Utley	2B	42.3	2003–2011
Dick Allen	3B	37.1	1963–1976
Johnny Callison	RF	35.0	1960–1969
Jimmy Rollins	SS	33.7	2000–2011
Del Ennis	LF	31.7	1946–1956
Chuck Klein	RF	30.9	1928–1944

(Source: Baseball-Reference.com)

41 Steve Carlton

The recent iterations of the Phillies may make you think otherwise, but acquiring an ace pitcher is difficult. For free agents, you must outbid several other interested teams; in trades, a team must sacrifice a portion of its farm system. On February 25, 1972, the baseball gods smiled upon the Phillies as they were able to acquire Steve Carlton from the St. Louis Cardinals in exchange for Rick Wise.

The two pitchers weren't all that different at the time. Up to the trade, Carlton had won 77 games while Wise had won 75; Carlton had a 2.1:1 strikeout-to-walk ratio, a hair below Wise's 2.2:1. Carlton, though, had a career ERA a half-run lower than Wise. However, the Cardinals did not intend to keep Carlton around after a disagreement over his salary, so they made the swap.

Carlton's first year in Philadelphia was, simply put, incredible. He went 27–10 with a 1.97 ERA en route to winning the NL Cy Young Award unanimously. As the Phillies grew as a team in the early 1970s, Carlton was the seasoned veteran leading the way. The Phillies broke a 25-year postseason drought in 1976, thanks in part

Steve Carlton deals to home plate in Game 3 of the 1978 NLCS against the L.A. Dodgers in Dodger Stadium. With the Phillies down 2–0, Carlton got the win and also hit a three-run homer in the second inning to help his cause.

to Carlton's 20–7 record and 3.13 ERA. There was much more to come from the lefty ace.

The Phillies stayed competitive in 1977, reaching the postseason in back-to-back years for the first time in franchise history. Carlton won his second Cy Young Award, finishing the year at 23–10 with a 2.64 ERA. In '78, when the Phillies reached the postseason for a third straight year, Carlton posted a 2.84 ERA, another good season for the lefty. However, he posted mediocre results in the playoffs again. After a complete game in Game 3 of the 1978 NLCS in which he allowed four runs against the Los Angeles Dodgers, Carlton had a career 5.53 ERA in four postseason starts as a Phillie.

Partially a result of his struggles and partially a result of a severed relationship with the media, Carlton began to receive a lot of criticism for his failure to show up when it mattered most for the Phillies. After all, what good is a Cy Young–caliber pitcher when he can't get it done in the playoffs?

Carlton had, by his standards, a down year in 1979, and the Phillies missed the postseason. The Phillies, however, clawed back in '80 as Carlton went 24–9 with a 2.34 ERA. He ended up winning his third career Cy Young Award, but more importantly, he was dominant in the postseason. The Phillies won all four of his starts, including the deciding Game 6 of the World Series against the Kansas City Royals. In the 1980 postseason, Carlton had a 2.30 ERA in four starts spanning 27⅓ innings. Mike Schmidt won World Series MVP, but a strong argument could have been made in favor of Carlton.

The 1981 season was arduous for Carlton as he missed time in the summer with an injury, but he came back with enough time to help the Phillies in the postseason. Despite quality starts in both of his starts in Games 1 and 5 of the NLDS against the Montreal Expos, the Phillies lost both games and the series. Carlton rebounded in 1982, winning his fourth career Cy Young Award with a 23–11 record and a 3.10 ERA. At that point in time, Carlton was the first pitcher in baseball history to win four career Cy Young Awards. Carlton cemented himself as one of the best left-handed pitchers of all time, but he was far from done.

The 1983 Phillies were affectionately referred to as "the Wheeze Kids," a play on the 1950 "Whiz Kids" Phillies pennant winners. Aside from right fielder Von Hayes, every Phillies regular was at least 30 years old, and the starting rotation was led by the 38-year-old Carlton. The end of the road was here; if the Phillies were going to win another World Series, it would have to be in 1983.

On the back of Steve Carlton, the Phillies made it to the World Series. Carlton had won Games 1 and 4 of the NLCS against the Dodgers, throwing 7⅔ shutout innings in Game 1 and six innings of one-run ball in Game 4. The Phillies ran out of steam in the World Series, though, despite Carlton's effort in Game 3.

The Phillies' run was over. They missed the playoffs for the remainder of Carlton's tenure, releasing him in 1986. Carlton played for the San Francisco Giants, Chicago White Sox, Cleveland Indians, and Minnesota Twins, but never had any success. He

Steve Carlton and the Cy Young Award

When he won his fourth Cy Young Award in 1982, Steve Carlton was the first pitcher to win four in a career. In the years since, however, he has been surpassed by Roger Clemens and Randy Johnson, and matched by Greg Maddux. Carlton retired a 10-time All-Star and one of the best left-handed pitchers of all time, having led the Phillies to six playoff appearances, two World Series appearances, and one championship.

Pitcher	CYAs	Years
Roger Clemens	7	1986, 1987, 1991, 1997, 1998, 2001, 2004
Randy Johnson	5	1995, 1999, 2000, 2001, 2002
Steve Carlton	4	1972, 1977, 1980, 1982
Greg Maddux	4	1992, 1993, 1994, 1995

retired in 1988 a 10-time All-Star with the record for most strike-outs in a career by a left-hander, with 4,136.

With 96 percent of the vote, Carlton was enshrined in the Baseball Hall of Fame in 1994. At the time he retired, his 329 career wins was ninth best in baseball history. He has since been passed by Greg Maddux and Roger Clemens.

Looking back, the Phillies' Wise-for-Carlton trade is one of the most lopsided in baseball history. It helped bring the Phillies to previously unattainable levels of success, setting the stage for the franchise's first championship.

42 Walking Off at 4:00 AM

The Phillies were scheduled to play a twinight doubleheader against the San Diego Padres on July 2, 1993. Three separate rain delays stalled the first game by nearly six hours, but the Padres eventually won 5–2 thanks to a Fred McGriff two-run home run. Given the time, nobody expected the second game to be played.

The players, however, were informed that the second game would be played. The previous game ended around 1:00 AM; the second game started around 1:20. The Padres staked themselves to a 5–0 lead after four innings against Phillies starter Jose DeLeon. The Phillies rallied for a run in the bottom half of the inning, then found themselves back in the thick of things when Ricky Jordan hit a three-run home run in the bottom of the fifth.

With an RBI single to right field, Darren Daulton tied the game at five apiece in the bottom of the eighth. The clock at Veterans Stadium read 3:16. The stadium was nearly empty for most of the game, but people were starting to come back. Recalling the game for MLB Network, Phillies reliever Mitch Williams noted that the bars in Philadelphia were closing, and people were allowed to come into the stadium without a ticket.

Williams was brought in to pitch the ninth inning and held the Padres scoreless. He did the same in the top of the 10th. In the bottom of the 10th, manager Jim Fregosi informed Williams, who was due up fourth in the inning, that if it got to him, he was hitting because the Phillies were out of position players. As a reliever, Williams didn't get to hit much, but he did have a home run to his name, hit in 1989 when he was with the Chicago Cubs.

Against future Hall of Fame closer Trevor Hoffman, Pete Incaviglia led off with a walk. Jim Eisenreich singled to right, putting runners on first and second with no outs and Daulton due up.

In a typical game where the home team has runners on first and second with no outs in extra innings of a tie game, the home team will usually bunt the runners over. However, with Williams on deck, Daulton had to take a normal at-bat and hope for a hit. Hoffman, though, struck out Daulton with a fastball. With a reliever due up, Phillies fans came to terms with a wasted inning and looked ahead to the 11th.

Williams took his spot in the batter's box. He recalled threatening to hit catcher Benito Santiago with his bat if he called for a forkball from Hoffman. Hoffman blew a chin-high first-pitch fastball by Williams for strike one. On his approach for the second pitch, Williams explained, "I cheated a bit 'cause I knew Trevor had good control. So I started early, and he just ran into my bat."

Hoffman threw a belt-high fastball that appeared to be several inches off the plate. Williams laced it into left-center where it skidded on the Astroturf. Left fielder Phil Clark judged it poorly, taking his momentum toward center field rather than toward home plate. Incaviglia, running as fast as his 6'1", 225-pound frame would allow, scored without a throw.

From the way broadcaster Harry Kalas called the play, you never would have known it was 4:41 in the morning. He exclaimed with all of his usual vim and vigor, "This game is over on an RBI hit by Mitchy-poo!"

And a nickname was born. From that point on, Williams was referred to as "Mitchy-poo." Williams explained that it was not the nickname he would have chosen for himself, but "when a legend gives you a nickname, you just kind of let it go." He added, "with Harry, anything he called me was fine."

Four forty-one AM remains the latest a major league game has ever been finished. The Phillies' win on July 3, 1993, is still one of the most memorable in their long history, and they have the vaunted bat of Mitch Williams to thank.

43 Scott Rolen

There was something about the way Phillies public address announcer Dan Baker introduced Scott Rolen that made every at-bat of his special, even in the dog days of an unforgiving summer at Veterans Stadium. Selected in the second round of the 1993 draft, the third baseman ascended quickly through the Phillies' minor league system, representing the hopes and dreams of a franchise that aimed to return to glory after the strike.

In his first full season as a Phillie in 1997, Scott Rolen was surrounded in the lineup by remnants of the 1993 World Series team and a hodgepodge of free agents acquired from the proverbial dumpster. As a result, the 22-year-old Rolen was thrust into the middle of the Phillies' lineup, expected to be a consistent run-producer. He did not disappoint. Along with stellar defense at the hot corner reminiscent of Mike Schmidt, Rolen hit 21 home runs and drove in 92 on his way to winning the NL Rookie of the Year award unanimously. He became the first Phillie to win the award since Dick Allen in 1964.

Scott Rolen played third base for the Phillies from 1997 to midway through the 2002 season. Rolen could have been one of the franchise's best third-baggers after Mike Schmidt, both offensively and defensively, but he turned down a lucrative offer from the Phils to pursue a deal with a contending team.

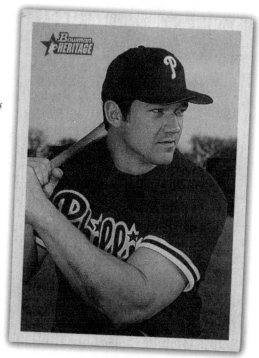

Rolen was only getting started. In 1998 he added 10 more home runs and 18 more RBIs, emerging as one of the best third basemen in baseball, alongside Chipper Jones of the Atlanta Braves. Rolen won his first Gold Glove, a trend that would become common over the span of his career.

After the 2001 season, Rolen had 133 home runs and nearly 500 RBIs. With the talk of Rolen having a career that could rival that of Schmidt, the Phillies focused on getting him signed to a long-term contract before he could become a free agent. In November, the Phillies offered him a 10-year contract with the potential to be worth $140 million. However, Rolen did not accept the deal, citing the Phillies ownership's lack of commitment to winning—the second such claim by a marquee player (the other being Curt Schilling) in the span of about two years.

The Phillies and Rolen entered the 2002 season bracing for the divorce. Rolen continued to play well, hitting 17 home runs with

66 RBIs in 100 games. On July 29, the Phillies and Cardinals reached an agreement on a trade that sent Rolen and prospect Doug Nickle to St. Louis in exchange for second baseman Placido Polanco, reliever Mike Timlin, and pitcher Bud Smith.

Just like that, it was over. One day, Rolen is on his way to becoming the next Mike Schmidt; the next, he is wearing a different shade of red for another team. All things considered, it was a necessary transaction for both sides: Rolen couldn't be expected to give it his all for an organization he didn't respect, and the Phillies couldn't keep a potentially toxic player around.

Rolen couldn't have sounded happier. Recollecting when he first heard the news, he said, "I felt as if I'd died and gone to heaven. I'm so excited that I can't wait to get on the plane [Tuesday morning] and get to Florida to join the Cardinals."

Scott Rolen's Defense

Scott Rolen drew comparisons to Mike Schmidt not just because of his offense—which, by the way, was great—but because of his incredible defense. Rolen was as steady as they come at the hot corner, finishing third among all third basemen in the years 1997 to 2002 in Total Zone, a defensive statistic that estimates a fielder's capabilities within his "zone." Over his career, Rolen won eight Gold Gloves, impressive in and of itself. However, he certainly could have won even more if he had managed to stay healthy in the latter half of his career, perhaps even surpassing the 10 Gold Gloves of Schmidt or matching the 13 of Baltimore Orioles third-sacker Brooks Robinson.

1997–2002 Aggregate

Player	Total Zone	Innings
Robin Ventura	80	6,583⅔
Jeff Cirillo	79	7,534⅓
Scott Rolen	65	7,487⅔
Matt Williams	38	5,898⅔
Scott Brosius	36	5,516

Sources: FanGraphs.com, Baseball-reference.com

While Rolen appeared in two World Series with the Cardinals, winning one of them (2006), he has been a shadow of his former self since 2005. Left shoulder issues dogged him for years with the Cardinals, forcing them to trade him to the Toronto Blue Jays for Troy Glaus in January 2008. Rolen spent a year and a half in Toronto before joining the Reds in another trade as back issues limited his abilities both offensively and defensively.

In retrospect, the Phillies dodged a major bullet when Rolen turned down the 10-year, $140 million contract. Since then, the Phillies opened a new ballpark, which gave them the flexibility to make other free agent signings while fostering one of the better minor league systems in baseball, which gave way to the likes of Chase Utley, Cole Hamels, and Ryan Howard. There is no way to know for sure, but if Rolen had signed that deal, the Phillies might never have had the chance to win a World Series in 2008.

To this day, Rolen remains a highly controversial figure in the city of Philadelphia. Fans still speak of him with contempt, and he still gets a round of boos when he takes his place in the batter's box at Citizens Bank Park. The boos, however, are considerably less passionate than they were in 2003. To Philadelphia, Rolen will always represent unreached potential.

44 Curt Schilling

If there was a way to put fans in the Veterans Stadium seats during the down years of the mid- and late 1990s, Curt Schilling was it. Schilling was the Boston Red Sox's second-round pick in the 1986 draft but didn't make his presence felt in the majors until 1992 with the Phillies, after they had acquired him from the Houston Astros for Jason Grimsley.

Entering 1992, Schilling was a reliever. He had started throughout his minor league career, but both the Orioles (who'd acquired him from Boston in 1988) and Astros used him out of the bullpen, and so the Phillies did to start the '92 season. Eventually, manager Jim Fregosi and pitching coach Johnny Podres felt that Schilling's talents were too good to be used just one inning at a time. On May 19, Schilling made his first start as a Phillie, hurling six shutout frames against the Astros in what kick-started a promising career. Schilling finished the season with a 2.35 ERA, cementing his status as a top-tier starter in the eyes of his manager.

Schilling's 1993 season was, in one word, inconsistent. He finished with a 4.02 ERA, but he had outings where he looked untouchable (such as a complete-game shutout against the Cubs on April 11) and others where he looked lost (seven earned runs in 2⅔ innings against the Cardinals on July 1). Meanwhile, the Phillies had a miraculous season, coming out of nowhere to reach the postseason. Fortunately for the Phillies, Schilling was ready for October baseball.

In two starts in the NLCS against the Atlanta Braves, Schilling won both games, striking out a total of 19 hitters and allowing just four runs (three earned). Two of the four runs were scored in the ninth inning, speaking more to Fregosi perhaps stretching him too long than Schilling's being ineffective. On the back of their ace, the Phillies advanced to their first World Series since 1983. They would be up against the defending champion Toronto Blue Jays.

Schilling's Game 1 was disastrous as the right-hander allowed seven runs and did not escape the seventh inning. John Olerud and Devon White tagged him for two home runs in what was a far cry from what the Phillies experienced in his previous two starts. However, as the Phillies faced elimination in Game 5, Schilling kept his team afloat. Heroically, Schilling tossed a complete-game shutout, outdueling Jays starter Juan Guzman for the 2–0 victory.

Although the Phillies were knocked out in the next game, Schilling's performances gave Phillies fans hope for the future.

Nineteen ninety-four saw a strike that cut the season short. For Schilling, it may have been a good thing—he was 2–8 with a 4.48 ERA. When play resumed in 1995, Schilling never looked back as he transformed into the ace the Phillies organization had always envisioned. His teammates, however, were not good enough, as the Phillies won fewer than 70 games in three straight seasons from 1995 to 1997.

As Schilling continued to lead the rotation, he moved ever closer to free agency. As such, the Phillies' clock on recouping value on the right-hander was winding down unless they could sign him to another contract. Schilling, however, requested a trade in 2000 when he made public his unhappiness with the direction in which the franchise was heading. On July 26, Schilling was traded to the Arizona Diamondbacks for starters Omar Daal, Nelson Figueroa, Vicente Padilla, and first baseman Travis Lee. It was the end of an era in Philadelphia as the Phillies used Schilling to help in the team's rebuilding effort.

Schilling went on to have great success in his new home, winning the World Series in one of his four years in Arizona, and two more World Series in his four years with the Boston Red Sox. Since retiring after the 2007 season, Schilling has enjoyed a career as a commentator with ESPN and as the founder of gaming company 38 Studios.

Schilling remains one of the most divisive players in recent baseball history, but specifically in Phillies history. Some fans have never forgiven him for what they perceive as abandoning the team in 2000 when he asked to be traded, while others sympathized with his desire to play for a contending team before his time in baseball was depleted. Walk into any Philadelphia bar and mention Curt Schilling, you are bound to start up a heated discussion.

45 Bobby Abreu

Bobby Abreu's career started unceremoniously. In 1990 he signed with the Houston Astros as an amateur free agent out of Venezuela. Between 1991 and 1997, Abreu toiled away in the Astros' minor league system. After the 1997 season, when Major League Baseball held an expansion draft to welcome in the newly minted Tampa Bay Devil Rays and Arizona Diamondbacks, the Astros left Abreu unprotected. The Rays took Abreu as the sixth pick, then traded him to the Phillies for shortstop Kevin Stocker on the same day.

Thus a legend was born. Abreu had a great showing for the Phillies in his first year in 1998, smacking 17 home runs and finishing with an OPS north of .900, which later became a trend. Abreu showed great plate discipline, ending the year with an on-base percentage over .400. He also had great bat control, giving him the ability to hit not only for a high average, but with power to all fields. His outfield defense left something to be desired, but there was no doubt he was on his way to becoming a force to be reckoned with at the plate.

Abreu had a career year in 1999. In another year, he may very well have won an MVP award, but he was part of a very crowded NL MVP race. Abreu hit 35 doubles, 11 triples, and 20 home runs and finished with a .335 average. Even more impressively, he finished with nearly as many walks as strikeouts, 109 to 113. However, Abreu finished 23rd in MVP voting—there was no way he was beating Chipper Jones, who hit 45 home runs and drove in 110.

From 2000 to 2003, Abreu continued to put up impressive numbers, but still managed to fly under the radar. In those four years, he hit a combined 175 doubles and 96 home runs with an aggregate .929 OPS, but he had yet to be nominated to an All-Star Game. In this span of time, Abreu had begun to draw the ire of Phillies fans. Certainly one component was the depressing performance of the team overall, but Abreu did not play right field well at Veterans Stadium, often appearing hesitant when he approached the wall in the outfield.

Abreu did his job at the plate as usual, though. In 2004 he had one of the best years of his career, earning his first All-Star selection, long overdue. He finished with a batting average over .300 and an on-base percentage over .400 for the third consecutive year and for the sixth year in his career to that point.

In 2005 Abreu put himself on the national radar. He made his second All-Star team, but was also added as a participant in the Home Run Derby, representing his home country of Venezuela. There, he demolished Derby records, hitting 24 homers in the first round and 41 overall, including one that went an estimated 517 feet. He bested New York Mets third baseman David Wright in the final round for the trophy, also becoming the first Phillie to win the Derby.

After the season, though, it became evident that Abreu's time with the Phillies was nearing its end. The Phillies hoped that they could stay in contention long enough to use Abreu for one magical postseason run, but a 9–18 June forced new GM Pat Gillick to recoup value for his soon-to-be free agent right fielder. On July 30, the Phillies traded Abreu and starter Cory Lidle to the New York Yankees for prospects C.J. Henry, Carlos Monasterios, Jesus Sanchez, and Matt Smith.

Abreu ended his time in Philadelphia as one of the franchise's most productive hitters ever. He has the fifth most Wins above Replacement (WAR) at 46.6, slightly behind Sherry Magee. More impressively, he finished with the fourth highest on-base percentage at .416 (the three players ahead of him each played in the dead-ball era in the late 1800s and early 1900s). He is also tied with Ryan Howard and Jim Thome for the second-highest OPS in Phillies history at .928, behind Chuck Klein at .935.

With the Yankees, Abreu could not help them escape the ALDS in 2006 and '07, and the Yankees missed the postseason for the first time since 1993 in '08. Abreu then signed with the Los Angeles Angels of Anaheim as a free agent, but he could not help them reach the promised land, either.

Abreu will end his career as a controversial player. While he was nothing short of outstanding offensively, he was subpar defensively, and many discredit him for intangible qualities. Some in the know claimed he was not a leader and detracted from clubhouse chemistry. Others did not think he was clutch, citing his .810 career postseason OPS, below his career average of .878. In the end, Abreu will be remembered as an offensive tour de force who could not overcome the faults of the Phillies of the late 1990s and early to mid-2000s. How much of that can be attributed to Abreu himself is up for debate and certainly will be when he becomes eligible on the Hall of Fame ballot.

46 Ryne Sandberg Trade

The Phillies have made quite a few trades with the Chicago Cubs over the years, but arguably none as bad as the Ryne Sandberg trade. Sandberg was drafted by the Phillies in the 20th round of the 1978 draft. In the minor leagues, he performed well enough to merit significant attention from other teams as a trade chip.

After the 1981 season, the Phillies and 36-year-old shortstop Larry Bowa could not reach an agreement on a new contract. Bowa requested a three-year deal, but team president Bill Giles had no intention of handing out a multiyear deal to an aging shortstop. When the team flat refused to grant Bowa the contract he desired, Bowa went on a tirade, accusing the organization of lacking class.

Bowa was still under his old contract, though, so the Phillies either had to keep a disgruntled player on their team or trade him to another organization. With a trade, however, the Phillies would not have any leverage, as their dispute with Bowa was in the public eye.

Former Phillies manager and newly installed Cubs GM Dallas Green saw an opportunity for his club. The Phillies wanted to swap Bowa for Ivan DeJesus, but Green knew he could extract more from the Phillies by playing on Bowa's shortcomings. Later speaking about the trade, Green said, "We knew we had them over a barrel." After a back-and-forth conversation, Green convinced the Phillies to include Sandberg in the deal.

On January 27, the two teams reached an agreement. The Phillies sent Bowa and Sandberg to Chicago, and the Cubs sent

Ryne Sandberg, from his playing days with the Oklahoma City '89ers, the Philadelphia Phillies' Triple A affiliate, before Cubs GM Dallas Green stole him away in one of the worst trades in Phillies franchise history.

RYNE SANDBERG INF

DeJesus to Philadelphia. While Sandberg went on to enjoy a highly successful career with the Cubs that would lead to enshrinement in the Hall of Fame, DeJesus had three very lackluster years with the Phillies, hitting just .249 between 1982 and 1984.

From 1984 to 1993, Sandberg made 10 consecutive All-Star teams. He won a Gold Glove at second base each year from 1983 to 1991 and was named the NL's Most Valuable Player in 1984. He finished his career with 62 Wins above Replacement (WAR). Prior to Chase Utley, the Phillies franchise leader in WAR for second basemen was Tony Taylor at 11.9. There is no doubt that, if Sandberg had stayed in the Phillies organization, he would have retired as the greatest second baseman in Phillies history.

They say hindsight is 20/20, but the outcome of this trade could have been seen coming from a mile away. Unfortunately, the Phillies were forced into action by an ugly contract dispute with one of the team's most recognizable players in Larry Bowa. Bowa, of course, would later return to the Phillies as a manager in 2001, but left at the end of the 2004 season after many clashes with his players, including third baseman Scott Rolen.

Bowa's fiery personality was one reason why he was and still is such a controversial figure in Philadelphia sports history, but the Sandberg trade is as big a part of it. Who knows just how good the 1984–1992 Phillies would have been with Sandberg—they may not have had to wait 10 years to reach the postseason.

47 Jim Thome

After the 2002 season, the Phillies looked forward to their final season at Veterans Stadium before ushering in a new era of baseball at Citizens Bank Park across the street. There was one thing notably absent at the time, however: fan excitement. Usually, when teams are ready to move into a new stadium, they expect a surge in income as fans recognize that their team is making a commitment to winning.

The Phillies finished the '02 season with 80 wins, a step down from the 86 games they'd won the previous year. They missed the playoffs again, and fans watched as third baseman Scott Rolen moved from Philadelphia to St. Louis after talks of a contract extension went nowhere. What if Rolen was right after all, that the Phillies organization was not interested in building a contender?

The off-season after the '02 season proved the skeptics wrong. On December 6, the Phillies made the biggest free agent signing in franchise history when they announced they had swept up free agent first baseman Jim Thome with a six-year, $85 million contract. The Phillies were going to close out the Vet with a bang, after all.

Thome had become a legend with the Cleveland Indians, starting out as a third baseman and moving to first base in 1997. At the time the Phillies signed him, Thome already had 334 home runs to his name and seemed to be a lock to finish his career with at least 500, health permitting. He was one of the best hitters in baseball. From 1995 to 2002, he had a .293 batting average, .426 on-base percentage, and .588 slugging percentage. The only hitter with better numbers in all three categories during that span was Barry Bonds (.308/.465/.664).

Needless to say, the city of Philadelphia was excited to have Thome on board. He was arguably the most well-respected player in baseball, not only because of his elite baseball skills, but because of his friendly demeanor both on and off the field.

Thome got to work right away, notching multi-hit games in four out of his first five games as a Phillie. He hit his first home run as a Phillie in a two-homer effort against the Atlanta Braves at home on April 9. They were Nos. 1 and 2 of what would be a total of 47 home runs on the year. Thome finished fourth in NL MVP voting,

Jim Thome was a Phillies fan favorite, slugging 89 homers and driving in 236 runs in 2003 and 2004, before injuries and the emergence of Ryan Howard eased him out of Philadelphia in 2005.

Jim Thome
PHILADELPHIA PHILLIES® • FIRST BASE

setting the stage for what appeared to be a long and prosperous career as a Phillie.

In 2004 Citizens Bank Park was officially open for business. The Phillies opened their new digs on April 3 with a whirlwind of excitement surrounding the team. Thome entered the season with 381 career home runs, so he would get to 400 at some point during the season, as long as he stayed healthy.

On June 14, the Phillies played a makeup game with the Cincinnati Reds. They opposed right-hander Juan Acevedo. Thome was on a home run tear, having hit six in his previous nine games, so it didn't appear as though there would be a long wait for No. 400. In the first inning, Thome took a Jose Acevedo curve ball to the gap in left-center field. If it was to reach the stands, it would be a wall-scraper. You could hear the uncertainty in the voice of broadcaster Harry Kalas, who—with audible excitement—said,

"Could it be? Could it be?" The ball landed in the first row above the 385' sign. Kalas continued, "It is outta here! Number 400 for Jim Thome!"

As Thome circled the bases upon reaching his milestone, the fans at Citizens Bank Park gave him a lengthy standing ovation, and his teammates all left the dugout to meet him by the on-deck circle after he touched home plate. Kalas, still beaming, gushed over Thome. "There is no more popular player in Phillies history than that big guy."

Thome finished the year with spectacular numbers, as usual. However, there was noise coming out of the Phillies' minor league system as prospect and first baseman Ryan Howard finished the year, spent between Double A Reading and Triple A Scranton/Wilkes-Barre, with 46 home runs and 131 RBIs. Scouts raved about the 24-year-old, harboring no doubt that he was ready for the major leagues. There was only one problem: he was road-blocked at first base by Thome.

Thome, dealing with a back injury, struggled to open the season, finishing April with a .651 OPS. He went on the DL on April 30 and returned on May 21. He would stay in the lineup through the month of June, but his production never improved. Eventually, he was shut down for the season after back spasms proved too much to deal with while playing every day.

That opened the door for Howard, who was remarkably productive en route to winning the NL Rookie of the Year award. The Thome era was over in Philadelphia. After the season, GM Ed Wade traded Thome to the Chicago White Sox for center fielder Aaron Rowand and pitching prospects Gio Gonzalez and Daniel Haigwood.

While Thome's time in Philadelphia ended on a rather somber note, he provided a lot of excitement in his two-plus seasons, helping the Phillies open their new ballpark with a bang and bridging the gap at first base for Ryan Howard. When Thome returned to Citizens Bank Park for the first time on June 13, 2007, he received a very respectful standing ovation from the crowd of nearly 43,000.

48 Hitting Streaks

Fans often argue about baseball's most unbreakable records. Cy Young's record of 511 career wins is often cited, as is Cal Ripken Jr.'s 2,632 consecutive games-played streak. Many a player has compiled a lengthy streak of hits in consecutive games, but none has come close to touching Joe DiMaggio's 56-game hitting streak. Willie Keeler holds the National League record with the second-longest streak at 45 games, and Pete Rose is right behind him at 44 games.

About the time a hitter reaches the 30-game plateau, fans start to really pay attention and chatter about the possibility of DiMaggio's record being broken. But 30 games is just barely more than half of DiMaggio's streak—astonishing, isn't it?

Nevertheless, hitting streaks are extremely fun to watch as they happen, and Phillies fans were treated to two in near-succession with Jimmy Rollins and Chase Utley in the 2005 and 2006 seasons.

Rollins' streak started on August 23 in San Francisco, just a short drive across the Bay Bridge away from his hometown of Oakland. The shortstop went 1-for-5 with an RBI in what appeared at the time to be a run-of-the-mill game. Rollins entered the game in a bit of a slump, racking up just six hits in his previous 53 at-bats.

Rollins notched a hit in each of the next 12 games, but surprisingly enough, he wasn't that productive in that span of time. He had multi-hit games only twice and hit a meager .254 overall.

Starting on September 7, Rollins turned on the afterburners. He had 15 multi-hit games in the 23 games until the end of the season, even getting three-plus hits in eight of them. The year ended with Rollins having hit in 36 consecutive games.

If Rollins was to challenge the NL record held by Keeler or the overall record held by DiMaggio, he would have to do it between two seasons. It was unprecedented that a hitter carried such a lengthy hitting streak into a six-month reprieve that is the off-season. Rollins was able to get hits in the first two games of the 2006 regular season, but it came to an end on April 6 in the series finale against the St. Louis Cardinals. In the end, Rollins' streak lasted 38 games, the eighth-longest streak in baseball history.

While one Phillie's hitting streak came to an end in 2006, another was born. On June 23 against the Boston Red Sox, Chase Utley went 1-for-4 with a home run. Like Rollins, the start of his streak was lackluster and didn't provide any foreshadowing of what was to come. As the calendar turned to July, though, Utley caught fire, starting the month with three consecutive multi-hit games. July ended with Utley on a 32-game hitting streak, 20 of them multi-hit games.

At this point, Utley was not only in hot pursuit of Keeler and DiMaggio, he was trying to catch up to his teammate Rollins, who was a short walk across the diamond at shortstop. Utley had three more multi-hit games to start August, bringing his streak up to 35 games, but he went 0-for-5 against the New York Mets on August 4, ending the chase (pun intended). Utley's 35-game hitting streak put him in a five-way tie for the 11th longest in baseball history.

Before Utley and Rollins, the longest hitting streak in Phillies history was held by Ed Delahanty, who hit in 31 consecutive games 1899.

Ultimately, both Rollins' and Utley's hitting streaks provided great entertainment to Phillies fans, but they certainly put the difficulty of reaching DiMaggio's 56-game hitting streak in perspective. Utley described the streak as "unbelievable." Rollins, ever the showman, thought he had enough left in the tank to go on another run. "I still have another chance. I have a lot of games left," he said at the time.

In the years since, no Phillies have approached even Utley's streak, so we will have to look toward the future for a potential challenger.

49 Binoculargate

Baseball is known for its unwritten rulebook. Don't steal bases when you are ahead by a lot of runs (intentionally vague). Don't gawk at your home run after you hit it, else you show up the pitcher. Don't argue balls and strikes with the home plate umpire, lest you be immediately ejected from the game.

The Phillies ran afoul of the written rulebook on May 12, 2010, when, from the bullpen in the outfield at Coors Field, bullpen coach Mick Billmeyer was caught using binoculars, ostensibly to steal the signs the Rockies' catcher was relaying back to the pitcher. The Rockies' television broadcast also saw Shane Victorino surreptitiously on the bullpen phone in the second inning. Why would an outfielder need to call the bullpen? One can understand the Rockies' suspicion.

Major League Baseball's rules state that a team cannot use technological devises for reconnaissance during a game. The Phillies, naturally, denied any wrong-doing. Manager Charlie Manuel responded to the accusations by asking and then answering a rhetorical question: "Would we try to steal somebody's signs? Yeah, if we can. But we don't do that. We're not going to let a guy stand up there in the bullpen with binoculars looking in. We're smarter than that."

The Phillies split the two-game series with the Rockies, dropping the controversial game 4–3 in 10 innings. Logically speaking, the accusations of the Phillies stealing signs didn't quite add up. If the Phillies wanted to utilize the signs, they would need Billmeyer to see them from the bullpen and relay them back to the dugout, where they could then be relayed to the hitter, all in the time between when a pitcher nods in approval of his catcher's signs and when the ball arrives at home plate.

However, it wasn't the first time the Phillies had been accused of stealing signs. In 2008 the Boston Red Sox accused the Phillies of stealing signs in an interleague series in mid-June. The Phillies, though, lost two of three games.

In addition, in 2007 the New York Mets accused the Phillies of stealing signs with a center-field camera. Two thousand seven, of course, was a franchise-altering year for both clubs. The Phillies won 12 of 18 games against the Mets, including seven consecutive wins in the final five weeks of the season, in which the Phillies overcame the Mets' 7½-game division lead.

Even former manager Larry Bowa confirmed the Phillies' reputation for stealing signs. "There's rumors going around that when you play the Phillies, there's a camera somewhere or bullpen people are giving signs," Bowa said at the time. "And catchers are constantly changing signs. That's the rumor. Now, is it proven? No."

In the end, there was no conclusive evidence that the Phillies were subverting baseball's rules, so commissioner Bud Selig gave the Phillies a general talking-to and nothing more. Amid all of the positive storylines involving the Phillies between 2007 and 2010, it was quite surprising to see other teams question their integrity. The Phillies, as usual, barely acknowledged the naysayers, instead pressing on to more important stories—trying to bring home another championship.

50 Roy Halladay

The playoff-era Phillies of the late 2000s were known across baseball for their ability to score runs in bunches, thanks to the power of Ryan Howard, the speed of Jimmy Rollins, and the consistency of Chase Utley. As the Phillies aged and went through a regime change, however, they started to shift into a pitching-and-defense team, keyed by the acquisition of Roy Halladay after the 2009 season.

With the Toronto Blue Jays, Halladay had earned a reputation as the best right-handed starting pitcher in baseball. His work ethic was unparalleled, leading to his first Cy Young Award in 2003, when he finished with a 22–7 record and a 3.25 ERA. Throughout his career, Halladay was kept away from free agency with two multiyear deals that helped him earn $82 million total over seven years.

As the 2009 season came to a close, the Jays were not optimistic about their chances of keeping Halladay. They had been exploring trade possibilities, even with the Phillies during the summer prior to the July 31 deadline, but nothing came to fruition. The Jays fired GM J.P. Ricciardi after the season, starting another dreary October in Toronto. Alex Anthopoulos took Ricciardi's spot in the front office and immediately made his mark on the franchise.

Ricciardi had turned down a Halladay deal with the Phillies during the season because the Phillies refused to include top prospect Domonic Brown. The Phillies instead chose to acquire Cliff Lee from the Cleveland Indians, who did not require Brown in the deal. Anthopoulos, however, realized that the longer the Jays waited, the less leverage they had in negotiations.

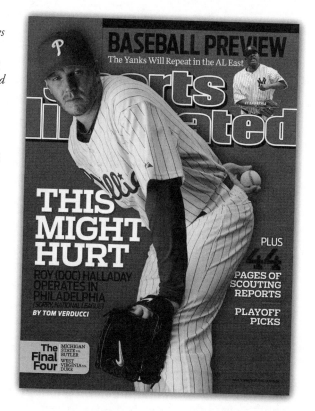

Roy Halladay graces the cover of SI on April 5, 2010. Big things were expected after the Phillies acquired the ace right-hander from Toronto, and Halladay delivered with a Cy Young Award–winning season.

On December 16, the Phillies and Jays reached an agreement, and it was a doozy. The Seattle Mariners were involved in what was not technically but essentially a three-team trade. The Phillies sent Cliff Lee to the Mariners for prospects Phillippe Aumont, Tyson Gillies, and J.C. Ramirez; the Jays sent Halladay to the Phillies for prospects Kyle Drabek, Michael Taylor, and Travis d'Arnaud. In the end, the Phillies swapped aces and prospects.

It was a bit of a head-scratcher for Phillies fans. They had grown fond of Lee for his nonchalant attitude and stellar performances. Why couldn't the Phillies have kept Lee and still acquired Halladay? In the end, though, no one could complain about Halladay donning Phillies red, so the fans welcomed their new ace with open arms.

Halladay got to work fast. He showed up at spring training at the crack of dawn, taking several of the Phillies younger pitchers, including Kyle Kendrick, under his wing. Halladay was not a vocal guy, but a leader nonetheless who directed the team with his actions and his approach to the game. The right-hander made his regular-season Phillies debut on April 5 in Washington against the Nationals, holding them to one run over seven innings.

He performed as advertised—his ERA didn't rise above 2.00 until his 10th start, a clunker against the Boston Red Sox. Across the entire season, he was simply dominant, rarely showing cracks in the armor. In fact, he tossed a perfect game on May 29 against the Florida Marlins, striking out 11 in the process. Halladay became the eighth pitcher to throw a perfect game in the National League; the second Phillie to do so, joining Jim Bunning, who tossed a perfect game on Father's Day in 1964.

Halladay finished 21–10 with a 2.44 ERA, setting a career-high with a 7.3:1 strikeout-to-walk ratio. So it was no surprise when Halladay won the NL Cy Young unanimously—the first Phillie to win the award since Steve Bedrosian in 1987.

The Phillies, however, did not acquire Halladay for gaudy regular season stats; they gave up a wealth of prospects so he could help them win a championship. There was one problem: Halladay had never pitched in the postseason before, how would he handle the new pressure?

With ease. Halladay made his postseason debut in Game 1 of the NLDS against the Cincinnati Reds on October 6. Already the author of a perfect game during the regular season, Halladay held the Reds hitless through all nine innings, becoming only the second pitcher in baseball history to throw a no-hitter in the postseason, joining New York Yankees hurler Don Larsen, who accomplished the feat in the 1956 World Series against the Brooklyn Dodgers.

Halladay finished the 2010 postseason with a 2.45 ERA. Unfortunately, the Phillies offense wasn't able to muster up enough runs against the San Francisco Giants in the NLCS. The Phillies were ousted from the playoffs one round too soon. The team went back to the drawing board, adding Cliff Lee to a staff chock full of aces behind Halladay.

Halladay was just as good if not better in 2011 than he was in 2010. He went 19–6 with a 2.35 ERA, setting a career-high strike-out rate, averaging 8.5 per nine innings. Halladay finished second for the NL Cy Young Award to Dodgers ace Clayton Kershaw (who won the triple crown in '11) and just ahead of teammates Lee (third) and Cole Hamels (fifth). In the playoffs, Halladay again shined, posting a 2.25 ERA in the NLDS against the St. Louis Cardinals. After winning the opener, however, he was once again victimized by his own team's lack of offense, as the Phillies fell in Game 5 to the eventual world champs 1–0.

51 Listen to the Phillies on the Radio

With the ubiquity of televisions these days, it's easy to forget that games are still broadcast on the radio. Phillies fans are already familiar with the TV crew of Tom McCarthy, Chris Wheeler, and Gary "Sarge" Matthews, who provide great insight and entertainment during the games, but the radio team does just as good a job.

Led by Scott Franzke and Larry Andersen, the Phillies' radio broadcasts are, quite often, tons of fun. Franzke's smooth play-by-play keeps fans informed while his chemistry with former Phillies reliever Andersen allows for levity when the game reaches a lull.

For example, during the eighth inning of a game on April 17, 2011, between the Phillies and Marlins, Andersen took what sounded like an on-air nap. Franzke was chuckling as he was describing the on-field action, followed by no response from Andersen. Finally, Andersen said, "What?" Franzke, still chuckling, responded, "Nothing. If I was another broadcaster in this town, I might have had a comment." Franzke was referencing the Sixers' broadcast when play-by-play man Marc Zumoff pointed out that his colleague Eric Snow had fallen asleep.

Andersen laughed as Franzke returned to play-by-play. The former reliever denied napping on-air and we, of course, take him at his word. But it is still an example of the unpredictable and entertaining nature of the Phillies' radio broadcast. For many fans, Franzke and Andersen are as much a part of the game as the players on the field.

A good color analyst is able to put himself in the fans' shoes. Few do that better than Andersen, who has a reputation for becoming audibly upset at umpires, just like the fans at home barking at their TV and radio sets. On August 24, 2010, Ryan Howard was ejected from a game against the Houston Astros by a minor league umpire recently "called up," as it were, to the majors named Scott Barry.

Andersen's rant was, in one word, epic.

> FRANZKE: [Barry has] just ejected Ryan Howard from the game.
> ANDERSEN: Why did he throw [Howard] out? He had no business to throw him out.
> FRANZKE: [not responding to Andersen but describing what is happening] ...Howard is going after Scott Barry.
> ANDERSEN (voice raised): And if these umpires put their hands on Howard, it's wrong. The umpires have no business pushing Howard.
> FRANZKE: Sam Holbrook, getting Howard pushed back. [Placido] Polanco pushing Howard back. Howard

couldn't believe it, and the Phillies don't have a first baseman now. They are going to have to get a pitcher into this game to play in the top of the 15th.

ANDERSEN (still with voice raised): He had no business— and they need to watch a replay of this and send this guy out. I'm telling you right now, this is a travesty, and that's what's wrong with these umpires today, is they can't control themselves; they got no composure. And that is wrong on Scott Barry's part, plain and simple, end of story. That's terrible.

FRANZKE: Two men left for the Phils, we go to the 15th still tied 2–2.

ANDERSEN: That's terrible.

If you haven't tuned in to a Phillies broadcast on the radio, put it on your bucket list. Franzke and Andersen will not disappoint.

52 Watch the Phillies on TV

There is nothing better than sitting on the couch after a hard day of work with a cold beverage and the Phillies game on the TV. For many Philadelphians, this is their daily routine between April and October and has been for many, many years.

For 27 seasons, from 1971 and 1997, Harry Kalas and Richie Ashburn called the action for Phillies fans. Ashburn passed away on September 9, 1997, and an era came to an end. In the ensuing years, Kalas was joined by a cadre of partners in the broadcast booth, including former players Larry Andersen, John Kruk, and Gary "Sarge" Matthews, as well as current broadcasters Chris Wheeler and Tom McCarthy.

The city of Philadelphia was shocked when Kalas passed away on April 13, 2009, in Washington, D.C. Kalas had finished calling the Phillies-Rockies series in Colorado but had been dealing with atherosclerosis and hypertension for several years. Another era in the Phillies' broadcast booth came to an end.

The Phillies mourned the passing of Kalas but had to press forward. McCarthy was chosen as the heir apparent to Kalas in the booth, joined by Wheeler and Matthews in three-inning intervals (Wheeler for innings 1–3 and 7–9, Sarge for innings 4–6). In every game, one can notice the impact that Kalas left on the broadcast team with catchphrases and mannerisms.

Let it not be lost that the Phillies' current team has developed their own unique styles. McCarthy's "Gone!" and "How about that?" calls are widely known throughout the area, while Wheeler was the genesis of both the website ChrisWheelerGlossary.com, which categorizes all of his sayings, as well as a bingo card that fans can play with during a game. The card includes such sayings as, "Oh Brother," "Dropped the Bat Head on It," and, "Likes the Ball Middle-in."

Meanwhile, Matthews has become known as a hat aficionado. He tries his best to wear a new hat for every broadcast. The trend was chronicled on the Phillies blog TheFightins.com, which found that from the start of the 2011 season to July 14, Sarge wore a navy blue kangol 18 times, the most of any other hat. Impressively, he only repeated a hat 14 times.

Needless to say, the Phillies television broadcast doesn't just show you the game; they entertain you. Few broadcast teams are as dedicated to their fans as the Phillies' is to theirs. If you happen to live outside of the Phillies' broadcast range, make sure to catch a game on MLB.tv or Extra Innings. You won't leave disappointed.

53 Chuck Klein

The story of how the Phillies acquired Chuck Klein simply screams "early 1900s baseball." Klein was signed to a minor league contract by the St. Louis Cardinals in the mid-1920s and eventually made it to Fort Wayne, one of the Cardinals' minor league affiliates. At the time, the Cardinals owned two teams in the same league—one in Fort Wayne, Indiana, and one in Dayton, Ohio. Commissioner Kenesaw Mountain Landis, historically known for ruling with an iron fist, ordered the Cardinals to sell off the Fort Wayne team and forfeit the right to the players.

The Phillies and New York Yankees were very interested in acquiring Klein, so they engaged in a bidding war. Eventually, the Phillies won, and Klein joined the team in July 1928, playing every day in right field.

Klein was what some call "really, really good." He finished his half-season in 1928 with a .360 average. He was not just a contact hitter, though; he could hit for prodigious power, get on-base at a high rate, run the bases well, and play high-quality defense with a great throwing arm. In short, he was the total package.

In 1929 Klein led the league with 43 home runs, while hitting .356 and driving in 145 runs. He topped that the next season with a .386 average and 170 RBIs (neither of which led the league, surprisingly enough). Klein also had 40 home runs and a league-leading 59 doubles and 158 runs scored.

Between 1929 and 1933, Klein led the league in home runs four times, RBIs twice, hits twice, runs three times, stolen bases once, slugging percentage three times, batting average and on-base percentage once each, and OPS twice. In 1933 Klein won the triple

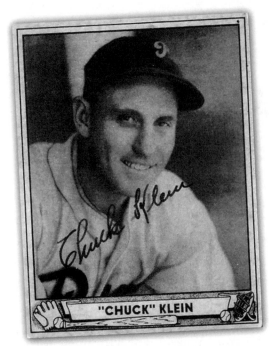

Chuck Klein, the only Phillie to ever win the triple crown (in 1933), was the Phillies home run king until Mike Schmidt came along and shattered his mark of 243 homers. Had the second half of his career matched the first, he'd be remembered as one of the game's all-time greats. As it stands, it was still enough to get him into the Hall of Fame.

"CHUCK" KLEIN

crown with a .368 average, 28 home runs, and 120 RBIs, one of only five National Leaguers to ever win the triple crown and the only Phillie.

Klein left Philadelphia after the '33 season, moving on to the Chicago Cubs. However, he had reached a plateau; he would never again replicate his production in his first six seasons. Klein did return to Philadelphia in late May of the 1936 season, but was already on the decline. He went to the Pittsburgh Pirates in early June 1939, then returned to the Phillies again after the season where he would play until 1944, when he retired.

Between 1934 and 1944, Klein racked up nearly 3,500 plate appearances, but hit just 109 home runs and drove in 474 runs while hitting .278. Compare that to the first six seasons of his career, when he batted just fewer than 3,400 times with 191 home runs, a .359 average, and 727 RBIs.

The Phillies were lucky to get six extremely high-quality seasons out of him when they did, but despite Klein's best efforts,

Four–Home Run Games

On April 17, 1976, Mike Schmidt became the 10th player in major league history to hit four home runs in one game, the first such occurrence in nearly 15 years. Since Schmidt's feat, only five players have matched it. Oddly enough, the Phillies needed each of Schmidt's four homers as they barely won that day, 18–16, having fallen behind 12–1 after three innings. Along with four home runs, Schmidt also singled and drove in eight runs. There are only 128 instances of a player driving in eight or more runs since 1919.

Players that have hit four home runs in one game:

Player	Team	Date
Bobby Lowe	Boston Braves	May 30, 1894
Ed Delahanty	**Philadelphia Phillies**	**July 13, 1896**
Lou Gehrig	New York Yankees	June 3, 1932
Chuck Klein	**Philadelphia Phillies**	**July 10, 1936**
Pat Seerey	Chicago White Sox	July 18, 1948
Gil Hodges	Brooklyn Dodgers	August 31, 1950
Joe Adcock	Milwaukee Braves	July 31, 1954
Rocky Colavito	Cleveland Indians	June 10, 1959
Willie Mays	San Francisco Giants	April 30, 1961
Mike Schmidt	**Philadelphia Phillies**	**April 17, 1976**
Bob Horner	Atlanta Braves	July 6, 1986
Mark Whiten	St. Louis Cardinals	September 7, 1993
Mike Cameron	Seattle Mariners	May 2, 2002
Shawn Green	Los Angeles Dodgers	May 23, 2002
Carlos Delgado	Toronto Blue Jays	September 25, 2003

Source: Major League Baseball

the Phillies were still a cellar-dwelling team. During Klein's best years, the Phillies were just a .403 team (which equates to 65 wins over a 162-game season).

To this day, however, Klein remains the franchise's leader in career OPS and, until Mike Schmidt came along, was the franchise leader in home runs with 243 (he's now fifth). The Phillies came to be in 1883, but had few star players in the years leading up to

Klein's arrival. Klein was certainly a star player and, at least in his first six seasons, was one of the premier players in the league.

The Phillies retired Klein's "number," but because he wore so many numbers in his career (3, 32, 36, 1, 26, 14, 29, 8), they simply used an Old English-style "P" in place of a number on his small banner in the outfield at Veterans Stadium. Klein's career was given its proper honor when he was posthumously inducted into the Hall of Fame in 1980, one of only six players inducted wearing a Phillies cap.

54 Ed Delahanty

Ed Delahanty was the first marquee player in Phillies franchise history. The right-handed hitter joined the club in 1888, but did not rise to stardom until 1892. Early in his career, he was a jack-of-all-trades, but as he became more established in the league, he settled in nicely as an outfielder.

In his first four seasons—which included one season with the Cleveland Infants of the Players League—Delahanty showed decent contact skills, but scant power. In 1892 he broke out with 57 extra-base hits and 91 RBIs. The next year, Delahanty barely missed out on the triple crown, leading the league with 19 home runs and 146 RBIs, but his .368 average trailed teammates Billy Hamilton (.380) and Sam Thompson (.370).

Delahanty hit .404 in each of the next two seasons. The trio of Delahanty, Hamilton, and Thompson are the only Phillies to hit over .400; no Phillie has accomplished the feat since the turn of the 20th century.

From 1893 to 1896, Delahanty hit .392 with a 1.069 OPS. He led the league in doubles, home runs, RBIs, and OPS twice.

Phillies Hall of Famer Ed Delahanty in 1889, from his Old Judge Cigarettes baseball card. A career .346 hitter, he hit over .400 in three different seasons and is one of only three Phillies to hit four home runs in a game, when homers were much less common than they would later become.

Delahanty did not slow down much as he aged. In 1899, at the age of 31, he led the league in average at .410 and RBIs at 137, missing out on the triple crown again. He also had an astonishing 238 hits. Impressively, Delahanty was also a great base runner, finishing his career with 455 stolen bases, averaging one every four games.

When Delahanty left the Phillies after the 1901 season, he was easily the best hitter in the Phillies' young history, but he still remains among the best in franchise history more than 100 years later. He ranks in the franchise's top 10 in batting average (2nd), on-base percentage (5th), slugging percentage (10th), OPS (6th), runs (2nd), hits (3rd), doubles (1st), triples (1st), RBIs (2nd), walks (7th), and stolen bases (2nd).

In addition, along with Rogers Hornsby, Delahanty is one of only two three-time .400 hitters. His career .346 average is fifth all-time in baseball history, behind Ty Cobb, Hornsby, "Shoeless" Joe Jackson, and Lefty O'Doul.

Along with his impressive numbers, Delahanty is remembered for one of "the most shameful home runs of all time." In 1892 the Chicago White Stockings (who later became the Cubs) were in Philadelphia at the Huntingdon Street Grounds. In the eighth inning, Cap Anson hit a fly ball to center field. The ball hit a pole and caromed into a "doghouse," where numbers were stored for the scoreboard.

Delahanty went after the ball but got stuck. His teammate, Sam Thompson, had to retrieve Delahanty with the ball, but Anson had already circled the bases by the time the two had emerged. The book *Baseball Hall of Shame* by Bruce Nash and Allan Zullo referred to the home run as an "inside-the-doghouse home run."

55 2011 Starting Rotation

In the span of two seasons, the Phillies went from having a mediocre starting rotation to having a historically great starting rotation. Along with bringing along young lefty Cole Hamels, GM Ruben Amaro acquired Cy Young winners Roy Halladay from the Toronto Blue Jays and Cliff Lee from the Cleveland Indians (who later re-signed with the Phillies as a free agent), as well as Roy Oswalt from the Houston Astros. With some of the best infielders in baseball in Ryan Howard, Chase Utley, and Jimmy Rollins, the Phillies became known as the class of the National League between 2009 and 2011.

In 2011 Halladay was coming off a season in which he had won his second career Cy Young Award, unanimously (the fifth pitcher to win the award in both the American and National Leagues), threw a perfect game in the regular season against the Florida Marlins, and threw a no-hitter in the postseason in Game 1 of the

NLDS against the Cincinnati Reds. Halladay led the league in a bevy of pitching categories, but most important was his 7.3:1 strikeout-to-walk ratio, also a career-best.

Meanwhile, Lee had helped bring the Texas Rangers to the World Series—Lee's second consecutive appearance in the Fall Classic with two different teams (the Phillies in '09; the Rangers in '10). Lee led all of baseball with a 10.3:1 strikeout-to-walk ratio, the second-best ratio in baseball history.

Cole Hamels rebounded from a shaky 2009 season, evolving from a two-pitch pitcher to a four-pitch pitcher. He improved his curveball significantly and added a cut fastball, both of which contributed to boosting his strikeout rate from 7.8 per nine innings in '08 and '09 to 9.1 in '10. Meanwhile, his change-up continued to grade as one of the best in baseball.

Roy Oswalt, who had been slowed by back problems, had a great showing in 2010, finishing with a 2.76 ERA, a career-low among seasons in which he made at least 21 starts. Not to be forgotten in the No. 5 spot was Joe Blanton, an underrated right-hander who helped the Phillies win the 2008 World Series.

Taken all together, the Phillies rotation was expected to compete with the Braves' rotations of the 1990s as one of, if not *the* best in baseball history. They did not disappoint.

Astonishingly, Halladay improved on his 2010 season, lowering his ERA about a 10th of a point to 2.35. He again led the league with a 6.3:1 strikeout-to-walk ratio while setting a career-high strikeout rate, averaging 8.5 per nine innings. He won 19 games, giving him 40 in his first two seasons as a Phillie.

Lee was just as good, finishing with a 2.40 ERA, a career low. He also set a career-high strikeout rate, averaging 9.2 per nine innings. Impressively, Lee threw six complete game shut-outs, best in baseball. Between Halladay and Lee, as well as Los Angeles Dodgers ace Clayton Kershaw, the Cy Young Award was expected to go to one of the three.

The 2011 Phillies Starting Rotation

Using Sabermetrics, we can get a deeper appreciation for the skill of the 2011 Phillies starting rotation. FIP is a stat like ERA that only focuses on events directly within a pitcher's control: strikeouts, walks, and home runs. This removes variables like the quality of defense and luck on batted balls. FIP− compares the team's FIP to the league average in a given season, setting an average at 100; the lower the number, the better. Going back to 1990, the 2011 Phillies rotation ranks the best by both FIP and FIP−.

Team	Year	FIP−	FIP
Phillies	2011	77	2.98
Braves	1997	78	3.30
Braves	1996	78	3.41
Braves	1998	79	3.38
Diamondbacks	2002	79	3.49
Yankees	2003	81	3.56
Red Sox	2002	81	3.60
Red Sox	1990	81	3.32
Braves	1995	81	3.45

Source: FanGraphs.com

Hamels had a career year, though it got lost in the excellence of two of his rotation mates. The lefty had a 2.79 ERA with a career-best 4.4:1 strikeout-to-walk ratio.

Oswalt's back problems flared up and caused him to miss some starts, while Blanton missed four months with an elbow injury. The Phillies took Oswalt's starts when they could get them, while they filled Blanton's spot with young right-hander Vance Worley. Worley was a top prospect, having been drafted in the third round of the 2008 draft. He threw well at Triple A Lehigh Valley in 2010 and '11, showing maturity and poise on the mound. With scant options, Worley was called up in late April.

Worley was impressive, using a herky-jerky, over-the-top delivery to hide the ball and deceive hitters. More than half of his strikeouts did not involve a batter swinging, illustrating the level of deception the right-hander possessed. In 25 appearances (21 starts), Worley went 11–3 with a 3.01 ERA, finishing third in the NL Rookie of the Year voting.

In aggregate, the Phillies' rotation finished the 2011 regular season with a 2.86 ERA, best in the league by far. The San Francisco Giants sat in second place at 3.28. Looking at Fielding Independent Pitching (FIP), a Sabermetric pitching statistic like ERA that only focuses on the events directly within a pitcher's control (strikeouts, walks, home runs), the Phillies finished at 2.98, the best mark among all teams since 1990. The second-best rotation by FIP was the 1997 Braves at 3.30.

The Phillies' rotation entered the 2011 regular season with a lot of hype. Many scoffed, citing long odds that they could actually live up to it. Statistically, they absolutely lived up to the hype and then some. There is a strong argument to be made that the 2011 Phillies starting rotation is the best of all-time.

56 Great Drafting in the 2000s

Pat Gillick and Ruben Amaro each received a lot of credit for the Phillies' immense success starting in 2007, and rightly so. Without scrap-heap pickups like J.C. Romero, the Phillies might never have won the World Series in 2008. Likewise, without trading for three aces, the Phillies probably wouldn't have set the franchise record for wins in a season at 102.

However, the table was set by the great scouting and drafting during the late-1990s and early 2000s. Under Ed Wade and Pat Gillick, Mike Arbuckle was assistant to the general manager who oversaw the drafting of core players including Chase Utley, Ryan

Howard, and Cole Hamels—all as important to the success of the Phillies as any free agents and trade acquisitions.

In 1998, a year after the Phillies were scorned by first-round draft pick J.D. Drew and his agent Scott Boras, Arbuckle continued to aim high, selecting then–third baseman Pat Burrell out of the University of Miami. Burrell spent very little time in the minors before earning a promotion to the majors and making his debut on May 24, 2000. As a left fielder, Burrell became one of the most prolific right-handed hitters ever to wear the red pinstripes, hitting 251 home runs in nine seasons, fourth most in franchise history.

The Phillies selected big right-hander Brett Myers out of high school with their first-round pick in 1999. Starting at rookie ball at the age of 18, Myers spent only one year at each level of the minors. The right-hander showed poise on the mound, decent control, and an ability to miss bats. Myers made his major league debut on July 24, 2002, and would become the front man for the rotation in the years to come, as well as a very effective closer in 2007.

The draft class in 2000 was historically weak, but the Phillies came away big winners. Chase Utley was selected 15th overall in the first round and, of course, went on to have a very prosperous career in a Phillies uniform. Of the 40 players taken in the first round (including supplemental picks), only 23 made the majors; of those 23, only four hitters took 1,000 or more at-bats, and only five pitchers pitched in 100 or more games. The most telling statistic, however, is that Utley is one of only four in the first round to compile at least 10 or more Wins above Replacement (WAR). Utley had 42.3, best in the class; Adrian Gonzalez was second at 28.2, Adam Wainwright third at 20.5, and Kelly Johnson fourth at 15.2.

Two thousand one was very kind to the Phillies. They selected Gavin Floyd in the first round (fourth overall) out of high school and Ryan Howard in the fifth round out of Missouri State University. Floyd showed ace potential in the minors, but was not able to put it together at the major league level between 2004 and

Phillies First-Round Draft Picks, 1998–2002

The Phillies had one of the most impressive runs of first-round draft picks between 1998 and 2002, when they drafted the bulk of the team's core. Pat Burrell became the team's left fielder for nine seasons; Brett Myers led an otherwise unimpressive rotation for eight years; Chase Utley quickly became the franchise's best second baseman of all-time; Gavin Floyd became a productive major leaguer; and Cole Hamels emerged as one of the best left-handed starters in all of baseball. All together, the five compiled 110 Wins above Replacement (WAR).

Year	Player	Career WAR
1998	Pat Burrell	18.7
1999	Brett Myers	14.1
2000	Chase Utley	42.3
2001	Gavin Floyd	12.0
2002	Cole Hamels	22.5

Source: Baseball-Reference.com

2006. The Phillies sent Floyd, along with prospect Gio Gonzalez, to the Chicago White Sox in the Freddy Garcia trade. Meanwhile, Howard became the key batter in the Phillies' lineup, supplanting the injured Jim Thome in 2005.

Cole Hamels was taken 17th overall in the first round by the Phillies in 2002. Considering other left-handed pitchers that were taken in the first—Adam Loewen (4th), Jeff Francis (9th), Joe Saunders (12th), Scott Kazmir (15th), and Royce Ring (18th)—the Phillies came out smelling like roses. Hamels put up ridiculous numbers in the minors (1.43 ERA in 201 innings) before being enthusiastically inserted into the Phillies' rotation in 2006. Hamels would go on to earn two All-Star nominations and the World Series MVP award in 2008.

Even as those draft picks matured, the Phillies continued to draft well, then use their prospects to acquire more established major leaguers. Michael Bourn was included in the Brad Lidge deal;

2004 picks Greg Golson, J.A. Happ, and Lou Marson helped bring John Mayberry Jr., Roy Oswalt, and Cliff Lee, respectively, to Philadelphia; 2005 10th-round pick Josh Outman was a part of the Joe Blanton trade, while 2006 first-round pick Kyle Drabek was the centerpiece of the Roy Halladay package.

Arbuckle left the Phillies after the 2008 championship season, joining the Kansas City Royals as a senior adviser to GM Dayton Moore. However, the Phillies have not forgotten his philosophies and have continued to put intelligent, talented people in positions to make sure the team continues to produce top-tier players. Scott Proefrock and Benny Looper assist Ruben Amaro while Pat Gillick and Dallas Green are senior advisors. Marti Wolever leads the team's scouting department.

As the Phillies have enjoyed more and more success over the years, their draft picks become lower and lower as a result, making it even more difficult to have a booming minor league system. Still, despite the odds, the Phillies continue to churn out prospect after prospect, allowing fans to both enjoy the present and have hope for the future.

57 Mike Schmidt's 500th Home Run

By the time Mike Schmidt was on the precipice of his 500th career home run, he had already become the best player the Phillies had ever seen. Del Ennis was the franchise leader in home runs prior to Schmidt with 259, but Schmidt eclipsed him in 1980, when he hit a career-high 48 and finished the season with 283 in his career.

When the 1987 season came around, Schmidt had won three NL MVP awards and had 495 career home runs to his name. There was absolutely no doubt that he would be a first-ballot Hall of Famer when the time came; getting to 500 was just the last thing Schmidt needed to do to top off one of the best careers in baseball history.

Schmidt started off the season on fire, hitting four home runs in the team's first 10 games. That, of course, left him at 499, on the doorstep of 500. The Phillies were in Pittsburgh for a three-game set with the Pirates at Three Rivers Stadium. With three more games in Montreal to follow, there wasn't any hope of Schmidt reaching the milestone at home, so he pressed forward at full speed.

The two teams played the second game of the series on April 18 as Phillies starter Don Carman opposed Bob Walk of the Pirates. Carman pitched well, holding the Pirates to two runs over seven innings while Walk was chased after three innings. Lance Parrish padded the Phillies' lead with a three-run home run in the third inning, putting them up 5–0.

Steve Bedrosian forked over the lead in the eighth inning, allowing four runs on a sacrifice fly followed by a three-run home run by Johnny Ray. If the Phillies were to come back, they would have to do it against starter-turned-reliever Don Robinson in the ninth inning.

After three batters, it looked like the Phillies would go down with a whimper, as Milt Thompson had singled in between two weak ground-outs. The speedy Juan Samuel, however, stood at first base as a result of a fielder's choice. Samuel knew he could put the Phillies in a position to tie the game with a single if he could steal second base, so he did just that. He quickly advanced to third when Robinson uncorked a wild pitch to Von Hayes. Eventually, he walked Hayes, putting runners on first and third for Schmidt, looking for his 500th home run.

All of the variables came together to foster one of the greatest calls broadcaster Harry Kalas ever made: "The stretch by Robinson. The 3–0 pitch. Swing and a long drive! There it is! Number 500!

The career 500th home run for Michael Jack Schmidt!" Not only did Schmidt reach his career milestone, he hit a go-ahead home run for his team. The Phillies went on to defeat the Pirates 8–6.

Schmidt finished the season with 35 home runs and 530 in his career, but 1987 was his last hurrah. The 1988 and 1989 seasons were not kind to him. Tearfully, Schmidt retired at the end of May 1989 with 548 career home runs. He was enshrined in the Hall of Fame in 1995, appearing on 444 of 460 ballots, one of the highest percentages of players in Cooperstown.

58 Charlie Manuel

When the Phillies chose Charlie Manuel to manage the team after Larry Bowa had been fired, no one expected him to become the greatest manager in the history of the franchise. In fact, many Phillies fans were upset that Jim Leyland or former manager Jim Fregosi were not selected. They viewed Manuel as a nobody from West Virginia with a lackluster track record. After all, Manuel did not have a great career as a player and only managed the Cleveland Indians for two and a half seasons before being fired.

However, the Phillies were looking for someone on the other end of the managerial spectrum from Bowa. Bowa was feisty and combative—with umpires, with the media, and even with his own players. Manuel was calm and even-keeled, known as a players' manager and an all-around nice guy. As such, Manuel was tabbed as the right guy for the job, and he took the reins after the 2004 season.

The Phillies had been competitive under Bowa but were labeled under-achievers, racking up several second- and third-place finishes in the division. It was looking like more of the same under Manuel:

the Phillies won 88 games in 2005 and 85 in 2006, finishing second both times. It got worse when GM Pat Gillick traded away right fielder Bobby Abreu at the trade deadline in '06, even foreseeing doom in the Phillies' immediate future, warning fans it would "be a stretch" to expect the team to compete in '07.

Through the first half of the '07 season, the Phillies played .500 ball, living up to the limited expectations of the fan base and the national media. Entering the season, few had called for the Phillies to win the NL East; those who did were making gigantic leaps of faith. Manuel, though, had control of his clubhouse, something with which many managers struggle. Under Manuel's calm leadership, the players never lost faith and continued to play each regular season game as if it was their last.

The Phillies played .608 baseball in the second half. On August 25, the Phillies were seven games behind the first-place New York Mets in the NL East. Memorably, the Phillies swept the Mets both in a four-game series at the end of August and in a three-game series in mid-September. Winning 13 of their final 17 games, the Phillies overcame the Mets on the last day of the regular season to take the NL East.

As the Phillies celebrated on the field, they showered their manager with champagne. It spoke to the level of respect they had for him. Other mangers found it necessary to trade friendliness for clubhouse control, but Manuel did not. The players viewed Manuel as an equal, just as critical a component in the team's success as anyone else.

Manuel was not just a manager, though; he at times acted as a hitting coach. When hitters slumped, Manuel would spend a lot of time trying to fix whatever was ailing them, whether it was footwork, the swing itself, timing, among many other variables. In particular, Manuel is credited for helping Ryan Howard find his swing when he lost it at times early in his major league career. The Phillies had one of the league's most prolific offenses between 2006 and 2009, partially due to Manuel's knowledge of hitting.

Impressively, from 2006 to 2011, the Phillies improved their regular season win total each year. For a team consistently above .500, that is incredible. Starting in '06, the Phillies wins total went: 85, 89, 92, 93, 97, and 102. The 102 games the Phillies won in 2011 set a franchise record and, at the same time, allowed Manuel to pass Gene Mauch for the most wins by a manager in franchise history with 646.

Under Manuel, the Phillies won five consecutive NL East crowns, reached the NLCS in three consecutive years, reached the World Series in two consecutive years, and won the World Series once. The Phillies fan base went from loathing the fact that he was not Jim Leyland to flat-out loving the guy because he is Charlie Manuel.

There is no doubt that Manuel will be remembered as the greatest manager in Phillies history. The 2007–2011 era was the greatest in the franchise's history dating back to 1883, and Manuel was a sizable part of that.

59 Larry Bowa

How likely would it be for a player to have a 16-year major league career and a managerial/coaching career afterward, despite never having made his high school baseball team and going undrafted? Astronomically unlikely? Many would agree, but Larry Bowa defied those long odds against him.

Bowa signed with the Phillies for $2,000, playing in the minors from 1966 to 1969 and making his major league debut in 1970. He was not exactly the most gifted hitter to don Phillies pinstripes—he lacked power but had good enough bat control and speed to make up for it. In addition, he was renowned for his defense. Along with

Larry Bowa, pictured in his 1973 baseball card. The five-time All-Star and two-time Gold Glove shortstop helped the Phillies to four NL East titles and one World Series championship. Later, as the Phillies' manager, he had an up-and-down tenure from 2001 to 2004.

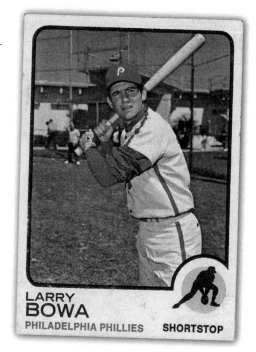

Mike Schmidt at third base, the Phillies had one of the best defensive shortstop–third baseman combinations in baseball for many years.

Both on and off the field, Bowa had a reputation as a fiery personality and a vocal player in the clubhouse. Every team needs someone like that and, although he was no Mike Schmidt in terms of on-field talent, Bowa assumed that responsibility.

In the mid-1970s, the Phillies were going through a transformation. Longtime players were discarded as the Phillies moved into a new era and attempted to end a playoff drought going all the way back to 1950. Between 1976 and 1980, the Phillies made the postseason in four out of five seasons, winning their first ever championship in 1980, in part due to Bowa's glove work.

Bowa set a record for best fielding percentage for a shortstop in a single season in 1979 at .991. When he retired, he also had the best career fielding percentage at the position with .980. Bowa was among the leaders in career assists (6,857) and double plays

(1,265), as well. However, he only won two Gold Gloves because much of his career overlapped with Ozzie Smith, who won the award at shortstop every season between 1980 and 1992. That Bowa had so few Gold Gloves severely underrates how good he was defensively.

In 1982 at the age of 36, Bowa and the Phillies argued back-and-forth about a contract, resulting in his trade to the Chicago Cubs, led by former Phillie Dallas Green. The Cubs received Bowa and prospect Ryne Sandberg. The Phillies received Ivan DeJesus. In retrospect, it is quite possibly the worst trade in franchise history.

Bowa retired in 1985, but he had a managerial career ahead of him. He was named manager of the San Diego Padres in 1987, but was fired in '88 with an 81–127 record at the helm. Bowa returned to the Phillies as a coach in '89, a position he held through '96. He then moved on to the Angels for three seasons and the Mariners for a year in 2000.

The Phillies fired manager Terry Francona after the 2000 season. Immediately, Bowa was suggested as one of the top candidates. He had certainly paid his dues as a member of the franchise dating back to 1966 and had accrued a tremendous amount of managerial and coaching experience. Surprising no one, Bowa was named as Francona's replacement going into 2001.

The Phillies went 65–97 in Francona's final year. Under Bowa, the Phillies improved by 21 games, going 86–76. Bowa's fiery personality was cited as a big reason for the team's turnaround, earning Manager of the Year in the Baseball Prospectus Internet Baseball Awards. In the years that followed, the Phillies remained competitive, but a late-season swoon in 2003 and several tiffs between Bowa and his players created a toxic atmosphere in the clubhouse. In 2004, although the team was several games over .500, the Phillies fired Bowa after the 160th game of the season.

In four seasons under Bowa's leadership, the Phillies went 337–308, certainly not bad numbers. The Phillies never reached the playoffs, but they were attempting to overtake the Atlanta Braves who, with the likes of Chipper Jones, Andruw Jones, Greg Maddux, John Smoltz, and Tom Glavine, were considered the greatest (regular season) dynasty since the New York Yankees of the 1920s.

Bowa moved on to coach the New York Yankees for two years and the Los Angeles Dodgers for three seasons. Two thousand eleven was the first time in a long time that Bowa did not have a job within major league baseball, but he did take a job as a studio analyst for the relatively new MLB Network, where he remains very fiery and outspoken. They say a tiger never changes his stripes; neither did this Phillie.

60 Dallas Green

Dallas Green epitomized Phillies baseball in the 1970s and '80s. Not only was Green a diligent worker, he was very rough around the edges, willing to say whatever was on his mind. Signed by the Phillies as an amateur free agent, Green pitched for the Phillies from 1960 to 1964 and again in 1967, managed the Phillies from 1979 to 1981, and worked in the Phillies' front office at various times between the 1970s and the present. Quite simply, he has earned his red pinstripes.

It was as a manager that Green truly made his mark on the franchise. Danny Ozark was fired before the end of the 1979 season, the first time the Phillies would miss the playoffs in four years. Green moved from the front office to the dugout, taking over the team with 30 games remaining in the season. The Phillies won 19 of 30 games the rest of the way under Green, an improvement from losing 18 of 29 in August under Ozark.

During the 1980 season, Green didn't hold back when he felt like his team wasn't playing baseball the right way. He was openly critical of his players in the media and even more abrasive in the clubhouse. Green was not popular.

"We hated him," catcher Bob Boone said. "He was driving us. I don't know if it was a unique approach, but it was a relationship that worked."

Ozark's Phillies were comprised mostly of veterans who felt they had earned their autonomy. Green came in and removed that autonomy, which clearly didn't sit well. Furthermore, Green, having been director of the minor leagues and scouting, cut into the veterans' playing time with call-ups such as Keith Moreland, Marty Bystrom, and Lonnie Smith.

"I knew [Ozark] had been partial to the older guys and that I'd have to infuse some of the kids in there to create competition. Luckily for me, the kids performed," Green said.

Greg Luzinski referred to Green as the Gestapo. In response, Green showed up in the clubhouse wearing a Nazi armband. Luzinski and Green never got along. The Phillies' former left fielder still harbors some ill will and does not wish to give Green credit for the team's success under his leadership. "Personally, I always thought he just happened to be in the right place at the right time," Luzinski said in 1989.

Regardless of Green's lack of popularity in the clubhouse, the Phillies succeeded. They responded to missing the playoffs in 1979 to winning it all in 1980. The Phillies won the NL East by one game over the Montreal Expos. Then, the Phillies emerged victorious in a grueling five-game NLCS with the Houston Astros in which the final four games each went extra innings. Finally, they defeated the Kansas City Royals in six games for the World Series, barely outscoring them 27–23.

After the strike-shortened season in 1981, Green left Philadelphia to become GM of the Chicago Cubs. He took with him a lot of the Phillies' staff, including Lee Elia, John Vukovich, and Gordon Goldsberry. Green also acquired several former Phillies such as Keith Moreland, Dickie Noles, and Dan Larson. Most importantly, he swindled top prospect Ryne Sandberg from the Phillies in the Larry Bowa trade, one of the worst trades the Phillies ever made.

With the Cubs, Green oversaw the development of future major league contributors Greg Maddux, Jamie Moyer, Shawon Dunston, Mark Grace, and Rafael Palmeiro. However, after engaging in battle with the city of Chicago over stadium ordinances, Green left the Cubs, moving to New York to manage the Yankees for one season. Green also managed the Mets from 1993 to 1996. Green returned to the Phillies in 1998, where he remains to this day. He has served as a senior advisor to GMs Ed Wade, Pat Gillick, and Ruben Amaro.

Green may not have been the most popular guy in baseball, but he certainly had the attention and respect with most of the people who dealt with him on a day-to-day basis. "I know what you can accomplish through sacrifice and determination," he said. "It's that message I've always tried to get across."

61 Gene Mauch

Gene Mauch won 645 games as manager of the Phillies from 1960 to 1968, a franchise record held for more than 40 years until Charlie Manuel eclipsed it at the end of the 2011 season. But Mauch isn't remembered for that first and foremost; instead, he has been for nearly 50 years linked with one of the worst collapses of all-time.

On September 17, after the 147th game of the 1964 regular season, the Phillies were in first place with a 6½-game lead on the

St. Louis Cardinals in the National League. The Phillies, however, would lose 12 of their next 13 games and relinquish control of first place with six games left in the season. To add insult to injury, the Phillies lost four of their final six, even falling down to third place for a short period of time.

Mauch received blame for the collapse as he chose to start his two aces, Jim Bunning and Chris Short, in seven of the team's final 10 games, often on nothing more than two days' rest. The Phillies lost three consecutive starts by both pitchers going into game 161, but won the final two games of the season. By then, though, it was too late.

Although Mauch's Phillies never reached the postseason, they were successful. In six of eight seasons, they finished with a winning record, but with such talented players as Bunning and Short, as well as Dick Allen and Johnny Callison, the Phillies were considered underachievers.

Mauch was fired during the 1968 season. The next year, he moved on to the expansion Montreal Expos, but he would not have as much success. The Expos never reached .500 under Mauch and went on one of the longest losing streaks in baseball history, losing 20 games between May 13 and June 7 in 1969. That was not the most consecutive games a team had lost under Mauch, surprisingly enough—the 1961 Phillies had lost 23 in a row between July 29 and August 20.

The Expos and Mauch parted ways after the 1975 season. The veteran manager signed on with the Minnesota Twins, where he stayed until 1980. He managed them to an above-.500 record in three of five seasons, but in 1980, the Twins missed the playoffs for the 10th consecutive year, and Mauch packed his bags.

Mauch's final stop would come with the California Angels. After the strike-shortened season of 1981, Mauch managed the Angels to a 93–69 record in '82, bringing them to the Championship Series, where they gave away a 2–0 lead in the best-of-five series. Mauch's reliance on aces was again the focus as he chose to start Tommy John and Bruce Kison on short rest.

The Angels reached the playoffs again in 1986, but more tragedy would befall Mauch's squad. In the best-of-seven ALCS, the Angels won three of the first four games against the Boston Red Sox, needing to win just one of the next three games to advance to the World Series. The Angels brought a 5–2 lead into the ninth inning of Game 5, but the Red Sox scored four runs in the ninth inning. Although the Angels tied it in the bottom of the ninth, the Sox won in extra innings and went on to win the final two games to advance to the World Series.

Mauch stopped managing after the 1987 season due to health issues. He had 1,901 wins to his name, which placed him in the top 10 among all managers in baseball history (he has since been passed by Tony LaRussa, Bobby Cox, and Joe Torre). Unfortunately, his name is associated more with failure than with success, as his 1961 and '64 Phillies teams can attest.

Mauch died on August 8, 2005. In the years since, he has been on the Veterans Committee ballot for Hall of Fame induction, and a grassroots movement has emerged to get him inducted. However, he has not received the posthumous honor yet, remaining with arguably the most mysterious managerial career in baseball history.

62 1964 Collapse

Between 1964 and 2006, the word "collapse" when used in the same sentence as "Phillies" referred to only one thing: the end of the 1964 regular season. Gene Mauch's Phillies held a 6½-game lead with 12 games remaining in the season, almost guaranteed to play in the World Series.

However, Mauch had made a habit out of using his starting pitchers on short rest, particularly his two aces Chris Short and Jim Bunning. In fact, Mauch used Short and Bunning as relievers when he deemed it necessary. However, the aces usually had at least three days of rest in between starts. Excluding relief appearances, the two never pitched in fewer than three days' rest entering September.

Mauch wanted to guarantee that his team advanced to the World Series, so he relied extra heavily on his starters. On September 16, Bunning started against the Houston Colt .45s just three days after a 10-inning start against the San Francisco Giants. Bunning lasted only four and one-third innings while allowing six runs.

Entering September 25, the Phillies had lost four games in a row and seven of their last nine. Their lead shrunk to three games. Mauch pressed harder on his aces. Short started on two days' rest against the Milwaukee Braves. He pitched well, but the Phillies lost in 12 innings on account of relievers Bobby Locke and John Boozer.

Bunning started on September 27 on two days' rest against the Braves. The future politician was chased after three innings, having surrendered seven runs on 10 hits. The Phillies lost, and they fell out of first place, one game behind the Cincinnati Reds.

Mauch was not deterred by his failing strategy. Short started the next day against the St. Louis Cardinals, but he was inefficient, unable to finish the sixth inning. The Phillies' offense could muster just one run. The Phillies lost again—their eighth in a row—and the Phillies fell to third behind the Reds and St. Louis Cardinals.

Dennis Bennett pitched game No. 159 and lost, the team's ninth in a row. With three games remaining, having already squandered away a sizable first-place lead, Mauch continued to ask his aces to perform. Bunning would start two of the final three games, and Short started the other.

Game 160 was played on September 30. Bunning was again on two days' rest, and it showed. He failed to make it through the fourth inning against the Cardinals, surrendering six runs in the process. The Phillies' losing streak increased to 10 as they remained in third place, 2½ games behind the now-first place Cardinals. At 2½ games behind with two games to go, the Phillies still had a chance as the Cards still had three games to play.

Short started game 161 on three days' rest against the Reds, who were just a half-game out of first place. Short was not particularly sharp, but good enough, allowing three runs in 6⅓ innings as the Phillies ended their slide and won 4–3. The Cardinals lost that night, and the next day as well, while the Phillies and Reds were idle, so they went into the final day of the season tied with the Reds. If the Phillies beat Cincinnati and St. Louis lost, there would be a three-way tie for first place.

Bunning made the final start of the year on three days' rest. The extra day might have helped as he threw a masterpiece against the Reds, shutting them out over nine innings. But the Cardinals won, eliminating both the Phillies and Reds, and earning the right to move on to the World Series to play the New York Yankees, which they would eventually win in a grueling seven games.

Sadly, the Phillies stayed home after what appeared to be a free ticket to the World Series. The gritty performances by Bunning and Short, who started 19 of 33 games in September and October, went for naught. The *Playoff Odds Report* from Baseball Prospectus put the Phillies at 96 percent to reach the World Series after September 17. Over the next 15 games, the Phillies would win just three of 15 games to see those odds drop to zero—certainly one of the most memorable collapses of all time.

History paid the Phillies back more than 40 years later in 2007, when the New York Mets gave away a seven-game lead with 17 games left to play. At that point, the *Playoff Odds Report* gave the Mets a 98 percent chance to reach the postseason. The Mets,

The 1964 Collapse

Nineteen sixty-four is a year that lives in infamy for many veteran Phillies fans. With 15 games to go in the season, the Phillies had a 6½-game lead and seemed destined to play in the World Series. As manager Gene Mauch pressed on his two aces, Jim Bunning and Chris Short, however, the team began to falter, slowly watching first place slip out from underneath them. Bunning and Short started 19 of the Phillies' 33 games in September and October, but they could not stop the Phillies from bleeding.

Game	Date	Opponent	Result	W–L	Rank	Ahead/Behind
148	Sept. 18	@ LAD	L	89–59	1	+ 6
149	Sept. 19	@ LAD	L	89–60	1	+ 5½
150	Sept. 20	@ LAD	W	90–60	1	+ 6½
151	Sept. 21	CIN	L	90–61	1	+ 5½
152	Sept. 22	CIN	L	90–62	1	+ 4½
153	Sept. 23	CIN	L	90–63	1	+ 3½
154	Sept. 24	MLN	L	90–64	1	+ 3
155	Sept. 25	MLN	L	90–65	1	+ 1½
156	Sept. 26	MLN	L	90–66	1	+ ½
157	Sept. 27	MLN	L	90–67	2	− 1
158	Sept. 28	@ STL	L	90–68	3	− 1½
159	Sept. 29	@ STL	L	90–69	3	− 1½
160	Sept. 30	@ STL	L	90–70	3	− 2½
161	Oct. 1	@ CIN	W	91–70	3	− 1½
162	Oct. 2	@ CIN	W	92–70	2	− 1

Source: Baseball-Reference.com

however, lost 12 of their final 17 games while the Phillies won 13 of their final 17. The Phillies advanced to the playoffs for the first time since 1993 while the Mets, somehow, earned the right to stay home in October.

But for the Mets' terrible September in 2007, the word "collapse" would still be associated with the 1964 Phillies, manager Gene Mauch, and aces Chris Short and Jim Bunning.

63 204 Consecutive Sellouts

How the times have changed. At Veterans Stadium between 1996 and 2002, the Phillies felt extremely lucky if the stadium filled to half of its 62,000-plus capacity. During that time, the average attendance per season ranged between 18,000 and 23,000, disappointing numbers for a disappointing franchise.

Citizens Bank Park opened in 2004, and with it came a surge in attendance. At first, it was because of that "new ballpark smell" and some of the big-name players the Phillies had acquired, namely Jim Thome and Kevin Millwood. In the first three years of the Bank's existence, however, the Phillies continued to miss the playoffs. As a result, attendance dropped from more than 40,000 per game in the inaugural season to around 33,000 in the ensuing two seasons.

The expectations for the Phillies entering 2007 were not high; fans just wanted their team to be competitive for a playoff spot throughout the season. The Phillies did that and more, surpassing the New York Mets on the final day of the season, ending the team's playoff drought that extended all the way back to 1993. The average attendance on the season exceeded 38,000, the eighth best in baseball.

Citizens Bank Park became a common hangout for Phillies fans all around the area. Families, college kids, and even hopeless romantics showed up to the ballpark on a nightly basis for a good time out in the city of Philadelphia. In 2008 the Phillies' average attendance went beyond 40,000 fans per game, marking only the second time that has happened (the other being 2004, CBP's first year). The Phillies finished in the top five among major league teams in attendance.

Another late-season surge in 2008 brought the Phillies to the postseason, where they later emerged victorious with a world championship. Winning a World Series did wonders for attendance. With few seats left to fill on a nightly basis, the Phillies still somehow found a way to do that. Average attendance in 2009 improved to 44,000, the third-best mark in the majors. The Phillies returned to the World Series, but finished just short of defending their title.

It was not evident at the time, but a streak was born. From 2009 to 2011, the Phillies would enjoy 204 consecutive regular season sellouts at home, a mark exceeded only by the Boston Red Sox (712). Attendance would continue to amaze: 2010 saw an average of more than 46,000 fans per game, while 2011 saw more than 45,000. The Phillies had the second-best attendance in 2010 and the best in 2011.

In the five-year span from 2007 to 2011, the Phillies welcomed in nearly 18 million fans. As a result, the team's Opening Day payroll boomed from $89 million in 2007 to $98 million the following season. After the 2008 World Series, the Phillies opened up at $113 million, then $138 million, and finally $166 million in 2011.

For as much as the players on the field and the front office staff are credited with the team's immense success in recent years, the fans have a lot to do with it, as well. Without such impressive attendance totals, which subsequently has effects on concession and merchandise sales, the Phillies might not have been able to offer free agent Cliff Lee a five-year, $120 million contract. They may not have had the payroll space to bring on Roy Oswalt or Hunter Pence. The fans deserve a lot of credit for being crazy about their Phillies and helping the team afford to bring on the caliber of players we have seen in the past several years.

64 Roy Halladay's No-Hitter in the 2010 NLDS

Before Roy Halladay joined the Phillies after the 2009 season, he was already a very accomplished pitcher. He was the 2003 AL Cy Young Award winner, had won 20 games in a season twice, and was one of the few pitchers left who could reliably reach the 200-inning plateau in any given year. One thing, however, was missing from a potentially Hall of Fame–worthy résumé: playoffs.

Certainly not to his discredit, the Toronto Blue Jays hadn't reached the postseason since defeating the Phillies in the 1993 World Series. They were competitive throughout the early 2000s, but in a division that includes the New York Yankees and Boston Red Sox, competitive just doesn't cut it and never has.

When Halladay joined the Phillies, it was all but guaranteed that Halladay would get some much-needed and well-earned post-season experience. The media wondered how the veteran right-hander would handle the new environment, pitching on national television where every pitch is magnified and scrutinized to the umpteenth degree.

The Phillies easily won the NL East over the Atlanta Braves, matching up with the NL Central champion Cincinnati Reds, the league's best offense. With left-handed sluggers Joey Votto and Jay Bruce in the middle of the lineup, damage control was the key. With the Phillies as the league's second-best offense, the series was expected to be a slugfest.

Halladay got the nod in Game 1, and he had his stuff working early. From a tailing two-seam fastball to a disappearing cutter to an unfathomably good 12-6 curve, the Reds could not get a good

Roy Halladay delivers the ball against the Cincinnati Reds during Game 1 of the 2010 NLDS. He allowed no hits, no runs, and only one walk in his complete-game victory, earning his second no-hitter of the year (the first being a perfect game in the regular season), the first pitcher to ever accomplish the feat.

swing on Halladay. The Phillies' ace retired the Reds in order in the first two innings on characteristically weak ground balls.

Reds starter Edinson Volquez, on the other hand, did not bring his A-game. The Phillies took a 1–0 lead in the first inning on a Chase Utley sacrifice fly, then tacked on three more the next inning on a Halladay RBI single and a two-run single from Shane Victorino. A four-run lead with Halladay on the hill? The game could have been called there for all intents and purposes.

Halladay had only one strikeout through three innings, but like so many aces, his stuff gets better as the game progresses. In the fourth and fifth innings, Halladay's six outs came on four strikeouts and two weak grounders. The only blemish on his record was a two-out walk to Bruce. The Reds' line score was all zeroes, and the crowd at Citizens Bank Park began to buzz with excitement at the prospect of a no-hitter. Halladay had already thrown a perfect game in May against the Florida Marlins.

Perhaps accepting that Game 1 was in the bag for the Phillies, the Reds seemed to be focused simply on getting a hit so as not to go down on the wrong side of history. They expanded the strike zone and chased pitcher's pitches, which only increased the difficulty of their task. The first five outs in the sixth and seventh innings all came on batted balls: two easy fly balls and three grounders. Halladay finished off the seventh by striking out former Phillie Scott Rolen, keeping his no-hitter intact.

Halladay was in a rhythm all night with catcher Carlos Ruiz. Ruiz would throw down the signs, and Halladay nodded immediately. Rarely are two battery mates in such sync with each other, but Ruiz is renowned for his game-calling abilities, and it particularly showed in this game.

Halladay was six outs away from a no-hitter. The eighth inning was the final hurdle as it was the middle of the Reds' batting order, Nos. 5, 6, and 7. Halladay struck out Jonny Gomes, forced a weak grounder back to the mound from Bruce, and struck out Drew Stubbs. Three left.

The ninth seemed just as easy as any other inning. At least, that is how Halladay made it look. He got Ramon Hernandez to pop up to Chase Utley, then forced a foul pop-out from pinch-hitter Miguel Cairo. One to go, lead-off hitter Brandon Phillips. Halladay quickly got ahead in the count 0–2. Ruiz called for a curve low and outside the strike zone.

Halladay hit his mark, and Phillips offered at the pitch, which was about six inches off of the outside corner. He tapped it weakly in front of home plate. Ruiz burst out from behind the plate, ripping off his face mask. It was tougher than advertised as Phillips had dropped his bat in fair territory, nearly hitting the ball. Ruiz fell to his knees, avoiding the bat. In nearly one motion, he picked up the ball and fired to first baseman Ryan Howard for the 27th out.

The full house at Citizens Bank Park whipped their white rally towels in celebration as Halladay embraced his catcher. Soon, Ryan Howard and the rest of the team mobbed the two by the pitcher's mound. Halladay joined Don Larsen as the only other pitcher to throw a no-hitter in the postseason (Larsen's was a perfect game). Halladay was the only pitcher ever to throw no-hitters in both the regular season and playoffs in the same year.

65 Roy Halladay's Perfect Game

When the Phillies acquired Roy Halladay from the Toronto Blue Jays, he went from a relatively small market in another country to one of the biggest markets with the most infamous fan base in sports. Needless to say, as Halladay arrived in Philadelphia to much fanfare, the expectations were high.

Through 10 starts in red pinstripes, Halladay had lived up to the hype. He had a 2.22 ERA and made just two mediocre starts to that point. Prior to his start on May 29, 2010, in Florida, the Phillies had just ended a five-game losing streak in which their lead in the NL East dropped from 4½ to 1½ games. The Marlins scheduled Josh Johnson to start, so a pitchers' duel was expected.

The game would live up to the billing and then some. The Phillies were able to hit Johnson a bit early, but as aces do, he played damage control and worked around doubles in the first and second innings. In the third, the Phillies got to him—or, rather, got to the

Marlins' defense. Wilson Valdez, hitting second in the lineup, singled with one out to bring up Chase Utley.

On the seventh pitch of the at-bat, Johnson threw a low two-seam fastball that could have been ball three. Utley swung and lined the pitch to center fielder Cameron Maybin. Initially, Maybin came in on the ball, but upon realizing he misjudged it, ranged back. He stuck up his glove, but the ball glanced off and bounced toward the fence. Valdez raced around the bases, scoring the Phillies' first run from first base. That was the extent of the offense the Phillies would muster against Marlins pitching.

Halladay, meanwhile, was on fire. Half of his first 12 outs came on strikeouts. When the Marlins did make contact, it was not good contact. First baseman Gaby Sanchez made the best contact of anyone, lining out to center in the fourth. With the combination of Halladay throwing strikes and the general impatience of the Marlins' lineup, Halladay kept his pitch count low, throwing between nine and 12 pitches each inning between the second and sixth innings.

Not having seen a no-hitter since Kevin Millwood in 2003, Phillies fans were hoping for offense. That Halladay was on the precipice of a perfect game didn't truly register until the seventh inning against the top of the Marlins order. The Marlins worked the count for the first time since the first inning, but Halladay still emerged on top. Chris Coghlan led off and quickly went ahead 2–0, but struck out. Sanchez hit another line drive, but left fielder Raul Ibanez was able to track it down. Hanley Ramirez went ahead 3–1, but Halladay eventually struck him out, as well.

The play of the game was made to lead off the bottom of the eighth. Jorge Cantu hit a sharp ground ball to third base. It took a short hop but Juan Castro, filling in for Placido Polanco, stayed with it, catching the ball in the webbing of his glove. He stayed calm and fired to first base for the out. If any ball was destined to

Halladay's No-Hitter and Perfect Game

In 2010 Roy Halladay became the only pitcher to throw no-hitters in both the regular season and playoffs. On May 29 he tossed a perfect game in Florida against the Marlins. Then, on October 6 in his first career playoff start, Halladay threw a no-hitter at Citizens Bank Park against the Cincinnati Reds. Halladay joined Don Larsen as the only other pitcher to throw a no-hitter in the postseason (Larsen's was a perfect game in the 1956 World Series).

The following shows the progression of Halladay's perfect game against the Marlins and his no-hitter against the Reds.

Batter No.	@ FLA	vs. CIN
1	K	6-3
2	K	F8
3	4-3	4-3
4	K	K
5	K	5-3
6	5-3	4-3
7	F4	F3
8	F8	2-3
9	K	L9
10	4-3	K
11	L8	K
12	K	6-3
13	4-3	K
14	F8	K
15	3U	BB
16	K	6-4 FC
17	6-3	F9
18	F7	6-3
19	K	F9
20	L7	4-3
21	K	5-3
22	5-3	K
23	K	K
24	F6	1-3
25	F8	K
26	K	F4
27	5-3	F5
28	–	2-3

Source: Major League Baseball

be a hit that night, that was it. Halladay struck out Dan Uggla and forced a weak pop-up to shortstop from Cody Ross, walking to the dugout three outs away from history.

The Phillies went down quickly and in order against Marlins closer Leo Nunez, content with sending Halladay back out to the mound with the narrowest of leads, 1–0.

Everyone who witnessed the ninth inning remembers to this day where they were. With the bottom of the Marlins' lineup due up, Phillies fans could feel history at their fingertips. Halladay started the inning by getting Mike Lamb to fly out to center, then struck out Wes Helms. At 111 pitches, Halladay was still remarkably sharp.

The 27th batter, Ronny Paulino, fell behind in the count—as most Marlins did that night—1–2 before rolling a grounder in the hole between third base and shortstop. It was too far to the left for shortstop Jimmy Rollins, so Castro ranged over, corralling the ball in his glove. He wheeled around and fired to first baseman Ryan Howard for the final out.

Halladay had done it: he had become the 20th pitcher (eighth National Leaguer) to throw a perfect game. Typically quiet and reserved, Halladay simply smiled as he walked off the mound, waiting to be mobbed by Ruiz and the rest of his teammates. A sea of red and road gray poured from the dugout, spilling onto the infield at Sun Life Stadium.

It took just two months for the Phillies' trade for Halladay to be graded a huge success, but there was much more in store. Halladay would win the NL Cy Young Award that year, becoming just the fifth pitcher to win the award in both leagues. More impressively, Halladay threw a no-hitter in his first-ever playoff start in Game 1 of the 2010 NLDS against the Cincinnati Reds. Not a bad start to a career with a new team.

66 Kevin Millwood's No-Hitter

Along with Jim Thome, Kevin Millwood was the face of a franchise attempting to turn itself around in the mid-2000s. Since losing the 1993 World Series to the Toronto Blue Jays, the Phillies had not been very competitive, losing 85-plus games each year from 1996 to 2000. However, the Phillies were set to open a new ballpark in 2004, so they signed Thome as a free agent and traded with the Atlanta Braves to acquire Millwood.

Millwood had shown promise with the Braves, winning 18 games in both 1999 and 2002. In between, though, was marked by inconsistency as the right-hander's ERA settled in the 4.50 area. Now in Phillies red pinstripes for the 2003 season, Millwood threw quality starts in three of his first five outings leading up to his April 27 start against the San Francisco Giants to close out the month of April.

Although the Giants had an above-average offense at the time, most of that could be credited to Barry Bonds. At the end of the season, the OPS of their everyday players sans Bonds ranged from .632 to .807. Bonds finished at 1.278, winning the third of four consecutive, and seven career, NL MVP awards.

Millwood did not have what is known as "no-hit stuff." No one doubted his ability to pitch effectively, but he at times lost the feel for his pitches, becoming very home run-prone. April 27 was looking like one of those days as Millwood started the game with a lead-off walk to Ray Durham. Durham would get erased attempting to steal second and Millwood finished the inning with a strikeout and a fly-out. The Phillies would take the lead in the bottom half on a Ricky Ledee solo home run off of Giants starter Jesse Foppert.

In the second inning, Millwood got Bonds to pop out to third base, then finished the inning with two more strikeouts. The movement on Millwood's pitches looked more crisp than usual; in retrospect, it was a clear indicator he would be nearly untouchable on that afternoon. Millwood was at 42 pitches through three innings, not exactly a great pace for a complete game. As the game progressed, however, the Giants became more and more impatient.

Millwood worked around a two-out walk in the fourth, tacking on only 13 pitches to his total. The next four innings would be a cakewalk for Millwood, retiring all 12 hitters in order, requiring only 44 pitches to do so. He entered the ninth inning at 96 pitches with 10 strikeouts and two walks. If Millwood could notch the final three outs without surrendering a hit, he would become the first Phillie to throw a no-hitter since Tommy Greene accomplished the feat in 1991 against the Montreal Expos.

Neifi Perez and Marvin Benard both grounded out weakly to the right side of the infield for the first two outs. The fans at Veterans Stadium rose to their feet in anticipation of the final out as Durham strode to the plate. Millwood went ahead 1–2, but Durham showed good plate discipline, taking three consecutive balls for the walk. A walk, however, is not a hit, so the fans continued to buzz in anticipation.

Marquis Grissom took his place in the batter's box. With a tired pitcher on the verge of a historic achievement, probably more nervous than he was in his major league debut, the modus operandi should have been to take a lot of pitches. Grissom went ahead 1–0 but then offered at a 93 mph fastball high and outside, hitting a fly ball to center field.

Phillies broadcaster Harry Kalas shouted, "Should be it! Should be it!" as Ricky Ledee settled under the ball, holding out his left hand to ward off right fielder Bobby Abreu. Kalas continued, "Ricky Ledee is there. He puts it away, and Kevin Millwood has pitched a no-hit, no-run game at Veterans Stadium!"

As is tradition, the rest of the Phillies bolted from the dugout to swarm Millwood on the field. Fans were still on their feet clapping and cheering what they had just witnessed. Hugs started to be exchanged on the field. One in particular was memorable between Millwood and his new pitching coach Joe Kerrigan. On the television broadcast, you could see Kerrigan happily say a few words of encouragement to his new disciple.

Millwood's career with the Phillies was short-lived, just two years, but he made a lasting impact on the city of Philadelphia with his start on April 27 against the Giants.

67 Cole Hamels

There was a time that Cole Hamels didn't think he'd ever throw a pitch again. Hamels broke his arm playing football, but kept the injury a secret out of embarrassment. Some time later, Hamels toed the rubber in a summer league game, and his future could have ended right there. His arm snapped, requiring some extensive surgery which knocked him out of his junior year of high school baseball.

"It sounded like a tree branch snapping," Hamels said.

If one drew a line graph of Hamels' career since high school, it would be strewn with peaks and valleys. Hamels was on the national baseball radar prior to his arm injury, but soon disappeared after that fateful summer day. Hamels, however, worked his way back into pitching shape more than a year later. As a draft prospect, teams were hesitant to take a risk with him. Sixteen teams, in fact, passed on Hamels before the Phillies took the leap of faith in the 2002 draft.

Hamels made his professional debut with Class A Lakewood in 2003 and quickly ascended to Clearwater. The Phillies' investment

Lefty Cole Hamels lets fly against the Tampa Bay Rays during the first inning of Game 5 of the 2008 World Series on October 27, 2008, in Philadelphia.

in Hamels appeared to have paid off as he averaged better than 13 strikeouts per nine innings at both levels combined.

In January 2005 Hamels was at a bar and found himself in a shouting match with someone there. There are conflicting stories as to what specifically occurred, but at the end of the night, Hamels had a broken hand. It was certainly possible that, if Hamels pitched well enough early in the season, he could have earned a promotion to the majors later, perhaps as a September call-up when rosters expanded. Instead, Hamels had to recover from an unnecessary injury and made only six starts that season.

Entering the 2006 season, Hamels had about 150 innings of work in three seasons of professional baseball, but his stats were outstanding and he was about as major league–ready as he was ever going to get. The Phillies promoted him to the big show, and he made his big-league debut on May 12 in Cincinnati against the Reds. He hurled five impressive scoreless innings, striking out seven batters. He showed some butterflies, as well, walking five. He made another less-impressive start against the Milwaukee Brewers on May 18 before being demoted.

The Phillies' starting rotation, though, was in shambles, so Hamels was quickly brought back. He made his third start on June 6 and would remain in the rotation until the end of the season. The Phillies used 12 starters that season, and just one of them—Brett Myers—posted an ERA under 4.00. Hamels wasn't far off, at 4.08. At the end of the season, Hamels averaged more than a strikeout per inning with a 3:1 strikeout-to-walk ratio, impressive to say the least.

Hamels took it to the next level in 2007. While Myers earned the Opening Day nod from manager Charlie Manuel, it wasn't long before Hamels became the ace of the staff. Myers disappointed early and was moved to the bullpen when Tom Gordon was sidelined with an injury. Just like that, the 23-year-old lefty was the ace of the Phillies' rotation. He did not disappoint, finishing the season with a 3.39 ERA.

Hamels continued to improve in 2008, finishing with a 3.09 ERA. More importantly, Hamels took control in the postseason, shutting out the Brewers for eight innings in Game 1 of the NLDS, leading the Phillies past the Los Angeles Dodgers in the NLCS, and earning World Series MVP honors against the Tampa

Bay Rays. All together, Hamels posted a 1.80 ERA in 35 postseason innings in 2008.

Just as quickly as Hamels earned the adoration of Phillies fans, he lost it. Two thousand nine was, in all facets, a terrible year; he just could not gather any momentum. As soon as he strung together a good start or two, he followed it up with two bad starts. He finished with a 4.32 ERA and did not pitch well in the postseason. Hamels even said, after a bad start in Game 3 of the World Series against the New York Yankees, "I can't wait for it to end," adding more fuel to an already spreading fire that was his reputation.

During the off-season, Hamels made strides to improve himself. He spent the off-season learning a cut fastball and improving his curveball, then considered far below his fastball and change-up. The hard work paid off. Hamels finished 2010 with a 3.06 ERA and improved his strikeout rate immensely. It continued in 2011 when he posted a 2.79 ERA and established himself, along with Clayton Kershaw and teammate Cliff Lee, as one of the top-three left-handed starters in baseball.

Hamels' time in Philadelphia has certainly been topsy-turvy, but it appears the corner has been turned. The lefty has certainly paid his dues and earned—re-earned, in fact—the respect and admiration of Phillies fans. When his career is over, he very well could surpass Steve Carlton as the best southpaw starter the Phillies have ever had.

68 Lenny Dykstra

For kids born after 1993, or at least too young to have enjoyed that year, it may be difficult to understand why Lenny Dykstra is a legendary part of Philadelphia sports history. He was originally brought up as a New York Met, and his post-baseball life has been wrought with controversy. But as a Phillie from 1989 to 1996, Dykstra gave the game of baseball everything he had on a daily basis, earning him the nickname "Nails" (as in "tough as nails").

With the Mets early in his career, Dykstra showed gap-to-gap power and great speed on the bases. In the first five years of his career, he hit 124 doubles and stole 133 bases. In addition, he was a key contributor in the Mets' magical postseason run in 1986, hitting a walk-off, two-run home run off of Dave Smith in Game 3 of the NLCS against the Houston Astros. He tacked on two more home runs in Games 3 and 4 of the World Series against the Boston Red Sox, both games resulting in Mets wins.

In 1989 the Phillies were in the market for a center fielder, and Dykstra caught their eye. Eventually, a trade was worked out in which the Phillies sent Juan Samuel to the Mets and received Dykstra and reliever Roger McDowell. Initially, Dykstra didn't live up to expectations, finishing the season with a meager .626 OPS in red pinstripes.

In 1990, however, Dykstra was one of the most productive hitters in the league, finishing ninth in NL MVP voting. The gritty outfielder posted a .325 batting average with a league-leading 192 hits and a .418 on-base percentage. He also hit 35 doubles and stole 33 bases in 38 attempts.

In early May of 1991, Dykstra drove his car under the influence of alcohol and crashed it into a tree, injuring both himself and teammate Darren Daulton. Dykstra fractured several ribs, his collarbone, and his cheekbone. Many players would have been sidelined for the rest of the season, but Dykstra missed 61 games, or just slightly over two months.

Dykstra returned on July 15 and immediately caught fire, compiling multiple hits in six of his first eight games. It wasn't long before Dykstra found himself on the sidelines again. On August 26, during a game in Cincinnati, he broke his collarbone a second time, crashing into the outfield wall attempting to catch a fly ball. Dykstra missed the final 38 games of the season.

Yet more injury befell the outfielder. On Opening Day in 1992, Chicago Cubs starter Greg Maddux hit Dykstra in the hand with a pitch, just the second pitch thrown to the first batter in the bottom of the first. Dykstra stayed in the game, even scoring before the inning was over, but went on the 15-day disabled list after evaluations of his hand. Dykstra returned on April 24 and had another productive season.

But wait, there's more. In New York to play the Mets on August 15, Dykstra slid into first base attempting to beat out an infield grounder and broke his hand. He missed the final 46 games of the season. If only the guy could stay healthy for one season, there was no telling what he could accomplish.

Nineteen ninety-three was Dykstra's year. He hit .305 with a .420 on-base percentage, leading the league in plate appearances, runs, hits, and walks. His OPS crept past the .900 plateau, earning him second place in NL MVP voting. More importantly, he helped the upstart Phillies reach the postseason for the first time in 10 years. For as good as Dykstra was in the regular season, he was even better in October.

Dykstra notched at least one hit in the Phillies' first 10 games in the playoffs, including a crucial tie-breaking, 10th-inning solo home run in Game 5 of the NLCS against the Atlanta Braves. The series was tied 2–2 going into the game, so Dykstra's home run provided a huge pendulum shift in momentum. Dykstra hit another two home runs in Game 4 of the World Series against the Toronto Blue Jays, but it was not enough, as the Phillies surrendered a 14–9 eighth-inning lead, losing 15–14.

Dykstra hit what at the time appeared to be a series-changing home run in Game 6. The Phillies were down 5–1 in the seventh, but he hit a three-run home run to bring them back to 5–4. The Phillies tacked on two more and ended the inning up by one run with nine outs left. Of course, Phillies fans remember how that story ended—certainly not Dykstra's fault, as he did all he could.

Injury issues, as well as a work stoppage, interrupted the final three seasons of Dykstra's career. Between 1994 and 1996, he compiled just 703 at-bats. He gave baseball one last shot in '98, but it was not enough. Although his career was not long, and he played in Philadelphia for just eight years, he easily became one of the most unique and memorable characters to ever wear the uniform.

69 1993's Macho Row

There was simply no way that team, rife with mullet-wearing no-goodniks and the stench of cigar smoke and cheap beer emanating from the clubhouse, could be a World Series contender. Right?

That was what everyone thought in 1992, when first baseman John Kruk referred to the team as "24 morons and one Mormon" (the Mormon being Dale Murphy at the end of his career). The team had gone 70–92, good for last in the NL East, 26 games behind the first-place Pittsburgh Pirates.

The Phillies welcomed in a few new faces and said good-bye to some others going into '93. Pete Incaviglia, Milt Thompson, Jim Eisenreich, and Larry Andersen joined the squad and fit in seamlessly. Incaviglia and Thompson took turns in left field, combining for a .786 OPS. Eisenreich and Wes Chamberlain platooned in right field, finishing with an aggregate .847 OPS. Andersen slotted into the bullpen led by Mitch Williams. Everyone had a role; no one was insignificant.

Somehow, the lineup amalgamations worked out. The Phillies had a powerhouse offense despite having just the fifth-highest home run total in the league. Rather than relying on the longball, the Phillies scored runs with seemingly endless strings of walks and hits. They finished the year with a league-best .351 on-base percentage and averaged 5.4 runs per game, well ahead of the second-best Giants at 5.0. John Kruk, Kevin Stocker, and Lenny Dykstra had individual on-base percentages in excess of .400, quite a feat. Those three and Eisenreich also finished the year with a .300 or better batting average.

On the pitching side of things, they were not too impressive. The up-and-coming Curt Schilling had a mediocre season after what appeared to be a breakout in 1992. Overall, the Phillies were in the middle of the pack when it came to ERA in both the starting rotation and in the bullpen. The trio of Andersen, David West, and Mitch Williams in the bullpen helped the Phillies lock down wins late in the game.

Despite their appearance and previous history, the Phillies pressed forward as if none of it mattered. They trampled through the National League, winning 97 games, earning the right to play the Atlanta Braves in the NLCS.

The Braves took a 2–1 lead in the series after two convincing wins in Games 2 and 3, outscoring the Phillies 23–7. But the Phillies rattled off three wins in a row, including two nailbiters in Games 4 and 5. In total, three of the Phillies' four wins in the series were by a single run. Nonetheless, they had overcome a tough opponent and moved on to battle the Toronto Blue Jays, hoping to take home their first championship since 1980.

The Jays were a lot like the Phillies: they were heavy on the offense and left a little to be desired when it came to pitching. John Olerud was a heavy MVP candidate, posting a .363 batting average and .473 on-base percentage. Second baseman Roberto Alomar and designated hitter Paul Molitor joined him in the .400 OBP club. If the World Series was expected to be anything, it was a slugfest.

It *was* a slugfest. The first four games saw 65 runs scored between the two teams, a fraction over 16 runs per game, on average. Game 4 was the craziest of the bunch, a fervent tug-of-war that ended 15–14 in the Jays' favor thanks to a six-run eighth inning.

With the Phillies on the brink of elimination going into Game 5, Curt Schilling turned in a gem of a start in the biggest game of his career. He shut the Jays out for all nine innings; the two runs the Phillies scored were more than enough to bring the series back to 3–2 as the teams traveled back to Canada.

Anyone old enough to remember the 1993 World Series will likely be able to recall exactly where they were when Game 6 ended. It is still a memory that haunts many Phillies fans, even after the 2008 World Series. The Phillies, down 5–1 in the seventh inning, scored five runs in the seventh to take a 6–5 lead with nine outs left to bring the series to a deciding Game 7. At this point, the Phillies' entire bullpen was gassed, but they managed to get six of those outs going into the ninth.

Manager Jim Fregosi called upon his closer, Mitch "Wild Thing" Williams, to finish it out. Williams had done yeoman's work all season long, but he had nothing left in the tank. He walked the speedy Rickey Henderson to lead off the inning. After retiring Devon White on a fly out, DH Paul Molitor singled to put runners at first and second with one out for Joe Carter, the Jays down by one run.

Williams fell behind 2–0, but battled back to 2–2, getting Carter to whiff at what would have been ball three. Catcher Darren Daulton threw down one finger and Williams nodded, putting everything he could on the pitch. It was a thigh-high inside fastball. Carter turned on it, sending the ball down the left-field line, over the fence for the walk-off, World Series–clinching win. Carter hopped around the bases as Williams solemnly walked back to the dugout, the last Phillies fans would see of this great team.

70 Game 4 of the 2008 NLCS

The 2008 season was magical for a vast array of reasons, but perhaps no one game was more iconic than Game 4 of the 2008 NLCS between the Phillies and Los Angeles Dodgers. The Phillies held a 2–1 series lead as they called upon Joe Blanton to oppose Derek Lowe at Dodger Stadium in front of nearly 57,000 fans.

The Phillies got to Lowe early, scoring two runs in the top of the first thanks to three straight hits to start the frame. The Dodgers got one back in the bottom half on a James Loney double. Both teams limited the damage until the fifth. After walking leadoff hitter Rafael Furcal, Blanton allowed two consecutive singles as the Dodgers tied the game at 2–2. Catcher Russell Martin gave the Blue Crew the 3–2 lead on an RBI ground-out before the inning was over.

Quickly, the Phillies brought the game back to a tie at 3–3 when Chan Ho Park uncorked a wild pitch with runners on second and third with two outs in the top of the sixth. Blanton was pinch hit for by So Taguchi, who flew out to end the inning.

"Big Joe" was relieved by workhorse right-hander Chad Durbin, who didn't have his best stuff. Casey Blake led off the bottom of the sixth with a solo home run. Juan Pierre doubled, and Matt Kemp walked to put runners on first and second with no outs. Charlie Manuel took the ball from Durbin, bringing in southpaw Scott Eyre.

Furcal laid down a sacrifice bunt down the first-base line, but Ryan Howard made an errant throw to Chase Utley covering the bag, allowing the run to score. Kemp advanced to third, and Furcal scampered to second base. Fortunately, the Phillies were able to get out of the inning without any further damage on two line drives, one a double play from Ryan Madson that ended the frame.

The Dodgers were up 5–3, and the Phillies were tasked with mounting a comeback against their vaunted bullpen. They had finished the regular season with the second-best (behind the Phillies) bullpen ERA at 3.34, miles below the league average of 4.09.

Enter the top of the eighth. Dodgers manager Joe Torre had called upon lefty Hong-Chih Kuo in the seventh, and he'd retired the top of the Phillies lineup—Jimmy Rollins, Jayson Werth, and Chase Utley—in order. Thinking he had the advantage with a southpaw pitching to the left-handed-hitting Ryan Howard to lead off the eighth, Torre left Kuo in. After a three-pitch at-bat, Howard singled up the middle. Torre emerged from the dugout and replaced Kuo with right-hander Cory Wade. He retired Pat Burrell on a fly ball. With the heart of the Phillies' lineup out, it was looking like a wasted opportunity.

In what was an anomaly of an at-bat, Wade threw a first-pitch curveball to center fielder Shane Victorino. Somehow, Victorino timed it perfectly, lifting the knee-high pitch up and over the fence in left field for a two-run, game-tying home run. Wade stayed in the game, getting the second out of the inning on a Pedro Feliz line drive. However, Carlos Ruiz singled to left, and Torre again made a pitching change. With a 5–5 game and a runner on first with two outs in the eighth, closer Jonathan Broxton entered the game to face pinch-hitter Matt Stairs.

Stairs had just one hit in his previous 10 postseason at-bats, last taken in 2000 with the Oakland Athletics. The 40-year-old had just one thing missing from an otherwise successful, lengthy career in the majors: a significant postseason contribution. After falling behind 0–1, Broxton struggled to find the plate, throwing three straight balls. Stairs knew he could look for a fastball, and he got one. Broxton grooved a belt-high fastball over the plate. Fox broadcaster

Joe Buck called it, "Stairs rips one deep into the night! Deep into right, way outta here."

The homer gave the Phillies a 7–5 lead, one that Brad Lidge closed out with relative ease. The closer finished off the eighth and had a 1-2-3 ninth inning, giving the Phillies a 3–1 series advantage. They, of course, would close out the series the next night in front of a disappointed Los Angeles crowd, earning the privilege of playing in the World Series.

71 Game 5 of the 2008 World Series

Some day, I will tell my grandchildren that Game 5 of the 2008 World Series took three days to complete. Then I will pull up the game on our hologram display and replay the memorable final game of the Series.

Game 5 really was memorable for many reasons. Chief among them was that the Phillies won, of course, but another was the weather. Meteorologists forecast heavy rainfall in the Philadelphia area as temperatures fell to 40 degrees. Players donned long-sleeved undershirts and added flaps to their hats to cover their ears from the cold wind. It was football weather, not baseball weather.

Regardless, the game went off as scheduled, with Cole Hamels opposing Scott Kazmir. Hamels had been enjoying a fine postseason, holding a 1.55 ERA over 29 innings.

Kazmir was a bit hit-or-miss, carrying a 4.15 playoff ERA into the night. He was much more "miss" that night. The Phillies took advantage of some early wildness as Kazmir walked two batters and hit another with a pitch, loading the bases with two outs for Shane Victorino. Victorino lined a single to left field, scoring two runs, providing a quick, early lead for their ace starter.

Through three innings, Hamels stymied the Rays, inducing weak grounder after weak grounder. In the top of the fourth, however, the Rays broke through. Carlos Pena doubled to right and was driven in quickly by Evan Longoria in the next at-bat.

Fast-forward to the top of the sixth with the score still 2–1. Rain was starting to fall more and more heavily. The field at Citizens Bank Park was a sloppy mess, with puddles forming across the infield dirt. The Fox television broadcast saw mud build up in the players' cleats, just a small illustration of the less-than-favorable conditions in which the game was being played. Still, the players attempted to do their jobs.

Hamels seemed to be on his way to an easy inning and, perhaps, a rain delay as the lefty got two quick outs on seven pitches. The speedy B.J. Upton kept the inning alive with an infield single to shortstop. Taking advantage of the wet baseball, Upton easily took second base, sliding feet-first through a puddle to get to the second-base bag. Now with a runner in scoring position, Pena lined a single to left field. Pat Burrell charged the ball and threw home as best as he could, but Upton scored the tying run, knotting the score at 2–2. Hamels exited the inning with no further damage.

After the top of the sixth, the umpires called for a rain delay as the field was in tatters. Forecasts did not call for a rain stoppage, but everyone hoped for the best. Eventually, the game was postponed to a later date. But the rain never stopped, pouring through October 28 and into the 29th. Finally, in the evening, the game was resumed after nearly 48 hours of delay.

The starters were both gone, so a potential World Series–clinching game would be decided by the bullpens. The Rays sent right-hander Grant Balfour out to start the bottom of the sixth against the 9-1-2 part of the Phillies' batting order. Geoff Jenkins pinch-hit for Hamels, crushing a double to right-center. As Jenkins pulled into second, he clapped his hands in intense celebration.

Jimmy Rollins moved him over to third base with a sacrifice bunt, then Jayson Werth drove him in with an infield hit.

Ryan Madson took the hill for the seventh inning, but just as quickly as the Phillies took the lead, they gave it back. With one out, Rocco Baldelli sent a first-pitch fastball over the left-field fence for a game-tying solo home run. Jason Bartlett followed with a single to left and was promptly moved to second base on a sacrifice bunt from relief pitcher J.P. Howell. Madson was replaced with J.C. Romero as Charlie Manuel wanted the lefty-on-lefty matchup. That set up one of the greatest plays of all-time.

Iwamura hit a ball up the middle. Chase Utley ranged to his right, snagging the ball in his glove. Realizing that Iwamura was fast and a play at first base would be tough, Utley faked to first and looked toward Bartlett rounding third base. Bartlett continued running, stampeding his way toward home plate. Off-balance, Utley whipped the ball to catcher Carlos Ruiz, who dived forward and tagged Bartlett out before he could wrap his hand around home plate. There was no doubt at the time that it was a game-changing play.

Pat Burrell led off the bottom of the seventh, looking for his first hit of the Series. If the Phillies won, it was likely his last at-bat as a Phillie, as the left fielder was eligible for free agency after the season. Burrell went out in style, doubling to left-center before being pulled for pinch-runner Eric Bruntlett. The Rays brought in right-hander Chad Bradford, who retired the first batter he faced to bring up Pedro Feliz. Feliz gave the Phillies a 4–3 lead with a line-drive single to center, scoring Bruntlett. If the Phillies could get six more outs, they would once again be world champions.

Romero did his job in the eighth, facing the minimum three batters. The Phillies looked for more insurance runs in the eighth frame, but did not find any as they moved into the ninth. Brad Lidge took the hill, looking for the last save in a perfect season. The right-hander was 47-for-47 in save opportunities to that point.

Closer Brad Lidge (arms raised), catcher Carlos Ruiz, and first baseman Ryan Howard converge in front of the pitcher's mound to celebrate clinching the 2008 World Series victory versus the Tampa Bay Rays at Citizens Bank Park.

Lidge had two outs with a runner on second as pinch-hitter Eric Hinske came to the plate. The crowd at Citizens Bank Park anticipated the 27th and final out of the game, all 46,000 of them on their feet. Lidge quickly went ahead in the count 0–2. Ruiz called for a slider low and outside, setting up for another memorable Harry Kalas call.

"The 0–2 pitch—swing and a miss! Struck him out! The Philadelphia Phillies are the 2008 world champions of baseball!"

72 The Drought Ends

In previous seasons, the end of September was an awful time of the year. The Phillies had been either completely out of the race for a while, or they had just been mathematically eliminated. Two thousand seven was a different animal. A year after GM Pat Gillick advised fans to lower their expectations for the '07 Phillies, his team was in a position to win the NL East and advance to the postseason.

The Phillies played extremely well down the stretch, picking up seven games on the New York Mets after September 13. Entering September 30, the final day of the season, the Phillies had won 12 of their last 16 games while the Mets had lost 11 of their previous 16 games. The two teams were tied for first place after 161 games.

Both the Phillies and Mets were scheduled for afternoon games against the Nationals and Marlins, respectively. Everyone anticipated a day of scoreboard-watching as they vied for first place in the NL East. That wasn't the case as the Mets, behind starter Tom Glavine, fell behind early and never recovered. The Marlins scored seven runs in the first inning. Since the Mets-Marlins game started about 25 minutes earlier, the Phillies started their game with the knowledge that the Mets were getting trampled.

Forty-four-year-old Jamie Moyer started the game for the Phillies, opposed by the Nationals' Jason Bergmann. The Phillies took a 1–0 lead in the first inning on a Chase Utley sacrifice fly, then tacked on two more in the third on a two-run single from Ryan Howard. Meanwhile, Moyer limited the damage on a day in which he did not have his best stuff. The Nationals managed just one run in the top of the fourth even though they were hitting Moyer hard all day long.

Moyer put runners on first and second with one out in the top of the sixth before giving way to reliever Tom Gordon. Gordon ended the inning by inducing a ground-ball double play from Austin Kearns. In the bottom of the sixth, the Phillies added some insurance runs on a So Taguchi sacrifice fly and an RBI triple from Jimmy Rollins. The triple was Rollins' 20th of the season, entering him into the exclusive 20/20/20/20 club, joining Willie Mays, Frank Schulte, and Curtis Granderson as the only players to hit 20 or more doubles, triples, and home runs, and steal 20 bases in the same season.

Howard tacked on another run with a solo home run in the bottom of the seventh, but the Phillies had more than enough, now leading 6–1. Entering the ninth, the Phillies called on closer Brett Myers for the final three outs. Myers had started the season in the rotation, but moved to the back of the bullpen when Tom Gordon was injured earlier in the season.

If the Phillies were to celebrate, Myers would have to handle the Nationals' 4-5-6 hitters. Myers struck out Dmitri Young to start the bottom of the ninth on the right foot. After a strenuous at-bat, Kearns flied out to left. With a sellout crowd at Citizens Bank Park on their feet, Myers peered in to catcher Chris Coste for his signs. Myers went ahead 1–2. Coste called for Myers' trademark 12-6 curve. The pitch hit the black on the outside corner. Wily Mo Pena stood in the batter's box as the home-plate umpire signaled for strike three.

Myers threw his glove in the air as the Phillies rushed onto the field, newly minted NL East champions. The Phillies' playoff drought was over. Deservedly, the Phillies celebrated their achievement, even including the fans as Myers sprayed champagne into the stands at Citizens Bank Park.

Little did the Phillies know they were on the verge of something big as 2007 was the start of a five-year playoff run in which they became the class of the National League and playoff titans.

The Phillies would win the World Series in 2008 and return to the Fall Classic in '09, but it all started with their late-season drama in '07.

73 Create a Fan Group

In the late 1990s and early 2000s, the Phillies were practically (but not mathematically) out of playoff contention before the end of July. The summer had meaningless game after meaningless game, and attendance dwindled as a result. This left many seats at Veterans Stadium, particularly the upper-level seats, empty.

With the freedom of space and the desire to make the games interesting, fans started attending games in groups named after particular players. The first incarnation of the Veterans Stadium fan group was the "Schillometer," a group of fans that showed up for Curt Schilling's starts and posted a piece of paper with a K on the wall behind the seats.

After that, the fan groups sprouted up in great numbers. There was "Person's People," named after Robert Person. Brandon Duckworth's group was "The Duck Pond." Even Vicente Padilla, a hard name with which to make a pun, inspired "Padilla's Flotilla." Perhaps the most memorable was Randy Wolf's "Wolf Pack," in which fans showed up to his starts wearing wolf masks.

Of course, there were some less-inspiring, short-lived groups, such as Chad Ogea's "Ogea's Oranges," Jim Thome's "Thome's Homies," Terry Adams' "Adams Family," and Jeremy Giambi's "Giambi's Zombies."

Even backup catcher Sal Fasano had a fan group at Citizens Bank Park, "Sal's Pals," which perched in the second deck in left field. Fasano was known for his facial hair, a fu manchu, so the group donned fake fu manchus. Not a star by any means, Fasano enjoyed the attention. "It's not easy being a jet-setting baseball player," he said.

As a result of the Phillies' success, finding a seat at Citizens Bank Park is difficult. The team has enjoyed more than 200 consecutive home sellouts, and it doesn't figure to end anytime soon. Finding a single ticket is a task in and of itself, let alone trying to find space for 15-plus people. The fan groups have mostly been phased out, but it would be nice to see them make a resurgence to show the players how much the city of Philadelphia supports their players.

Feel free to use this one for outfielder Ben Francisco: "Francisco's Treats." Or, how about "Pence's Hunters" with fans showing up in orange vests and camouflage hats? I never said I was creative!

Of course, Philadelphians prefer year after year of incredible success, but few things breathed life into a crowd the way the fan groups did in the dog days of summer at the Vet.

74 Attend a Minor League Game

Few things rival the electricity in Citizens Bank Park in September during a pennant race. This new era of Phillies baseball with top-tier pitching and fundamentally sound baseball is a joy to watch.

However, there's a lot of fun to be had at the Phillies' minor league games, as well. If you're not much of a crowd-surfer, the crowds are smaller and you have more space to yourself—and less competition for foul balls. It's a more family-friendly atmosphere, as well. Given the lower prices, it's a perfect retreat with your family for a day.

You will also get a chance to witness the stars of tomorrow. Believe it or not, Chase Utley was once in the minor leagues working long hours for a shot at a major league career. Fans in 2003 could catch him tear it up at Scranton/Wilkes Barre (the Phillies' old Triple A affiliate, which later became a part of the New York Yankees organization), batting .323 with 18 home runs.

In the upcoming years, fans can witness the ascent of Freddy Galvis, Domonic Brown on the comeback trail, and bullpen prospect Phillippe Aumont. In lower levels, pay attention to Matt Rizzotti, Austin Hyatt, Sebastian Valle, Trevor May, Domingo Santana, and many others. Injured major leaguers will make rehab appearances at various times during the season, as well.

Given the relaxed atmosphere and smaller crowds, minor league games are a perfect place to seek autographs from your favorite future stars. Get there early to hang out down the foul lines, and you may even get a batting practice ball.

The Iron Pigs play at Coca-Cola Park in Allentown, Pennsylvania. It is a bit of a hike for Philadelphia natives, roughly an hour and a half to two hours, but it is a good excursion to experience baseball in a different atmosphere.

The Reading Phillies call FirstEnergy Stadium home in Reading, Pennsylvania. From Philadelphia, the trip is about as long as it is to Lehigh Valley—it's a haul—but they have some of the best promotions in all of baseball, major or minor league. For instance, on Sundays at FirstEnergy Stadium in 2012, the Reading Phillies will be giving away bikes and flat-screen TVs and selling hot dogs for the low, low price of $1. On Thursdays starting in June, every game wraps up with a fireworks show.

If you're in New Jersey, you're in luck, as the Lakewood Blue Claws (Class A) call Jersey home. It's a 90- to 120-minute drive from Citizens Bank Park, depending on traffic. At the moment, the Phillies' Class A teams are loaded with high-upside talent, so make sure to get to a Blue Claws game during the season.

The Clearwater Threshers are only an 18-hour drive away from Philadelphia, according to Google Maps. In the mood for a road trip? Go see the Threshers! On a more serious note, the Threshers' home at Bright House Field becomes the Phillies' home during spring training starting in late February. The clear blue skies and bright sun of Clearwater are great reasons to escape the cold snow and ice of Pennsylvania.

Whether it's the smaller crowds, the relaxed atmosphere, the lower prices, or the overall convenience, there are many reasons to check out a Phillies minor league game. If you haven't, you're missing out!

75 Phillies Defense 2007–2011

The 2007–2011 era Phillies get lauded for many things. Between '07 and '09, they led the league in many offensive categories, including on-base percentage, slugging percentage, OPS, stolen bases, stolen-base success rate, doubles, triples, home runs, runs scored, and so on. Starting in '09, the Phillies stocked up on pitching, acquiring Cliff Lee, then Roy Halladay, Roy Oswalt, and Lee again. In 2011 the Phillies led the league in wins, ERA, complete games, shutouts, and strikeout-to-walk ratio.

One underrated aspect of the Phillies in that era is defense. According to Ultimate Zone Rating (UZR), a Sabermetric defensive statistic, the Phillies have had the best defense in the National League the last five years (prorated to 150 defensive games). The stat credits the Phillies with about five plays (4.8) made above what an average defense would have made. The only team in the majors better than the Phillies in that span of time is the Tampa Bay Rays at 5.6.

The biggest contributors on defense have been Chase Utley at second base and Jimmy Rollins at shortstop. Since 2007, no second baseman has been better than Utley, according to UZR. At 14.8, Utley leads second-place Brandon Phillips by about four plays above average. In fact, only four shortstops are even above 10.0 in this span of time, with the others being Dustin Pedroia at 10.7 and Mark Ellis at 10.0.

Somehow, Utley has not won a Gold Glove award in his career. Since he started playing every day in 2005, the winners have been Orlando Hudson and Phillips three times each and Luis Castillo once.

Jimmy Rollins has been the third-best defensive shortstop in baseball from 2007 to 2011, per UZR. J.J. Hardy leads the way at 10.8, while Rollins trails at 7.0, just ahead of Troy Tulowitzki at 6.9. Perhaps just as important, Rollins also has racked up the third most defensive innings at shortstop, trailing only Derek Jeter and Yuniesky Betancourt.

Unlike Utley, Rollins received recognition for his defensive prowess, taking the Gold Glove award in three consecutive years from 2007 to 2009.

Other positive contributors include Jayson Werth (11.1 UZR/150) in right field, Pedro Feliz (9.9) and Placido Polanco (13.7) at third base, and Shane Victorino (1.5) in center. Only four Phillies have logged 1,000 or more defensive innings at one position and posted a negative UZR/150: Pat Burrell (–20.5) and Raul Ibanez (–8.6) in left field, Greg Dobbs (–5.7) at third base, and Ryan Howard (–3.6) at first base.

The numbers are backed up by some very memorable plays. Aaron Rowand made a fantastic catch in center field, robbing Xavier Nady of a three run extra-base hit in 2006, breaking his nose in the process. Jayson Werth and Shane Victorino made a habit of throwing runners out at third base and home plate; Victorino even preserved Brad Lidge's perfect saves streak, ending a game with an assist to home plate. And, perhaps most memorable of all, Utley made a game-saving play at the plate in Game 5 of the 2008 World Series, faking a throw to first before nailing Jason Bartlett at the plate.

Make no mistake: the Phillies teams of the 2007–2011 era were the most complete, well-rounded teams in franchise history. They could do it all. While the defense did not get much press, it was arguably the part of the game the Phillies did best.

Phillies 2007–2011 Defense

With strong up-the-middle players and some smart bargain-bin signings by Pat Gillick, the Phillies were one of the best defensive teams in baseball every year from 2007 to 2011. In fact, over the span of those five years, the Phillies were best in the National League according to Ultimate Zone Rating (UZR). The chart below lists every Phillie who logged 1,000-plus defensive innings at one position in that era along with their UZR, as well as their UZR prorated to 150 defensive games. Astonishingly, only four Phillies finished with a negative mark, while seven finished with an above-average grade, including Chase Utley, the best defensive second baseman in baseball.

Player	Pos.	Innings	UZR	UZR/150
Chase Utley	2B	5,814	60.9	14.8
Placido Polanco	3B	2,120	24.0	13.7
Jayson Werth	RF	3,567	27.0	11.1
Pedro Feliz	3B	2,320	18.6	9.9
Jimmy Rollins	SS	5,925	29.9	7.0
Aaron Rowand	CF	1,373	4.5	4.5
Shane Victorino	CF	4,957	4.5	1.5
Ryan Howard	1B	6,570	−19.7	−3.6
Greg Dobbs	3B	1,064	−4.6	−5.7
Raul Ibanez	LF	3,614	−21.1	−8.6
Pat Burrell	LF	2,226	−29.9	−20.5

76 Check Out Ashburn Alley

A fan could drift away for hours, enjoying everything Ashburn Alley has to offer. A part of Citizens Bank Park located beyond center field, it is named after longtime Phillies center fielder and Hall of Famer Richie Ashburn. "Whitey" played 12 seasons in Philadelphia and broadcast their games between 1963 and his death in 1997. Ashburn is memorialized with a bronze statue in Ashburn Alley.

There are a plethora of features at Ashburn Alley. The most popular seems to be the ability to hang out above both the home and visiting team bullpens in left-center. With the visiting team's bullpen on higher elevation than the home team's, fans can lean over the railing and let the opposing pitchers know what is on their minds—perhaps the most unique use of home-field advantage in baseball.

By the left-field gate, the Phillies' lineup is displayed on 10' x 5' placards hung on the wall. They can then proceed to Harry the K's Bar and Grille, named after late broadcaster Harry Kalas. Or, if fans would rather get food they can carry back to their seats, Ashburn Alley is littered with great food amenities, including Season's Pizza, Planet Hoagie, Campo's, and Tony Luke's.

For barbecue enthusiasts, a stop by Bull's BBQ is a must. Named after and partially owned by former Phillies left fielder Greg Luzinski, it is a meat-lover's heaven. Walking within 50 feet of Bull's BBQ is enough to make one's mouth water.

After some fine dining, fans can literally walk down Memory Lane. Memory Lane details the highs and lows of Phillies baseball dating back to the 1800s, capturing all of the important moments

Phillies Wall of Fame

The Phillies Wall of Fame, located in Ashburn Alley in center field at Citizens Bank Park, displays plaques of the franchise's most notable players, including many Hall of Famers and contributors to successful teams. At Veterans Stadium, the team honored players from both the Phillies and the Athletics; once the team moved to Citizens Bank Park, they no longer inducted Athletics. Below are the inductees since the opening of the Phillies' new home in 2004.

Year	Name	Position
2004	Billy Hamilton	OF
2005	Bob Boone	C
2006	Dallas Green	P, MGR
2007	John Vukovich	INF, coach, executive
2008	Juan Samuel	2B
2009	Harry Kalas	Broadcaster
2010	Darren Daulton	C
2011	John Kruk	1B

in the history of the franchise. The Phillies Wall of Fame is also nearby, displaying plaques of the most notable players in Philadelphia baseball history. Ashburn, of course, is among those as is his longtime broadcast partner Kalas. The most recent inductee is John Kruk, whose acceptance speech on August 12, 2011, was incredibly inspiring.

The All-Star Walk has a similar theme to the Wall of Fame, but it honors Phillies who have played in the All-Star Game since 1933, running the length of Ashburn Alley. In addition, the Phillies have flags commemorating all of the team's playoff appearances, including the 1980 and 2008 World Series teams. Ashburn Alley proudly flies the American Flag, a POW/MIA flag, and the flags of the Commonwealth of Pennsylvania and the City of Philadelphia.

Finally, there are the Rooftop Bleachers. An attempt to capture the style of older ballparks, including Shibe Park and Wrigley Field, these seats are offered to fans at cheap prices and with additional food and event perks.

While enjoying everything Ashburn Alley has to offer, don't forget there is a game going on! There are great views of the field from Ashburn Alley, so don't simply camp out at your seat.

77 Richie Ashburn

Richie Ashburn could do it all. "Whitey" finished third in National League Rookie of the Year voting in 1948, hitting a cool .333 with a .410 on-base percentage and 32 stolen bases. The speedy center fielder also played Gold Glove–caliber defense—though, of course, the Gold Glove award was not created until 1957.

Ashburn made a habit out of hitting .300 and getting on base in roughly two out of every five plate appearances. He twice led the league in batting average and four times led the league in OBP. His presence in the lineup was a big reason why the 1950 Phillies, known as the "Whiz Kids," were so successful. That team won 91 games en route to winning the National League pennant, but they were swept in the World Series by the New York Yankees.

Whitey was part of one of the strangest stories to come out of major league baseball. In 1957 the Phillies hosted the New York Giants at Connie Mack Stadium. During the game, Ashburn hit a foul ball into the stands, striking Alice Roth, the wife of a Philadelphia sports editor. While Roth was being carried off in a stretcher, Ashburn hit another foul ball into the stands, hitting Roth a second time. To this day, people are still astonished at the statistical improbability of such an event.

Aside from 1950, the Phillies as a team did not enjoy any more success in Ashburn's tenure, certainly not his fault. Ashburn left the Phillies after the 1959 season, playing three more seasons in the majors before retiring at the age of 35.

Richie Ashburn played center field for the Phillies from 1948 to 1959, leading the "Whiz Kids" to the World Series in 1950. After retiring, the Hall of Famer spent 34 years broadcasting Phillies games until his death in 1997.

A colorful character, Ashburn had a bright post-baseball career ahead of him. In 1963 he became a broadcaster for the Phillies, joining Bill Campbell and By Saam. In 1971 Campbell was replaced by Harry Kalas. Saam retired in '76, leaving Ashburn and Kalas to themselves. As a result, a legendary broadcast duo was born. The two would become great friends, adding to the quality of their on-air banter.

One memorable feature of their broadcasts involved Ashburn ordering pizza while on air. As they went deeper and deeper into the game, Ashburn would get hungry, so he would mention Celebre's, a South Philly pizzeria, on air. Soon after, pizza showed up in the radio booth. The Phillies did not enjoy this practice, as Celebre's wasn't an official sponsor, but Ashburn continued anyway, hiding a pizza order in on-air birthday wishes: "I'd like to send out a special birthday wish to the Celebre's twins—Plain and Pepperoni," Ashburn would say.

Ashburn received many honors. Most importantly, he was enshrined in the Hall of Fame in 1995 alongside Mike Schmidt, thanks to a grassroots campaign with a memorable slogan, "Richie Ashburn: Why the Hall Not?"

Ashburn died on September 9, 1997, but he was never forgotten. He was posthumously inducted into the Philadelphia Sports Hall of Fame in 2004 and had two parts of Citizens Bank Park named after him: Ashburn Alley beyond the center-field fence, and the Richie "Whitey" Ashburn Broadcast Booth for the Phillies' radio broadcasts.

For 12 years as a player and 34 years as a broadcaster, Ashburn endeared himself to the city of Philadelphia, bringing happiness and laughter into many homes. While the days of Ashburn and Kalas are over, they have left a lasting impact on a very appreciative fan base.

78 Whiz Kids

Going into 1950, the Phillies had made it to the postseason exactly once, dating back to the team's founding in 1883. In 1915 they lost the World Series in five games to the Boston Red Sox. From 1916 to 1949, there was a whole lot of nothing. In that span of time, the Phillies had finished above fourth place three times in 34 seasons while finishing in seventh or eighth place 24 times.

With catcher Andy Seminick, starters Robin Roberts and Curt Simmons, and a bona fide outfield of Richie Ashburn, Del Ennis, and Dick Sisler, the 1950 Phillies finally gave the fans something to be proud of.

After a sluggish start in April, the Whiz Kids went 17–9 in May, battling with Jackie Robinson's Brooklyn Dodgers for first place in the National League. The Phillies kept their foot on the gas in June and early July, leading into the All-Star break, finishing with a 44–29 record at the break, narrowly holding onto first place.

Four Phillies were named to the All-Star team: Roberts as the starting pitcher, Willie Jones at third base, and Sisler and reliever Jim Konstanty as reserves. The National League won 4–3 in 14 innings. Had the game been played in the 2000s, the win may have been useful as the NL would have earned home-field advantage in the World Series.

The Phillies appeared to have lost momentum after the All-Star break as they lost seven of their first 10 games in the second half. However, they never fell behind by more than one game, so they remained heavy contenders in the pennant race. Between July 25 and August 25, the Phillies rattled off three unique winning streaks of at least four games while losing back-to-back games only once.

After defeating the Pittsburgh Pirates on August 25, the Phillies were 74–45 with a five-game lead. August was a very prosperous month for them, winning 20 of 28 games (.714).

September, however, wasn't so kind to them. The Phillies were swept in consecutive doubleheaders against the New York Giants on September 4 and against the Brooklyn Dodgers on September 6. However, they had built up a 7½-game lead by the middle of the month, a nearly unbreakable lead with 11 games remaining.

On September 30, the Phillies dropped their fifth consecutive game in a series opener with the rival Brooklyn Dodgers, leaving them with a paltry one-game lead with one game remaining. If the Dodgers beat the Phillies in the final game of the season, the two teams would play a three-game playoff to decide the National League champion.

Manager Eddie Sawyer tabbed his ace Robin Roberts with the crucial start. Roberts would be opposed by Don Newcombe, the reigning NL Rookie of the Year with 19 victories to his name on the season. The final game had all the makings of a pitchers' duel, and that's exactly what it was.

Through nine innings, both pitchers had allowed just one run in the sixth and otherwise held the opposition silent. Newcombe took the hill to start the 10th and was quickly victimized by the Phillies. Roberts led off with a single and advanced to second on a follow-up single by Eddie Waitkus. Richie Ashburn attempted to sacrifice bunt the runners over, but Roberts was forced out at third as runners remained on first and second. The bunt didn't prove to be of any importance as Dick Sisler hit a three-run home run.

With the Phillies in the driver's seat, Roberts returned to the mound for the bottom of the 10th to face the bottom of the Dodgers' lineup. Roy Campanella lined out to left for the first out. Roberts followed up with a four-pitch strikeout of pinch-hitter Jim Russell before notching the final out on a ground-out to first base.

The Phillies advanced to the World Series, but were swept in four close games by the New York Yankees. The first three games were each decided by one run with both teams combining to score nine runs. The Whiz Kids dropped the fourth and final game 5–2, a disappointing end to a great season.

From 1951 to 1975, the Phillies would suffer another playoff drought before the Mike Schmidt and Steve Carlton–led Phillies broke the spell in '76. The drought left fans wondering what might have been if the Phillies had managed to take the 1950 World Series. At any rate, the Whiz Kids took the city of Philadelphia on a wild ride experienced just once in the preceding 66 years.

79 Pennant Races at Citizens Bank Park

Media types often talk about "electricity in the stadium" when the fans are excited, or "the air being let out of the stadium" when they are disappointed. They seem like empty phrases attempting to anthropomorphize the stadium, and they generally are. Having taken in a game at Citizens Bank Park during a pennant race, however, I can say that the stadium certainly felt like it took on some of those human qualities.

In the days leading up to September 29, 2009, the Phillies were almost guaranteed a postseason spot. I spent those days trying to map out when the Phillies would clinch the division so I could attend. The lowly Houston Astros came into town for a four-game series starting on the 28th, so that seemed like the time. Assuming Cole Hamels would beat Astros starter Yorman Bazardo, I chose the 29th as "clinch night" with J.A. Happ against Wilton Lopez.

The Phillies lost Hamels' start, so the 29th could not be clinch day. Disappointed, my friend and I trekked down to Philadelphia, anyway. It was a windy, chilly night with temperatures starting in the low 60s and dropping into the low 50s. Fans bundled up in sweatshirts and jackets, protecting their faces from the chilly wind.

In the bottom of the fourth, with the score tied, the bases were loaded with no outs. Third baseman Pedro Feliz crushed a first-pitch slider to left field for a grand slam, landing several seats to our right. Citizens Bank Park came alive. Fans stood up, whipping their white rally towels around, cheering at the top of their lungs. As uncomfortable as the weather was, positive energy reverberated throughout the stadium.

I remember sitting in my seat, taking it all in, astonished at the electricity and excitement flowing from seat to seat. In another situation, if I sat in sub-60-degree temperatures with 15 to 20 mph winds for three hours, I would have been a grumpy mess. Not with the Phillies.

The Phillies tacked on two more runs on a Jayson Werth home run in the fifth, padding their lead to 7–2. The Astros scored two on a Kaz Matsui two-run home run, but they dropped the game, bringing the Phillies' magic number to one. If they could win on the 30th, they would win the NL East.

I have been to many Phillies games in my lifetime, but that was my first in the midst of a pennant race. Even as fans filed out of the stadium, they were buzzing with excitement. I couldn't help but be impressed with how much a city could rally behind its sports teams.

If you have seen late-season Phillies games on TV recently, you have seen the outpouring of fan support the team has enjoyed since becoming contenders in 2007. If you haven't been to Citizens Bank Park in late September, you're missing out on one of the most unique feelings. To be a part of more than 45,000 people all trying to will their favorite players toward a common goal is an incredible feeling. You must go. Of all of the suggestions I will make in this book, this may be the one I recommend most.

80 Mets-Phillies Rivalry

It seems like a laughable notion now, but there was a time when the Mets-Phillies rivalry was burgeoning and expected to be among the most heated in baseball. Ever since the Phillies took advantage of a historic late-September collapse by the Mets in 2007—and again, to a lesser extent, in 2008—the two teams and their fan bases were at each others' throats.

A lot of the growing rivalry had to do with off-the-field bravado. Prior to the 2007 season, when the Mets were on the verge of playing in the World Series and the Phillies stayed home in October as they had every year since 1993, Jimmy Rollins called the Phillies "the team to beat in the NL East."

Rollins elaborated, saying, "For the first time since I've been here, I can say I know we have the pitching to get us there. Our offense has been productive the last couple years, but it's tough when it's 6–0 in the third inning." His prognostication turned out to be true, as the Phillies clinched the NL East crown on the last day of the regular season in 2007.

Mets outfielder Carlos Beltran fired back at the Phillies going into the 2008 season. After praising teammate Johan Santana, Beltran quipped, "So this year, to Jimmy Rollins, we are the team to beat."

Naturally, the media flocked to Rollins for a response. The charismatic shortstop did not disappoint. Targeting Beltran, Rollins asked the media, "Has anyone ever heard of plagiarism?" He added, "There isn't a team in the National League that's better than us."

Rollins also predicted that the Phillies would win 100 games. He was right if you stretch the rules. The Phillies won 92 regular season games, but if you include the 11 they won in the postseason, he was right.

After the Phillies' championship season in 2008, World Series MVP Cole Hamels went on a much-publicized media tour. One particular stop included WFAN, New York's 24/7 sports radio station. Hamels was asked if he and his teammates thought the Mets were choke artists. "Last year and this year I think we did believe that [they were choke artists]," Hamels said.

The media couldn't help but fan the flames, so they went to Beltran for a response. "The only thing that I know is he will be watched every time he faces us," he said. "Hopefully we kill him, and then he'll have to deal with the situation."

Recently acquired closer Francisco Rodriguez, signed to a three-year, $37 million contract, joined in the preseason prognostications, labeling the Mets "the team to beat" in 2009. "Of course, we're going to try to win the division. Of course, we're going to be the front-runner. Of course, we're going to be the team to beat," he said.

The Mets were supposed to hang tough with the Phillies in 2009, but they finished the season 72–90 in fourth place, 23 games behind the Phillies. Trash-talking between the two teams ended abruptly. The Mets hit the skids again in 2010, winning 79 games and remaining in fourth place. Two thousand eleven was no better, another sub-80-win season in fourth place.

As a baseball fan, it is unfortunate that the Mets' fall from grace has been so steep. A Mets-Phillies rivalry would have been great not only for both teams and their fan bases, but for major league baseball in general, which only has Red Sox–Yankees, Cardinals-Cubs, and Dodgers-Giants as lively, major rivalries.

For the Phillies, though, they emerged from all of this trash talk having backed up every single word of it, even the seemingly outlandish prediction of 100 wins. In fact, prior to the 2011 season, Rollins predicted another 100-win season for the Phillies. To beat writer Matt Gelb of the *Philadelphia Inquirer*, Rollins wrote, "We'll win 100 games. I really plan on going after, what is it, [the Seattle Mariners] won 114 [sic] or something…. We'll go get somewhere hopefully in that range. But that requires everybody doing their job." The Phillies won 102 games—a franchise record—in the regular season and two more in the playoffs.

A Mets-Phillies rivalry certainly would have been fun to watch with the cast of colorful characters on both sides. Perhaps in the future, the rivalry will be reignited, or another team will jump in the fray.

81 Mike Schmidt's Four-Homer Day

Entering 1976, Mike Schmidt had already established himself as a premier power hitter. He led the National League in home runs in the two previous seasons. The sky was the limit for the 26-year-old; he could accomplish anything as long as he continued to work hard and stay healthy.

On April 17, 1976, Schmidt accomplished something that had more to do with good timing than anything else. The Phillies, at 1–3, were in Chicago at Wrigley Field for the first of a two-game series, looking for their second win of the season. Phillies ace Steve Carlton opposed Cubs starter Rick Reuschel. In what had the makings of a pitchers' duel, the two teams put together something completely different.

The game looked like a lost cause after the second inning, when the Cubs victimized Carlton for seven runs. The Phillies' lefty exited the game with two outs in the second, giving way to Ron Schueler. It got worse in the third, when the Cubs threw up a five-spot to increase their lead to 12–1. Both teams managed another run, making it 13–2 after four innings.

If it was later in the season (and, perhaps, played in this era), the Phillies may have conceded the game by taking out their regulars for some rest. Down 11 runs, the Phillies put their nose to the grindstone and attempted a comeback. Mike Schmidt hit a two-run home run off of Reuschel in the fifth to bring the score to 13–4. The Phillies went down in order in the sixth.

On an RBI triple by Jay Johnstone and a sacrifice fly from Greg Luzinski, the Phillies inched closer at 13–6. Before the inning was over, Mike Schmidt hit his second homer of the game, this time a solo homer, to make it 13–7.

In the eighth, with Reuschel out of the game, the Phillies had two innings to score at least seven runs against the Cubs bullpen, starting with Mike Garman. The Phillies accepted the challenge, loading the bases with no outs on two singles and a walk. However, Johnstone hit a weak fly ball to left, and Luzinski struck out. It looked as if the Phillies would squander their best opportunity of the game. Dick Allen kept the inning alive with a two-run single, allowing Mike Schmidt to take a trip to the plate with the score 13–9 Cubs.

With runners on first and third, Schmidt crushed a three-run home run to left field, his third home run of the game. It was a ballgame; the Cubs' lead shrunk to one run, 13–12.

Going into the top of the ninth, the Phillies were still behind 13–12 facing Darold Knowles. As impressive as their rally was, they were still three outs away from a crushing defeat that would send them to 1–4 on the season. Bob Boone wasn't about to let the Phillies lose, as he completed the comeback, leading off the inning with a solo home run that knotted the game at 13–13. The Phillies added two more on an RBI triple from Larry Bowa and a suicide squeeze from Johnstone. At the end of the inning, the Phillies miraculously led 15–13.

Tug McGraw came in to lock down the win for the Phillies, but the Cubs had a rally of their own. With two outs and runners on second and third, catcher Steve Swisher singled to left, scoring both runners and retying the game at 15–15.

If there was good news to be had, it was that Schmidt would get another at-bat in which to hit his fourth home run of the game, joining a very select group. In the top of the 10th, Knowles walked Dick Allen before being pulled for Paul Reuschel as Cubs manager Jim Marshall wanted the right-on-right matchup against Schmidt.

It didn't matter. Schmidt hit his fourth home run of the game. At the time, only nine players had accomplished the feat, including Hall of Famers Ed Delahanty, Lou Gehrig, Chuck Klein, and Willie Mays. Schmidt was also the third Phillie to hit four homers in one game (joining Delahanty and Klein); the Phillies were the only team with more than one player on the list.

Just for good measure, the Phillies scored one more run before the inning was over, taking an 18–15 lead into the bottom of the 10th. The Cubs again rallied, scoring a run on two doubles against Tom Underwood, but Jim Lonborg recorded the 30th and final out for the 18–16 victory. On the day, Schmidt was 5-for-6 with four home runs and eight RBIs. It was just one of many great days in the career of the future Hall of Fame third baseman.

23–22

As far as crazy games go, the craziest may have been played on May 17, 1979, in Chicago between the Cubs and Phillies. Nineteen seventy-nine was an otherwise disappointing year for the Phillies, as it was the first time in four years they did not win 90-plus games with a postseason ticket punched. At the very least, they could hang their hat on their grueling victory over the Cubs on this afternoon in May.

Phillies starter Randy Lerch opposed Cubs hurler Dennis Lamp, but their respective shifts were over quickly. Lamp allowed two three-run home runs to Mike Schmidt and Bob Boone in the top of the first, giving way to reliever Donnie Moore after having retired just one batter. Lerch (a pitcher, remember) hit a solo home run before the frame was over to give the Phillies a 7–0 lead. In Lerch's frame in the bottom half, he surrendered four runs on a Bill Buckner RBI single and three-run home run by Dave Kingman. Like Lamp, he recorded just one out before being lifted. Doug Bird entered in relief of Lerch, but allowed runs five and six on an RBI single and RBI triple. At the end of the first inning, the Phillies narrowly led 7–6.

The second inning could have been charged with false advertising. With both offenses on fire and the bullpens being worked early, both teams preemptively braced for another explosion of runs that never happened. Both sides put up goose eggs in the second frame.

With Moore still in the game for the Cubs, the Phillies went to work figuring him out in the third. Recording just one out, Moore was chased after allowing four runs on five hits and a walk, giving way to Willie Hernandez. The Phillies now led 11–6, the inning seemingly a crushing blow to the Cubs' faithful. Hernandez intentionally walked Mike Schmidt to load the bases—can you blame him? A run scored on a ground-out to first base, bringing Garry Maddox to the plate. Maddox hit what at the time appeared to be the killing blow, a three-run home run that pushed the Phillies' lead to 15–6.

In the bottom of the third, Doug Bird set the Cubs down quietly, bringing the Phillies back to the plate much to the chagrin of the fans at Wrigley Field. The Phillies tacked on two more runs on two RBI doubles in the top of the fourth, extending their lead to 11 runs.

The Cubs started the slow crawl back to an even game. In the bottom of the fourth, Dave Kingman slugged his second homer of the game, a two-run shot, followed by a solo shot from Cubs third baseman Steve Ontiveros. The Phillies took the runs back about as quickly as the Cubs scored them. This time, their weapon of choice was small-ball, putting up a four-spot on an RBI double, an infield error, and two sacrifice flies. Their lead increased to 21–9.

With Tug McGraw in the game to start the bottom of the fifth, the Cubs loaded the bases with no outs. McGraw forced in a run by walking Ivan DeJesus. Not long after, Bill Buckner crushed a McGraw fastball well into the stands in left-center for a grand slam, bringing the score to 21–14. Center fielder Jerry Martin added a two-run home run before the inning was over, and the Cubs pulled to within five runs.

Between the sixth and eighth innings, the Cubs small-balled their way to a tie game, with Kingman's third home run of the game thrown in for good measure. The Cubs scored six runs in that time, with five coming on RBI ground-outs (two) or RBI singles (three). After eight innings, the score was knotted at 22–22. Cubs closer Bruce Sutter and Phillies reliever Rawly Eastwick held the opposing offenses at bay in the ninth, but Schmidt broke the tie in the top of the 10th with a solo home run. Eastwick again held the Cubs scoreless for the win, 23–22.

The teams combined for 45 runs on 50 hits and 15 walks (the Phillies had 12 of them). Surprisingly, the teams combined to use just 11 pitchers and 25 position players. The 11 combined home runs tied a National League record, while the combined 45 runs was just four runs off of the major league record also set by the Phillies and Cubs in 1922.

Needless to say, it was a thriller of a game, one that would be remembered fondly (by Phillies fans) for many years. Few games have been able to match the offensive explosion and excitement created by the Phillies and Cubs on this mid-May game in 1979.

May 17, 1979

On this date, the Phillies and Cubs played an afternoon game at Wrigley Field. A crowd of only 15,000 fans was in attendance, unaware of the fireworks display they were about to witness. The two teams combined for 45 runs, four runs shy of the MLB record for combined runs scored in a game (coincidentally set by the same two teams on August 25, 1922). Here's a summary of how the scoring went down:

Inn.	Hitter	Pitcher	Result	Phillies	Cubs
T 1	Schmidt	Lamp	3-R HR	3	0
T 1	Boone	Lamp	3-R HR	6	0
T 1	Lerch	Moore	HR	7	0
B 1	Buckner	Lerch	RBI 1B	7	1
B 1	Kingman	Lerch	3-R HR	7	4
B 1	Sizemore	Bird	RBI 1B	7	5
B 1	Moore	Bird	RBI 3B	7	6
T 3	Boone	Moore	RBI 1B	8	6
T 3	McBride	Moore	RBI 1B	9	6
T 3	Rose	Moore	2-R 2B	11	6
T 3	Unser	Hernandez	RBI 3U	12	6
T 3	Maddox	Hernandez	3-R HR	15	6
T 4	Rose	Hernandez	RBI 2B	16	6
T 4	Maddox	Hernandez	RBI 2B	17	6
B 4	Kingman	Bird	2-R HR	17	8
B 4	Ontiveros	Bird	HR	17	9
T 5	Bowa	Hernandez	RBI 2B	18	9
T 5	Rose	Hernandez	RBI E6	19	9
T 5	Unser	Hernandez	Sac Fly	20	9
T 5	Gross	Hernandez	Sac Fly	21	9
B 5	De Jesus	McGraw	RBI BB	21	10
B 5	Buckner	McGraw	GS HR	21	14
B 5	Martin	McGraw	2-R HR	21	16
B 6	Vail	Reed	RBI 6-3	21	17
B 6	Buckner	Reed	RBI 6-3	21	18
B 6	Kingman	Reed	HR	21	19
T 7	Boone	Caudill	RBI 2B	22	19
B 8	Buckner	Reed	RBI 1B	22	20
B 8	Martin	Reed	RBI 1B	22	21
B 8	Foote	Reed	RBI 1B	22	22
T 10	Schmidt	Sutter	HR	23	22

Sources: Retrosheet.org and Baseball-Reference.com

83 Von Hayes and the 305-Mile Walk

The Phillies traded for Von Hayes after the 1982 season and got exactly what they expected out of him for nine seasons. In return, the Phillies sent five players to the Cleveland Indians, including Manny Trillo and Julio Franco—quite a hefty price for an outfielder. A left-handed hitter, Hayes had gap-to-gap power and was even adept at drawing walks. He found himself involved in the middle of quite a few interesting games, but one in particular stood out.

The date was June 8, 1989, and the Pittsburgh Pirates were in Philadelphia to wrap up the series at Veterans Stadium. The Phillies had won the previous two games, but very early on, it appeared that a sweep was not in the cards. In the first inning, the Pirates scored 10 runs against Phillies starter Larry McWilliams and reliever Steve Ontiveros. In the frame, the Pirates drew five walks and hit six singles, a double, and a home run.

Pirates broadcaster Jim Rooker, a major league pitcher from 1968 to 1980, thought the game was wrapped up. Who could blame him? Rooker said, "If we don't win this one, I don't think I'd want to be on that plane ride home. Matter of fact, if we don't win, I'll walk back to Pittsburgh."

A former player, Rooker should have known not to tempt the baseball gods. Hayes got the Phillies on the board in the bottom of the first with a two-run home run off of Pirates starter Bob Walk. He added another two-run home run in the bottom of the third to bring the score to 10–4. From there, the Phillies gradually clawed their way back into the game.

Steve Jeltz entered the 1989 season with one home run in 1,612 major league plate appearances. The baseball gods smiled on him this evening. He stepped to the plate with a runner on first base with two outs against Walk in the fourth and quickly made the score 10–6 with his second career home run. Jeltz hit his second homer of the game—and third of his career—in the sixth, a three-run shot that cut the Pirates' lead to two runs at 11–9. Ricky Jordan added an RBI single to make it 11–10.

The Phillies' pitching had kept the Pirates mostly in check after the first inning. Between the second and eighth innings, the Pirates managed only one more run. In the bottom of the eighth, the Phillies broke through, posting a five-spot on a wild pitch, a two-run single, and a two-run triple by Curt Ford that was almost an inside-the-park home run. With three outs left, the Phillies had finally taken the lead, 15–11. Closer Steve Bedrosian had an easy ninth inning, nailing down the win.

After the game, it wasn't Hayes or Jeltz at the center of attention for their combined four home runs; it was Rooker for, somehow, losing his bet. He did not walk home to Pittsburgh from Philadelphia that night, but fans were very outspoken that they wanted Rooker to make good on his bet.

It was a lesson well-learned for Rooker. Shortly after the 15–11 game, the Pirates went up 10–0 on the St. Louis Cardinals. Rooker's broadcast partner asked, "And if we lose this game?" Humbly, Rooker said, "Yes, if we lose this game…our road record will be 11–23."

After the season, Rooker paid his debt and used the trek as a way to help charity, walking 305 miles between the two cities while raising more than $100,000 in the process.

Hayes retired after the 1992 season having never recovered from being hit by a Tom Browning pitch. He went on to manage several teams in the minor leagues as well as the Lancaster Barnstormers and Camden Riversharks of the Atlantic League.

84 Jimmy Rollins

Jimmy Rollins was never expected to win an MVP award. On his way through the Phillies' minor league system, the undersized shortstop impressed with his defensive abilities, but scouts wondered if his bat would play at the major league level. Between Double A and Triple A at the age of 20, Rollins hit .268, but he earned a promotion to the majors in mid-September 2000. In 53 at-bats, Rollins hit .321.

He kept his major league spot in 2001, earning an everyday job out of spring training. For many years, Rollins lived up to the scouting reports: he was tremendous defensively, had great speed, and possessed gap-to-gap power. However, Rollins' power progressed rapidly, defying expectations. His season-high home run total in the minors was 12; he equaled or surpassed that total in nine of his 11 full seasons over his career.

Entering 2007, Rollins had led the league in triples three times and stolen bases once. He was a lock for at least 700 plate appearances every year, speaking to his durability. Rollins took it to another level in 2007. He set career highs in runs (139), hits (212), triples (20), home runs (30), RBIs (94), batting average (.296), slugging percentage (.531), and OPS (.875). In addition, he stole 41 bases in 47 attempts (87 percent) and continued to play stellar defense. Along with Curtis Granderson, Willie Mays, and Frank Schulte, Rollins joined the exclusive 20/20/20/20 club of players who have hit 20 or more doubles, triples, and home runs, and stolen 20 or more bases in the same season.

Having sparked the Phillies to end their playoff drought extending back to 1993, Rollins received a lot of support for the

Jimmy Rollins has achored the shortstop position for the Phillies since 2001, winning NL MVP honors in 2007, after joining the exclusive 20/20/20/20 club. Through 2011, he's proven himself to be the greatest shortstop in Phillies franchise history.

2007 NL MVP award. He narrowly defeated outfielder Matt Holliday, then of the Colorado Rockies, in a controversial finish. Rollins also won his first Gold Glove and Silver Slugger awards at shortstop.

Whether he intended to or not, Rollins assumed a leadership role with the Phillies, acting as the team's mouthpiece. At the top of the lineup, it seemed that, as Rollins went, so went the team. The shortstop continued to speak his mind, engaging in more preseason smack-talk and prognostications.

One year after having correctly pegged the Phillies as the "team to beat" in the NL East, Rollins had clearly gotten underneath the skin of the New York Mets. Outfielder Carlos Beltran used Rollins' words to call the Mets the "team to beat" in 2008. Rollins said the Phillies would win 100 games. And they did.

While Rollins wasn't as good in 2008 as he was the previous year, he was still more than good enough at a position where it was hard to find quality players. Rollins continued to set the table at the top of the lineup, then cause havoc on the base paths. Under the tutelage of first-base coach and base-running guru Davey Lopes, Rollins stole 47 bases in 50 attempts, an incredible 94 percent success rate.

The Phillies reached the postseason again and eventually proved Rollins correct. Winning the requisite 11 games for a championship, along with the 92 regular season wins, the Phillies had won 103 games total. Rollins was proven correct again.

The following three years were marked by decline and injury. While Rollins hit 21 home runs in 2009 as the Phillies returned to the World Series, he posted a sub-.300 on-base percentage for the first time in his career. Rollins' 2010 season was ravaged by injuries—to his calf on Opening Day, to the same calf again later in the season, and to his thigh after that.

Rollins had his best showing in three years in 2011. It was bittersweet for Phillies fans, though, who knew it was potentially his last season in Philadelphia as he would soon be eligible for free agency. At the end of the season, there was no doubt Rollins was the best shortstop the Phillies had ever seen. With 34 Wins above Replacement (WAR), Rollins doubled Larry Bowa's 17.1 total and Granny Hamner's 16.1. A Wall of Fame induction awaits Rollins in the future.

85 Pat Burrell

One of the downsides—and there are few—of being a No. 1 overall draft pick is that your baseball career begins with tremendous expectations. You are considered a disappointment if you don't become the next Ken Griffey Jr. Pat Burrell, taken No. 1 overall in the 1998 draft out of the University of Miami, entered the Phillies organization and wasted no time getting to the majors.

Burrell hit 29 home runs with 94 RBIs, mostly with Double A Reading, in 1999. That was more than enough for the Phillies. Burrell was promoted to the majors in late May 2000 and did not disappoint, hitting 18 home runs in 408 at-bats. Although the early part of his career was spent with under-performing teams, Burrell became a fan favorite.

He seemed to reach his potential in 2002, finishing the season with a .920 OPS, 37 homers, and 116 RBIs. If this was the type of production the Phillies could count on every season, Burrell was on his way to a long and prosperous career. The Phillies gave Burrell a six-year, $50 million contract.

Burrell took a major step back the next year, however, perhaps under the weight of his new contract. Whereas his .920 OPS in 2002 was 46 percent better than the league average, Burrell's .713 OPS in 2003 was 10 percent below average. He hit 21 home runs and drove in just 64 runs, opening himself up to round-the-clock criticism on sports talk radio. Burrell's season-long slump resulted in boos and hecklers behind him in left field.

Still, the left fielder dealt with it in stride. He rebounded a bit in 2004, but because his home run and RBI totals (24 and 84) did not change much, the criticism endured. Burrell's motivation, attitude, and work ethic were called into question.

Burrell endured, putting up great numbers in the next four seasons, answering each and every one of his critics. From 2005 to 2008, Burrell hit 124 home runs with 395 RBIs and a .890 OPS. Perhaps most impressively, Burrell drew at least 98 walks in each of those seasons, contributing to a .386 on-base percentage.

In 2008, at 31 years of age and on the verge of free agency, Burrell made his final year in Philadelphia count. He hit 33 home runs and became a crucial component of the Phillies' playoff push. The left fielder hit two home runs against the Milwaukee Brewers in Game 4 of the NLDS and hit a solo home run that later became the winning run as the Phillies defeated the Los Angeles Dodgers 3–2 in Game 1 of the NLCS.

The World Series was trouble for Burrell, however. Tampa Bay's pitching had shut him down in 18 consecutive plate appearances. Burrell wasn't about to let his Phillies career end on such a sour note. In what would become his last at-bat as a Phillie, Burrell hit a double off of J.P. Howell in the seventh inning of Game 5. Burrell was replaced by pinch runner Eric Bruntlett, who later scored the World Series–winning run on a Pedro Feliz single.

Burrell went on to play for the Rays, but foot problems led to subpar production. The Rays released him in May 2010. Ten days later, he joined the San Francisco Giants. It proved to be a tremendous bargain-bin grab as Burrell found his swing again, hitting 18 home runs and helping the Giants win their first World Series since 1954.

Foot problems plagued Burrell throughout 2011, forcing him to spend time on the disabled list and forfeit his everyday spot in the Giants' lineup. He announced his retirement following the season. His career was a great success, though, having won two championships with two different teams while being regarded as one of the most fearsome right-handed hitters in baseball for eight seasons between 2001 and 2008.

Burrell ranks fourth on the Phillies' all-time list in home runs with 251, eight behind Del Ennis. He also ranks eighth in RBIs and fifth in walks. In retrospect, it is hard to imagine how Burrell could have deserved the rampant criticism he received early in his career. Like Bobby Abreu, who received similar criticism, Burrell's career was quietly very, very productive, perhaps best appreciated with time.

86 1994–2000 Phillies

Phillies history wasn't always littered with playoff appearances. There is a generation of fans that has grown up mostly on the 2007–2011 era Phillies, a team that has won the NL East five years in a row and reached the World Series twice. Even going back to 2003, the Phillies have won at least 85 games in each season.

Phillies fans growing up in the mid-to-late 1990s remember just how excruciatingly bad those teams were. In fact, some of us play games in which we name lesser-known Phillies from those teams, such as Garrett Stephenson, Chad Ogea, and Kevin Sefcik. When the team struggles to win 70 games, you find ways to amuse yourself.

Labor strife interfered with the end of the 1994 season and part of the '95 season, culling the momentum of the Phillies '93 team that reached the World Series. However, by the time the players were ready to get back on the field in '95, Darren Daulton was 33 years old, Jim Eisenreich was 36, and Lenny Dykstra was 32. Meanwhile, the Phillies were utilizing many younger players, particularly in the starting rotation. If the Phillies were going to make it back to the World Series, they would have to do so with a new cast of characters.

Needless to say, it never happened. The Phillies cobbled together rosters from a mediocre minor league system, free agent signings, and trades, but nothing worked. The 1996 and 1997 Phillies won 67 and 68 games, respectively, finishing dead last in the NL East. In '96, the veteran-laden team battled injuries and ineffectiveness, finishing with the run total and 11th-best ERA in the National League.

The '97 team had an infusion of youth as catcher Mike Lieberthal and third baseman Scott Rolen were given starting jobs. Of course, the two would become cornerstones of the team for years to come. Terry Francona took over as manager, replacing Jim Fregosi. It didn't matter, as the Phillies underperformed yet again.

Right fielder Bobby Abreu made his first splash in 1998, hitting .312 with a .409 on-base percentage, but it wasn't enough to make up for an otherwise shoddy team. Rolen was the only other regular to post an OPS above the league average. Meanwhile, Curt Schilling was the lone bright spot in the rotation. Five other starters made at least 15 starts; none posted an ERA lower than 4.44. Overall, the Phillies won seven more games than in '97, but they still needed a lot of work to become playoff contenders.

Pitching continued to be the Phillies' downfall in 1999. Six hitters reached double-digits in home runs, but Schilling was once again the only consistently good starter. Between Paul Byrd, Chad Ogea, Robert Person, Randy Wolf, and Carlton Loewer, the lowest ERA among the five was 4.27. Closer Wayne Gomes posted a 4.26 ERA while walking nearly as many hitters as he struck out (seven per nine innings).

In 2000 the offense took a big step backward. The Phillies had crept into the upper-third of the National League in average and on-base percentage the previous year, but a combination of injuries and poor performances resulted in the 2000 Phillies finishing with the 15th-best average and 14th-best OBP. The starting rotation improved, but the bullpen became a big issue. Among the 10 relievers who logged at least 20 innings of work, Ed Vosberg had the lowest ERA at 4.13. Seven of the 10 posted an ERA above 5.00. Francona was fired after the season, one of few symbolic gestures the front office could make to show Phillies fans they were committed to winning.

In total, the 1994–2000 Phillies won 475 games and lost 594, a .444 winning percentage. Some bright spots included Abreu,

Rolen, Lieberthal, and Schilling, but otherwise, the Phillies were desperate to field quality players at every position. The 1996 Phillies, for example, used 29 different position players and 25 different pitchers. As a comparison, the 2010 Phillies fielded 21 position players and 21 pitchers.

They say one must experience sadness to be able to experience happiness. I question the axiom's applicability to baseball, but the Phillies of the mid-to-late 1990s have helped me better appreciate the 2007–2011 era, which has truly been the "golden era" of Phillies baseball.

87 Ferguson Jenkins

"Fergie Jenkins, a Hall of Famer and Cy Young Award winner, pitched for the Phillies, won 20 or more games in six consecutive seasons…" That is a sentence that could have been written about Jenkins had the Phillies not decided to trade him to the Chicago Cubs early in the 1966 season. The Phillies sent Jenkins along with John Herrnstein and Adolfo Phillips to Chicago in exchange for Bob Buhl and Larry Jackson. To this day, fans argue that either that or the Ryne Sandberg trade is the worst in Phillies history, and among the worst in baseball history.

Buhl was at the end of his career, posting a 4.93 ERA in 135 innings for the Phillies. Jackson pitched well but was also at the end of his career. Still, he finished his career with a 2.95 ERA in Phillies pinstripes. Meanwhile, Jenkins went on to pitch incredibly well for the Cubs, then the Texas Rangers, Boston Red Sox, the Rangers for a second time, and the Cubs again.

From 1967 to 1972, Jenkins made 234 starts with a 127–84 record, while logging 1,836 innings in total and posting an even

3.00 ERA. Among those 234 starts were 140 complete games and 24 shutouts. In that span of time, Jenkins led the league in wins once, complete games three times, WHIP once, walk rate twice, and strikeout-to-walk ratio three times.

Jenkins won the 1971 Cy Young Award over Tom Seaver and Al Downing. In his career, Jenkins finished in the top three of Cy Young voting on four other occasions.

Jenkins didn't slow down until 1979, when he was 36 years old. From 1965 to 1978, Jenkins was 231–168 with a 3.19 ERA. Fans hoped he could continue to stay healthy and effective enough to reach 300 wins before he called it quits. However, over the next five years, Jenkins went 53–58, finishing his career 16 wins shy of 300.

Regardless, his sub-300 wins total was not enough to keep him out of the Hall of Fame. Jenkins was enshrined in Cooperstown in 1991, appearing on 75 percent of BBWAA ballots.

After trading Jenkins, the Phillies would continue their playoff drought extending back to 1950. They had narrowly missed the playoffs in 1964, but went downhill from there. During Jenkins' prime in 1967–1972, the Phillies won just 420 of 965 games (.435). Jenkins averaged 7.1 Wins above Replacement (WAR). Between 1968 and 1971, the Phillies' best pitcher finished at 5.0 or below. Jenkins would have been quite the asset to those Phillies teams.

After his career concluded, Jenkins was the only pitcher to finish his career with more than 3,000 strikeouts and fewer than 1,000 walks. He was later joined by Greg Maddux, Curt Schilling, and Pedro Martinez. Jenkins was also regarded as one of the better-hitting pitchers in baseball with 13 home runs during his career, six of which were hit in 1971 when he won his Cy Young Award.

One interesting thing to ponder, given chaos theory, is the Phillies' draft position in future years. Obviously, there is no way to know for sure, but if the Phillies had kept Jenkins, they may not have been able to draft Schmidt 30th overall. Perhaps they would have chosen George Brett (29th overall) instead, or maybe Ron Jackson (37th) would have been the only attractive player available.

At any rate, you want your team to make the best decisions possible at the time. In retrospect, trading Jenkins for two veteran arms for an incremental improvement in playoff odds was one of the worst decisions made in Phillies history.

88 Secretary of Defense

Garry Maddox was so swift in the outfield that Harry Kalas famously said, "Two-thirds of the Earth is covered by water, the other one-third is covered by Garry Maddox." The center fielder, acquired in 1975 from the San Francisco Giants for first baseman Willie Montanez, became a fixture of the Phillies teams, contributing to the championship team in 1980.

In recent years, the rise of Sabermetrics has shown us the fallibility of traditional defensive statistics. For instance, we now know that fielding percentage severely underrates better defenders and overrates worse defenders because the latter can make fewer plays on balls, meaning fewer errors. However, Sabermetric defensive stats are still in their infancy and rely on batted ball data that was not available for players in Maddox's era.

Consequently, we do not have a great way to numerically appreciate Maddox's defensive prowess. At the time of this writing, TotalZone (found on Baseball-Reference.com) is arguably the best for analyzing players of Maddox's era, and it speaks very highly of the "Secretary of Defense." From 1975 to 1982, when Maddox won the Gold Glove each season, TotalZone has Maddox at a total of 110 fielding runs above average, an average of about 14 runs per season. Based on run environments, it has been found that nine to

Garry Maddox crashes against the center-field wall after making a running grab of a drive off the bat of the Los Angeles Dodgers' Bill North during Game 3 of the 1978 NLCS on October 6 at Dodger Stadium.

10 runs is equivalent to one win, so Maddox's defense alone added about a win and a half per season and 11 over his defensive prime.

Maddox's eight NL Gold Gloves are tied for the fifth-most in baseball history among outfielders. He trails Roberto Clemente and Willie Mays (12 apiece); Andruw Jones, Al Kaline, and Ichiro Suzuki (10); and Torii Hunter (9). Barry Bonds and Andre Dawson are tied with him at eight.

In praising his defense, many often forget that he was also quite good at the dish. From the start of his career in 1972 through 1980, Maddox hit at least 25 doubles and stole 20-plus bases in all but his rookie season. His best season came in 1976, when he hit .330 and finished with an OPS (.833) 32 percent better than the league average. Maddox's performance at the plate was a big reason why the Phillies ended their playoff drought that year. Despite their center fielder's best efforts, the Phillies were taken out in the NLCS in three consecutive years from 1976 to 1978.

Maddox brought the Phillies to the World Series in 1980. The NLCS was as close as any Championship Series in baseball history as the final four games of the five-game series went into extra innings. In the fifth game, the two teams were tied 7–7 going into the 10th inning at the Astrodome. Del Unser had doubled against Frank LaCorte and remained on second base as Maddox came to the plate with two outs. Maddox brought Unser home with a double to center field, putting the Phillies up 8–7. Dick Ruthven tossed a scoreless bottom of the 10th as the Phillies punched their ticket to the World Series.

After winning a championship in 1980, Maddox declined precipitously due to injuries. From 1981 to 1985, Maddox played in 492 of 756 possible games (65 percent), hitting .271 with a stolen-base success rate barely above 60 percent.

Maddox retired early in 1986. He was able to hang his hat on being arguably the best defender in all of baseball, helping the Phillies reach the playoffs in six of eight seasons between 1976 and 1983, winning it all in 1980.

Since calling it quits, Maddox has had a diverse post-playing career. He was a successful businessman, a baseball broadcaster, and a spring training instructor for the Phillies. Maddox even made a name for himself in the world of barbecued foods, hosting the Garry Maddox Barbecue Challenge outside of Citizens Bank Park, which raises money for the Youth Golf & Academics Program, helping inner-city students.

While Greg Luzinski (of Bull's BBQ fame) might have something to say about the title of "Best Barbecue in Philly," no one can beat Maddox when it comes to covering ground in the outfield.

89 Robin Roberts

Entering the last day of the 1950 season, the Phillies' most-recent 20-game winner was Grover Cleveland Alexander, who had won 30 in 1917. By fending off the Brooklyn Dodgers in game 157, Roberts secured his team's spot in the World Series and won his 20th game of the season. Roberts was the ace of a staff that also included Curt Simmons. However, Roberts finished seventh in NL MVP voting behind three teammates, including closer Jim Konstanty, who won with 85 percent of the share.

Nineteen fifty was the start of a prosperous six-year run for Roberts. From 1950 to 1955, Roberts went 138–78 with a 2.93 ERA, 35 percent better than the league average during that time period. He completed 161 of 232 starts, including 24 shutouts. Roberts finished in the top 10 of NL MVP voting in five of those six seasons. Unfortunately, later iterations of the Phillies failed to succeed the way the 1950 squad did.

In the six seasons 1950 to 1955, Roberts led the league in wins four times, starts six times, complete games four times, innings pitched five times, strikeouts twice, WHIP once, walk rate three times, and strikeout-to-walk ratio three times. He was the most dominant pitcher in this six-year span. Of pitchers who logged at least 1,000 innings between 1950 and 1955, Billy Pierce of the Chicago White Sox was the only other hurler to post an ERA at least 30 percent better than the league average.

Unfortunately, the rest of Roberts' career was disappointing by comparison. Between 1956 and 1966, with the Phillies, Baltimore Orioles, Houston Astros, and Chicago Cubs, Roberts went 126–143 with a 3.78 ERA, exactly at the league average for that

Phillies right-handed ace Robin Roberts shows off a basketful of baseballs in the locker room after earning his 200th win on August 1, 1958, in Philadelphia, a 3–1 win over the Chicago Cubs.

period of time. Nineteen fifty-six—when Roberts posted a 4.45 ERA—marked the last time Roberts would be selected as an All-Star or included in MVP balloting.

Roberts finished his career with 286 wins, just a hair shy of the 300-win club. Nevertheless, Roberts was enshrined in the Baseball Hall of Fame in 1976, named on 337 of 388 ballots. Two years later, the Phillies inducted Roberts, along with Connie Mack of the Philadelphia Athletics, on the Phillies Wall of Fame in its first year.

Roberts was and still is considered the best right-handed pitcher in Phillies history. In fact, before Steve Carlton came along, Roberts was considered the best pitcher, period, in Phillies history. In 1969 the Phillies let the fans vote on players for their all-time

Best Right-handed Starter in Phillies History?

When Robin Roberts retired, it was universally agreed upon that he was the best pitcher in Phillies history. Of course, that changed to "best right-handed pitcher" when the Phillies traded for Steve Carlton in 1972. In the last 50 years, the Phillies have only had two right-handed pitchers who can even be considered in the same echelon as Roberts: Curt Schilling and Roy Halladay. Halladay, though, has only been with the Phillies for a short period of time, so he isn't eligible to be part of the discussion yet. So, how do Roberts and Schilling compare?

Player	Years	W	L	ERA	IP	ERA+	WHIP	BB/9	SO/9	SO/BB
Roberts	14	234	199	3.46	3,739⅓	114	1.17	1.7	4.5	2.6
Schilling	9	101	78	3.35	1,659⅓	126	1.12	2.3	8.4	3.7

Roberts had five years on Schilling and played in an era where bullpens were relied upon significantly less than they were during Schilling's time. Roberts averaged over 70 more innings per season than Schilling in their time with the Phillies, allowing Roberts to set marks in many counting categories.

Schilling grades out slightly better when using rate statistics and adjusting for era. Schilling's 3.35 ERA with the Phillies was 26 percent better than the National League average, while Roberts' 3.46 ERA was only 14 percent better. The results are inconclusive, but it is an interesting debate that isn't likely to be settled.

Source: Baseball-Reference.com

team. Roberts was named as the only right-handed pitcher and was voted the greatest player.

It wasn't until Curt Schilling came along in the early 1990s and settled in as a major leaguer by the late 1990s that the Phillies could lay claim to a right-handed starting pitcher who could be named in the same sentence as Roberts. Of course, the Phillies assembled a super-rotation in 2011, but Roy Halladay was only in his second year with the team as was Roy Oswalt. Roberts was a once-in-a-generation pitcher. They are even harder to find these days since players move around more frequently than they did in the 1950s.

The Throw That Saved Perfection

Many people say, often derisively, that hindsight is 20/20. In the case of a Phillies-Braves game played on June 6, 2008, hindsight gives us a much better appreciation for what was witnessed.

The Phillies took a 1–0 lead on Tim Hudson and the Braves in the first inning, but relinquished it when Brian McCann hit a two-run home run off of Jamie Moyer in the bottom of the sixth. Pat Burrell threw a runner out at home plate on a line drive to left field in the seventh inning to keep the score close at 2–1.

The Braves called on Blaine Boyer to get the final two outs in the ninth. Boyer quickly got the second out of the inning but walked the next two hitters, bringing up catcher Chris Coste with runners on first and second. Coste hit a pop-up down the right-field line behind first base. Kelly Johnson ranged after it, calling off first baseman Mark Teixeira. By his body language, it seemed like an easy play, but the ball went in and out of Johnson's glove. Eric Bruntlett scored the tying run. Behind him, Pedro Feliz was tagged out at the plate to end the inning.

Tom Gordon held the Braves scoreless in the bottom of the ninth, giving the Phillies a chance to take the lead in the 10th inning. Against flame-throwing Manny Acosta, Chris Snelling led off the inning with a double. So Taguchi pinch ran for Snelling, advancing to third base on a sacrifice bunt by Jimmy Rollins. Shane Victorino drove him in with a triple, chasing Acosta. Royce Ring relieved Acosta but allowed a second run on a double by Chase Utley. At the end of the inning, the Phillies were up 4–2 with a dominant closer on his way in to convert the save.

Lidge got the hardest out of the inning, striking out McCann to start the frame. Josh Anderson and Gregor Blanco both reached on singles, however, extending the threat. Lidge struck out Greg Norton for the second out, bringing up Yunel Escobar. The situation: runners on second and third, two outs, up by two runs in the bottom of the 10th.

Lidge got ahead of Escobar 0–1. Coste called for a slider low and away, but Lidge caught too much of the plate. Escobar lined the pitch up the middle to center fielder Victorino, who had given many third-base coaches pause due to his extremely strong and accurate throwing arm.

Anderson scored easily as Victorino fired home. The ball took a friendly hop for Coste, who snagged the ball and wheeled around to his left, tagging Blanco out as he slid feet-first into the plate. The third out was recorded as the Phillies won the game 4–3. At the time, the biggest gain from the victory was padding their division lead, which went from 2½ to 3½ games.

In retrospect, though, we know that Lidge had a perfect season in 2008, converting 41 of 41 regular season saves and an additional seven in the postseason. Little did they know at the time that Gregor Blanco's foot was inches away from tarnishing a historically great season for Lidge. Even more impressively, there is a very short list of outfielders who could have made an equal or better throw than Victorino.

91 1996 All-Star Festivities at the Vet

Phillies fans had very little to look forward to in 1996. The roster left little in the way of optimistic prognostications, and it lived up to its uncomplimentary billing. The Phillies went into the All-Star break with a 37–49 record, 16½ games back and in fifth place in the NL East.

Philadelphia was, however, the host of the All-Star Game and festivities for the first time in 20 years. Ricky Bottalico was the Phillies' lone representative, entering the break with 20 saves and a 3.61 ERA. With a shoddy baseball team taking the field every day, fans could at least look to the All-Star Game for some high-quality baseball.

The Home Run Derby was the appetizer before the main event. The American League sent out Mark McGwire, Brady Anderson, Jay Buhner, Joe Carter, and Greg Vaughn. The National League countered with Barry Bonds, Henry Rodriguez, Jeff Bagwell, Ellis Burks, and Gary Sheffield. Bonds went on to win the tournament, hitting 17 home runs—nearly three times as many as his NL teammates combined (six). McGwire finished with 15 longballs. Phillies fans happily watched as Carter—the man who hit the dagger of a home run in Game 6 of the 1993 World Series—floundered with a paltry two homers.

The main event featured the managers of the previous year's World Series, Mike Hargrove of the Cleveland Indians and Bobby Cox of the Atlanta Braves. Not coincidentally, the league's starters also hailed from the Indians and Braves: Charles Nagy and John Smoltz, respectively.

Smoltz held the AL scoreless in his two frames while Nagy surrendered a run on an RBI ground-out by Barry Bonds in the first and two more in the second on a Mike Piazza solo home run and a Henry Rodriguez RBI single.

Piazza padded the National League's lead to 4–0 with an RBI double off of Chuck Finley in the fourth. Bottalico entered the game to much applause in the fifth, facing two future Hall of Famers in Ivan Rodriguez and Cal Ripken Jr. He struck out Rodriguez and got Ripken to fly out to left field. Bottalico would have had a 1-2-3 inning but Ken Caminiti booted a ground ball at

1996 All-Star Game Starting Lineups

Philadelphia played host to the All-Star Game in 1996, welcoming in a cadre of talented players from both leagues. The NL won the game 6–0 thanks to home runs from All-Star Game MVP Mike Piazza and Ken Caminiti. It was the first time Philadelphia had been the All-Star locale in 20 years and has not hosted it since. The American League lineup featured three players since inducted into the Hall of Fame—Wade Boggs, Roberto Alomar, and Cal Ripken Jr. It remains possible that more could join the club, including Piazza, Ivan Rodriguez, Barry Bonds, Chipper Jones, Craig Biggio, Barry Larkin, and John Smoltz.

	AL All-Star	Pos.	NL All-Star	Pos.
1.	Kenny Lofton	CF	Lance Johnson	CF
2.	Wade Boggs	3B	Barry Larkin	SS
3.	Roberto Alomar	2B	Barry Bonds	LF
4.	Albert Belle	LF	Fred McGriff	1B
5.	Mo Vaughn	1B	Mike Piazza	C
6.	Ivan Rodriguez	C	Dante Bichette	RF
7.	Cal Ripken Jr.	SS	Chipper Jones	3B
8.	Brady Anderson	RF	Craig Biggio	2B
9.	Charles Nagy	P	John Smoltz	P

Source: Baseball-Reference.com

third base, allowing Brady Anderson to reach. The inning ended with no further damage when Buhner lined out to center.

Caminiti made up for his error in the sixth, pounding a solo home run against Roger Pavlik. Craig Biggio drove in the NL's sixth and final run with a ground-out. The combination of Steve Trachsel, Todd Worrell, Mark Wohlers, and Al Leiter held the AL scoreless in the final three innings, notching another victory for the National League, 6–0. Mike Piazza earned All-Star Game MVP, going 2-for-3 with a double, home run, and two RBIs.

The All-Star Game at the Vet marked the end of the era. The NL would not win the midsummer classic again until 2010, marking 14 years of futility. The All-Star Game in 2002 made the

NL's failure worse as the game ended in a 7–7 tie after 11 innings. Consequently, Commissioner Bud Selig implemented a rule change to make it a more meaningful exhibition: starting in 2003, the league that won the All-Star Game earned home-field advantage in the World Series. From 2003 to 2009, the AL earned that home-field advantage, going 13–5 in home games.

As strange as it sounds, National League players looked back fondly on their time in the Vet in 1996, wishing they could rely on hitters like Barry Bonds and Mike Piazza and pitchers such as Greg Maddux and John Smoltz to bring their teams the highly valuable home-field advantage.

Phillies fans remembered the event being two days of great fun. With hosts of the upcoming two All-Star Games set it stone— Kauffman Stadium in Kansas City in 2012, Citi Field in New York in 2013—Phillies fans are hoping that the All-Star Game will make its way back to Philadelphia, perhaps in 2015.

92 Dutch

For a player who logged 400 or more at-bats in a season only three times in a 14-year major league career, Darren Daulton certainly left a mark on the Philadelphia Phillies. Drafted in the 25th round of the 1980 draft, Daulton toiled the minor leagues from the age of 18 to 22. He got his first taste of the big leagues in 1983—a "cup of coffee"—and returned to stay in 1985. However, due to the presence of catchers Ozzie Virgil and Lance Parrish, Daulton's playing time was scant until 1989.

Dutch was behind the dish for one of the Phillies' few bright spots between 1984 and 1992. On August 15, 1990, Terry Mulholland toed the rubber for a start against the San Francisco

Giants. It was about as easy a start as they come. Mulholland faced the minimum 27 batters, holding the Giants hitless through nine innings as the Phillies won 6–0. The only blemish on his record was an error by third baseman Charlie Hayes, but it was quickly erased on a ground-ball double play.

Calling the no-hitter was nice, but Daulton hadn't done much with the bat through 1991. In 1992 Daulton put it together. The catcher slugged 27 home runs—more than twice his previous career high of 12—and drove in a league-leading 109 runs, finishing sixth in NL MVP voting. However, the Phillies lacked offensive consistency and had a revolving door in the starting rotation as 15 different pitchers made a start during the season. The Phillies finished with a lackluster 70–92 record.

Daulton continued to hit in '93. He slugged 24 home runs and drove in 105 runs as the Phillies took the league by storm. Daulton, having taken the position as the clubhouse leader, was one part of an unrelenting Phillies offense that paced the National League in on-base percentage while finishing second in batting average and slugging percentage. Defying preseason expectations, the Phillies won the NL East, moving into the postseason to face the Atlanta Braves in the NLCS.

"Dutch" entered Game 5 of the NLCS with one hit in 17 trips to the plate. Going into the top of the ninth with the Phillies up 2–0, he was 1-for-2 with a single and a walk but looking to help the Phillies add to their lead. He finally broke out of his slump, smoking a solo home run to deep right-center.

The big hits kept coming for Daulton in Game 6. Facing the inimitable Greg Maddux in the bottom of the third, Daulton broke a scoreless tie with a two-run double. The Phillies went on to win 6–3, earning the right to play the Toronto Blue Jays in the World Series.

Not surprisingly, Daulton played a role in Game 4 of the World Series, one of the craziest games—if not the craziest—game ever played. Tied 7–7 in the bottom of the fifth, Daulton hit a two-run home run, spurring the Phillies to a five-run inning. Despite his best efforts, the Phillies lost 15–14.

In 1994 Daulton appeared to be on his way to another great season. On June 28, Daulton was hitting exactly .300 with a .929 OPS, but a knee injury ended his season—made worse by the fact that the season was cut short by a strike. He wasn't the same when he returned the next year. After slugging between .482 and .549 in the previous three seasons, his percentage dropped to .401. Daulton played in just five games in 1996, forcing the Phillies to move on with a new catcher. The Phillies traded Daulton to the Florida Marlins for Billy McMillon.

In a case of "right place at the right time," Daulton played first base and pinch-hit for the Marlins, eventually contributing to their World Series victory over the Cleveland Indians. While Daulton's post-baseball career has been laced with controversy, he became the host of a Phillies show on 97.5 FM "The Fanatic" and was inducted onto the Phillies Wall of Fame on August 6, 2010.

For many players, it is easy and often trite to look back and ask "What might have been?" For Dutch, however, it seems fitting to wonder what he could have accomplished if he had not been road-blocked at his position and endured some devastating injuries. Offensive ability is incredibly difficult to find with a catcher; Daulton was a rare breed, indeed.

93 Pedro Martinez

When the Phillies assembled the starting rotation to end all start-ing rotations in 2011, it was the second time they had two Cy Young Award winners together (Roy Halladay and Cliff Lee). The first was Cliff Lee and Pedro Martinez in 2009.

Martinez was nearing the end of his career and was coming off a disappointing 2008 with the New York Mets. His entire tenure with the Mets was marked by inconsistency and injury, but as a free agent going into '09, teams could take a risk with him without spending too much money. Having his pick of several interested teams, Martinez chose the Phillies on July 15.

He would make his debut in red pinstripes on August 12 against the Chicago Cubs at Wrigley Field (a game which may be better remembered as the game in which Shane Victorino had a cup of beer thrown at him). Martinez threw 99 pitches over five innings, allowing three runs as the Phillies won convincingly, 12–5.

The most memorable regular season start came against the Mets in the second game of a doubleheader on September 13. The New York Mets were set to face the Phillies on national television with Martinez facing noted Phillie-killer Tim Redding. It was a particularly intriguing matchup as the Phillies-Mets rivalry was still hot at the time, despite the Mets' failure, and Martinez was facing his former team to boot.

Martinez was shaky in the first two innings, allowing five base runners total, but escaped both frames without allowing a run. Chase Utley put the Phillies on the board with an RBI single. From the third through the eighth, Martinez was unhittable. Only two runners reached second base; the second, Daniel Murphy, was thrown out trying to take third on a wild pitch. Martinez sat in the dugout having shut out the Mets through eight innings on 130 pitches. Ryan Madson finished the ninth with ease as the Phillies won 1–0, sweeping the doubleheader from their division rivals.

For as good as Martinez was that night against the Mets, he was even better against the Los Angeles Dodgers in Game 2 of the NLCS. Facing former Phillie Vicente Padilla, the game was yet another low-scoring affair. Ryan Howard broke a scoreless tie with a solo home run in the fourth, which seemed like just enough run support for a pitcher throwing as well as Martinez.

After seven innings, the small right-hander held the Dodgers scoreless through seven innings, allowing just three base runners on two hits and a hit batter. Martinez gave way to Chan Ho Park in the eighth. The Dodgers took the opportunity to rally. Casey Blake and Ronnie Belliard reached base on singles. Blake scored on a throwing error by Utley. Before the inning was finished, J.A. Happ walked in the go-ahead run. Jonathan Broxton had an easy 1-2-3 ninth as the Dodgers won 2–1 despite a gem of a performance by Martinez.

As fate would have it, the Phillies lost all three of Martinez's postseason starts, but it was because the offense gave him a total of just five runs. The Phillies lost the World Series in six games, but Martinez was one of the most interesting mid-season pickups the Phillies had made in franchise history. It is not often that a GM has the chance to pick up a three-time Cy Young Award winner for the prorated league-minimum salary to help out a World Series–contending team.

94 Wheeze Kids

Entering 1983, the Phillies had reached the postseason in five of the previous seven seasons, winning it all in 1980. By '83, though, the bulk of the team was on the wrong side of 30, and their "window," as they say, was closing. Of players to rack up 350 or more plate appearances, Von Hayes was the only player younger than 30. The right side of the infield, Pete Rose and Joe Morgan, was a combined 81 years old. The ace of the starting rotation, Steve Carlton, was 38, and an equally aged Tug McGraw had already relinquished his role as closer.

As a homage to the young 1950 Phillies team nicknamed the "Whiz Kids," the '83 squad was dubbed the "Wheeze Kids." Don't let the nickname fool you—these guys could still play baseball at a high level. The Phillies finished with the second-best staff ERA and got on base at the third-highest rate in the National League.

Their road wasn't easy, however. Throughout the season, the Phillies, Pittsburgh Pirates, and Montreal Expos traded control of first place in the division. With an 11-game winning streak from September 16 to 26, however, the Phillies raced ahead of the Pirates, clinching their postseason berth after the 160th game of the season with a victory at Chicago.

Third baseman Mike Schmidt represented most of the Phillies' offense, finishing the regular season with 109 RBIs and a league-leading 40 home runs. Schmidt also led the league in walks (128) and on-base percentage (.399). Joe Morgan hit just .230 but got on base 37 percent of the time, setting the table for Schmidt.

The Phillies played the Los Angeles Dodgers in the NLCS, a familiar matchup as the two teams battled in the playoffs in '77 and '78, as well, both times resulting in World Series trips for the Dodgers.

Game 1 of the NLCS was typical Wheeze Kids baseball. Schmidt put the Phillies on the board with a solo home run in the first inning, then Carlton shut down the Dodgers through seven and two-thirds innings. Al Holland got the final four outs to wrap up a nail-biting 1–0 victory.

The Phillies lost Game 2 by the score of 4–1, but Gary "Sarge" Matthews hit the first of three home runs in the series. In Game 3 Matthews hit a solo home run to increase the Phillies' lead to 4–2 in the fourth, then tacked on three more with a two-run single in the fifth and another RBI single in the seventh. Behind the hot bat of Matthews, the Phillies downed the Dodgers 7–2.

The Sarge show continued in Game 4 as Matthews gave the Phillies the lead with a three-run home run off of Jerry Reuss in the first inning. The Phillies went on to win 7–2. With a total of three homers, eight RBIs, and a .429 batting average, Matthews was named NLCS MVP. The Phillies moved on to face the Baltimore Orioles in the World Series.

With two future Hall of Famers in Eddie Murray and Cal Ripken Jr., the Orioles offense was frightening. Phillies starter John Denny was able to silence them in Game 1, allowing one run in seven and two-thirds innings as solo home runs from Garry Maddox and Joe Morgan gave the Phillies the 2–1 win and a 1–0 Series lead.

In Game 2 Phillies starter Charles Hudson was out-dueled by Orioles hurler Mike Boddicker, who threw nine innings of dominant baseball as the Orioles won 4–1 and evened up the series.

The Phillies couldn't capitalize on any scoring opportunities in Game 3, going 0-for-2 with runners in scoring position. Their two runs came on two more solo home runs from Sarge and Morgan, but it wasn't enough, as the Orioles took the game 3–2.

Game 4 was close but sloppy as both teams' starters—Denny for the Phillies and Storm Davis for the Orioles—couldn't get past the sixth inning. The Phillies entered the bottom of the ninth down 5–3 but put together a rally as Ozzie Virgil drove in Bob Dernier with two outs to make it 5–4. Joe Morgan ended the rally, lining out to second base, bringing the Phillies to within one game of elimination.

The Phillies ran out of steam in Game 5. Orioles starter Scott McGregor pitched well, but the Phillies went 0-for-6 with runners in scoring position. The Orioles slugged three home runs, including two by Eddie Murray, as they shut out the Phillies 5–0 for the World Series win.

Fans who had worried about the age of the team were proven right as the Phillies finished better than third place just once between 1984 and 1992, a span of nine excruciating playoff-less years. Familiar faces faded away, and new faces entered the frame as the first golden era of Phillies baseball came to a close. Fans were, however, extremely grateful for the great playoff runs between 1976 and 1983 that revived baseball in Philadelphia.

95 Dick Allen

Dick Allen remains one of the most controversial players in Phillies history, representing a dark time in baseball's history, but particularly so for the Phillies, as they were one of the last teams to get on board with the integration of African American players.

The Phillies signed him in 1960. By his fourth minor league season, he was promoted to their top minor league affiliate in Little Rock, Arkansas. Allen was the first black player in Little Rock's history. The fan base was not pleased, staging protests, but Allen endured, hitting 33 home runs with the Arkansas Travelers in 1963.

Allen earned an everyday job with the Phillies in 1964 and did not disappoint. Allen hit 29 home runs and drove in 91 runs, leading the league in runs scored (125), triples (13), and total bases (352), en route to winning the Rookie of the Year award with 18 of 20 first-place votes.

Nineteen sixty-four, of course, is a year that is infamous in Phillies history, as the team wasted a 6½-game lead with 12 games remaining. The Phillies lost 10 games in a row between games 151 and 160 as manager Gene Mauch pressed harder and harder on his aces Jim Bunning and Chris Short.

Allen hit .415 during his team's 10-game losing streak. His team's failure appeared to hamper his candidacy for the NL MVP award as he finished in seventh place behind Ken Boyer of the eventual World Series–winning St. Louis Cardinals, who overtook the Phillies with three games left in the season.

As Allen became a fixture in the Phillies' lineup, he continued to amaze players across major league baseball with his natural talent and far-traveling home runs. "Now I know why [Phillies fans] boo

[Allen] all the time," said Willie Stargell. "When he hits a home run, there's no souvenir." Stargell was referencing a 529-foot home run Allen hit at Connie Mack Stadium that cleared the Coke sign on the roof.

Allen's 1966 season was historically great. His 40 home runs and 110 RBIs were no doubt impressive, but his 1.027 OPS was incredible given the era. Adjusted OPS (or OPS+) accounts for the quality of the league and park factors, putting Allen's OPS at 81 percent better than the league average. In the last 50 years, only 57 players' seasons have been as much as 80 percent better than the league. Somehow, Allen finished fourth in MVP voting to Roberto Clemente, despite having better numbers in almost every category.

Controversy encapsulated Allen's 1965 season. He fought with Frank Thomas, a veteran outfielder and corner infielder who had made a habit out of making racist remarks to Allen. In anger, Thomas swung a bat, hitting Allen in the shoulder. Allen threw some punches, and ultimately the two players were separated. Thomas was released by the Phillies the next day, but Allen was not permitted to speak about the incident.

Callison, however, did speak about what happened. "Thomas got himself fired when he swung that bat at Richie. In baseball, you don't swing a bat at another player," he said.

Allen was suspended indefinitely in 1969 when he got stuck in traffic and did not show up for the Phillies' twinight doubleheader with the New York Mets. After the season, Allen demanded a trade, starting yet another controversy. The Phillies and Cardinals agreed on a deal that sent Allen, Cookie Rojas, and Jerry Johnson to St. Louis in exchange for Byron Browne, Joe Hoerner, Tim McCarver, and Curt Flood. Flood, however, refused to go to Philadelphia, so the Cardinals sent Willie Montanez and Jim Browning to the Phillies instead. Montanez would later be used by the Phillies to acquire outfielder Garry Maddox from the San Francisco Giants.

Allen would be traded twice more: to the Los Angeles Dodgers in 1971 and to the Chicago White Sox in 1972. It was in his first year with the White Sox that Allen would finally win an MVP award, hitting .308 and leading the league in home runs (37), RBIs (113), walks (99), on-base percentage (.420), slugging percentage (.603), and OPS (1.023). His 199 OPS+ was even more historically great than his 1966 season: in the last 50 years, only 21 players have had an OPS+ 95 percent better than the league average in a season.

At the end of his career, Allen returned to the Phillies in 1975 and '76 but wasn't nearly as good as he used to be, nor could he find

Dick Allen

Dick Allen's 1972 season was among the best offensive seasons in the last 50 years. Going by OPS, adjusting for league and park factors (OPS+), Allen had the 16th-best season since 1961. He was also just the 11th player in that time to have an OPS that was 99 percent better than the league average or more.

Best Seasons Since 1961 by OPS+

Player	OPS+	OPS	Year	Team
Barry Bonds	268	1.381	2002	SFG
Barry Bonds	263	1.422	2004	SFG
Barry Bonds	259	1.379	2001	SFG
Barry Bonds	231	1.278	2003	SFG
Mark McGwire	216	1.222	1998	STL
Jeff Bagwell	213	1.201	1994	HOU
Frank Thomas	211	1.217	1994	CHW
Willie McCovey	209	1.108	1969	SFG
Mickey Mantle	206	1.135	1961	NYY
Barry Bonds	205	1.080	1992	PIT
Barry Bonds	204	1.136	1993	SFG
Sammy Sosa	203	1.174	2001	CHC
George Brett	203	1.118	1980	KCR
Norm Cash	201	1.148	1961	DET
Mike Schmidt	199	1.080	1981	PHI
Dick Allen	**199**	**1.023**	**1972**	**CHW**

his way onto the field as frequently as before. Allen retired after the 1977 season with the Oakland Athletics.

Had he been able to be more productive after the age of 30, Allen may have been a shoe-in for the Hall of Fame. He retired with fewer than 2,000 hits, 351 home runs, and only 1,119 RBIs, missing many meaningful milestones that catch the eye of voters. Even if he is never enshrined, he will forever be a legend in Philadelphia.

96 Keep Score at a Phillies Game

One of baseball's most enjoyable pastimes, for fans, is keeping score at a baseball game. It has been around as long as hot dogs and Cracker Jack. As a kid, the first thing I did upon entering Veterans Stadium was purchase a program with a scorecard from the nearest vendor. It was then a race to the seats before the first pitch, so I had time to jot down the starting lineups, their positions, and their uniform numbers.

Keeping score is astonishingly complicated, so you must both pay close attention during the action and have a good understanding of the game of baseball. While scoring a ground-out to shortstop is easy ("6-3"), you may have to log the details of a rundown, which can become very messy, especially when it involves outfielders coming into the infield.

With the rise in popularity of the Internet, particularly with applications like Gameday on MLB.com that keep score for you, it may seem a trivial task to keep score at a game. However, it keeps you engaged for the duration of the game, which tends to span between three and four hours. At the end of the night, if you've been doing it right, you have a filled scorecard as a memento of your time at the ballpark. If you scored a particularly unique game, such as a no-hitter, having it autographed by relevant parties makes it all the better.

I risk sounding like an old fogey in saying this, but as someone who grew up watching baseball games before handheld devices were commonplace, it is odd to see people burying their faces in their smartphone screens instead of being engaged with the play on the field. There are scoring apps out there, but many people are incessantly checking Twitter, Facebook, email, and various other social media rather than keeping up with the on-field action. A baseball game is supposed to help you take your mind off of the rigors of the day. The next time you take a trip to Citizens Bank Park, keep the phone in your pocket and put a scorecard in your lap instead. You'll be surprised how much fun you have! And you might even learn some of the more intricate rules of baseball.

97 Pete Rose

Although he spent nearly four times as much time with the Cincinnati Reds as the Phillies, Rose is known almost equally as well in both shades of red. In Cincinnati, Rose won the NL Rookie of the Year award in 1963 and the NL MVP award in 1973. From 1965 to 1973, Rose hit .300 or better every year. After 16 seasons with the Reds, Rose had logged 3,164 hits.

After the 1978 season, at the age of 37, Rose elected to sign with the Phillies as a free agent. At the time, the Phillies had become a National League superpower, reaching the NLCS—but ultimately losing—in each of the three previous seasons. In Rose's first year with the Phillies in 1979, the Phillies finished barely above

.500, missing out on the postseason. Rose, however, hit .331 with a .418 on-base percentage.

Rose, or "Charlie Hustle" as he was known, gave his all on every pitch, on every play. It was a wonder he was able to play into his late thirties and early forties with how much effort he gave and how much wear and tear he had accumulated over the years.

He had already won two World Series with the Reds in 1975 and 1976, but hungered for another ring. In 1980 Rose led the league in doubles, played well defensively, and ultimately helped the Phillies reach the postseason to play the Houston Astros in the NLCS.

Unlike many players, Rose always showed up and performed in the playoffs. Going into the NLCS, Rose had a .318 average in 173 postseason at-bats, which included 17 extra-base hits. Rose hit .400 in the epic NLCS with the Astros, helping the Phillies rally in the eighth inning of Game 4 when they started the inning down 2–0 and came back to win 5–3 in 10 innings.

Rose also contributed to a big inning in Game 5. The Phillies started the top of the eighth down 5–2 against Nolan Ryan, but Rose forced in the Phillies' third run with a bases-loaded walk. At the end of the inning, the Phillies led 7–5, eventually winning 8–7 in 10 innings.

In the World Series, the Kansas City Royals were able to deal with Rose, holding him hitless in his first 12 trips to the plate in the first three games before Rose again helped the Phillies rally late in Game 3. The Phillies went into the eighth inning down 3–2 against reliever Renie Martin. With runners on first and second, Rose singled to right-center, tying the game at three apiece. Were it not for a walkoff RBI single by Willie Aikens in the bottom of the 10th, it could have easily gone the Phillies' way.

Rose had five hits in 12 plate appearances in the final three games of the series, as the Phillies defeated the Royals in six. Mike

Schmidt won World Series MVP honors with a .381 average, two home runs, and seven RBIs. If a consolation MVP could have been awarded, there was a solid argument for Rose.

In 1983 the Phillies (known as the "Wheeze Kids" due to their age) reached the World Series and ultimately lost to the Baltimore Orioles. Rose was 42 years old and at the end of his career. On the cusp of passing Ty Cobb for the all-time hits record (4,191 at the time, later adjusted to 4,189), Rose signed with the Montreal Expos going into 1984. After he hit just .259, the Expos traded him to the Reds. In 96 at-bats, Rose hit .365. After the 1984 season, Rose had 4,097 hits, just 95 hits away from breaking Cobb's record.

Knowing that he just needed to stay healthy and the record was his, Rose played in 1985 at the age of 44. He hit just .264, but finally broke the record of 4,191 hits on September 11 against San Diego Padres pitcher Eric Show. Rose finished the season at 4,204. Surprisingly, he came back in '86 and tacked on 52 more hits to his total. He retired after the season with 4,256 hits, a record that still stands today and figures to stand for quite some time, if not forever. The closest active player is 37-year-old Derek Jeter at 3,088.

Due to a betting scandal, baseball's all-time hits leader remains, very controversially, outside of the Hall of Fame. The cities of Cincinnati and Philadelphia, however, will always remember his relentless style of baseball that brought his teams three championships.

98 Pie Man

Every successful team will have a clubhouse leader, often chosen ad-hoc. Typically, the most successful player on a successful team is, by default, made the leader. Have you ever seen a .220 hitter take control of a clubhouse? Me neither.

The Phillies of the early 2000s were an exception. Curt Schilling was traded in 2000, leaving Scott Rolen and Bobby Abreu as the two possible clubhouse leaders. Neither of them had qualities of a leader. Abreu always kept to himself, rarely speaking, while Rolen led more by his play on the field, rather than firing his team up with a moving speech. Rolen went from Philadelphia to St. Louis during the 2002 season, so Abreu was all by himself.

That opened the door up for Tomas Perez. After the 2000 season, the Phillies endured their fifth straight season of 85 or more losses. More than someone to light a fire underneath them, the Phillies needed someone to bring excitement into the clubhouse.

Perez was not a future MVP; he was a jack-of-all-trades role player. From 2000 to 2005, he never reached 300 at-bats in a season but played all four infield positions and even served as an emergency pitcher. Perez started a tradition in which, after a Phillie got a key hit in the bottom of the ninth or in extra innings, he would throw a shaving-cream pie in the player's face during the postgame interview. He would have the biggest smile on his fast as he crept up and giggled as he ran off before the player could retaliate.

There is no stat that accounts for fun, but Perez certainly brought fun to the Phillies. With the controversies brewing between players (Schilling, Rolen) and the front office and the disappointing seasons, a little levity was exactly what the clubhouse—and the fans—needed. Perez had it in spades.

Perez does not show up on any franchise leader-boards. His home runs were, for the most part, unimportant, and he was not flashy with the glove. He was, however, exactly the type of player made for the 2000–2005 Phillies. Any fan who was old enough to appreciate (your definition of *appreciate* may vary) those teams will remember Perez fondly. What Pete Rose had in hustle, Perez had in thrill-seeking.

99 Phillie Killers

For some unknown reason, some players simply perform better against certain teams and in certain locations. Chipper Jones is a famous example of this. Over the course of his long, Hall of Fame–worthy career, Jones hit 19 home runs at Shea Stadium, the most in any non-home stadium. He enjoyed Shea Stadium so much that he named one of his sons Shea in honor of his immense success in Queens, New York.

Jones, however, is also known as a Phillies killer. He hit 13 home runs at Veterans Stadium, the third-highest total of any non-home stadium. On a per at-bat basis, however, the Vet has been slightly more friendly to Chipper than Shea Stadium. Chipper averaged a home run every 16.9 at-bats at the Vet, 17.0 at Shea Stadium, and 27.2 at Pro Player Stadium, the home of the Florida Marlins. He also hit .350 at the Vet, the most at any stadium in which he has logged 175 or more at-bats.

Jones' continued success—as well as that of the Atlanta Braves in general—led to Phillies fans derisively chanting his real name, Larry, when he would step to the plate.

Many Phillies fans will be able to rattle off a list—and even a complete lineup—of Phillies killers in recent years. One whom many will not remember is Erubiel Durazo, a former first baseman with the Arizona Diamondbacks. On May 17, 2002, Durazo hit three home runs in one game: two off of starter Terry Adams and one off of reliever Rheal Cormier. Over the course of his career, Durazo posted a 1.216 OPS against the Phillies, the third-highest OPS of any team against which he has logged 40 or more at-bats.

Fans certainly remember the way Juan Pierre and Luis Castillo terrorized the Phillies at the top of the Marlins' batting order early in the 2000s, particularly in 2003. Going into the final six games of the regular season, the Phillies and Marlins were vying for the NL wild-card. The Marlins were ahead by one game with an 86–70 record. The Marlins swept the Phillies in a three-game series, clinched the wild-card in their next game, and eventually went on to win the World Series.

In that three-game set, Pierre went 4-for-8 while Castillo had four hits in 10 at-bats. Over their careers, Pierre hit .310 against the Phillies with 40 stolen bases in 49 attempts. Castillo hit .273 with 24 stolen bases in 32 attempts.

Catcher Rod Barajas may be the most annoying of them all. Barajas spent one season with the Phillies in 2007, but his time in Philadelphia was summed up by one event in Florida on May 23, 2007. The Phillies went into the ninth inning ahead 7–3, but closer Brett Myers struggled, allowing three runs to score. Now ahead just 7–6, Myers faced Aaron Boone with runners on first and second. Boone singled to left. The speedy Hanley Ramirez wheeled around third base as left fielder Jayson Werth fired home. The ball took a perfect bounce to Barajas, but he did not block the plate, allowing Ramirez to slide underneath him to tie the game.

Phillies fans never forgave Barajas for not blocking the plate. Not only was it cowardly, but it led to Myers suffering a shoulder strain, sidelining him for two months. Overall, Barajas was not productive with the bat, hitting just .230 with four home runs.

In the years since, Barajas has spent time with the Toronto Blue Jays, New York Mets, and Los Angeles Dodgers. Since leaving Philadelphia, Barajas has been a pest when facing the Phillies. In 2008 he had four hits in seven at-bats, including two home runs and six RBIs. The next year, he went 5-for-10 with two home runs and four RBIs. In 2010 he had 10 hits in 25 at-bats with four

home runs and nine RBIs. The Phillies finally held him silent in
2011 when he went 1-for-14.

From 2008 to 2010, Barajas hit .452 with eight home runs and
19 RBIs in 42 at-bats versus the Phillies. That represents 1.3
percent of his career at-bats, but he hit 6.4 percent of his home runs
and drove in 4.2 percent of his RBIs in that three-year period.

There will always be players who perform better against the
Phillies than anyone else. For Barajas, this was inexplicably true and
incredibly annoying. As a result, fans now loathe Barajas more than
any other player in baseball.

100 Opening Day at Citizens Bank Park

The months between November and March are excruciatingly long
and boring for diehard baseball fans. *SportsCenter* is inundated with
football highlights as baseball news comes in short bursts. While
March features the return of baseball, the month is littered with
meaningless exhibition games involving many players who will not
be featured on the roster. As a result, March is more of a tease than
anything.

Opening Day at Citizens Bank Park is something to behold.
45,000 rabid baseball enthusiasts come out of their winter caves for
their first dose of meaningful baseball. A freshly manicured field
features the most vivid shade of green and the softest of browns as
white chalk lines the boundaries. The sun shines over the stadium
as brand-new uniforms are donned by players warming up in the
outfield. A sea of red—on shirts, jackets, and hats—lines the seats
around the stadium.

Leading up to the first pitch, a large American flag is unfurled
as members of the armed forces spread it out for a packed house to

honor. All of the players and coaches of both the visiting and home teams are introduced one-by-one as they line up on the first- and third-base lines, respectively. For the Phillies, the postseason success of the previous year typically involves a flag being raised at Ashburn Alley.

From there, you are just moments away from baseball. As is tradition, the national anthem is sung and the ceremonial first pitch is thrown. Suddenly, nine players—some familiar, some new—burst from the home dugout to thunderous applause and cheers.

Finally, baseball is back. The pop of a fastball into the catcher's mitt. The shouting from behind home plate as the umpire calls balls and strikes. The crack as a bat makes contact with the ball. The numerous times you will leap from your seat to cheer what is going on in front of you. The calls of beer and hot dog vendors announcing their presence.

All of it means baseball is back for another six months. For six months, you are allowed to lose yourself in the pendulum swings of a baseball season.

That is baseball in Philadelphia.